I0153151

THE
NORTH
AMERICA
DIVE
GUIDE

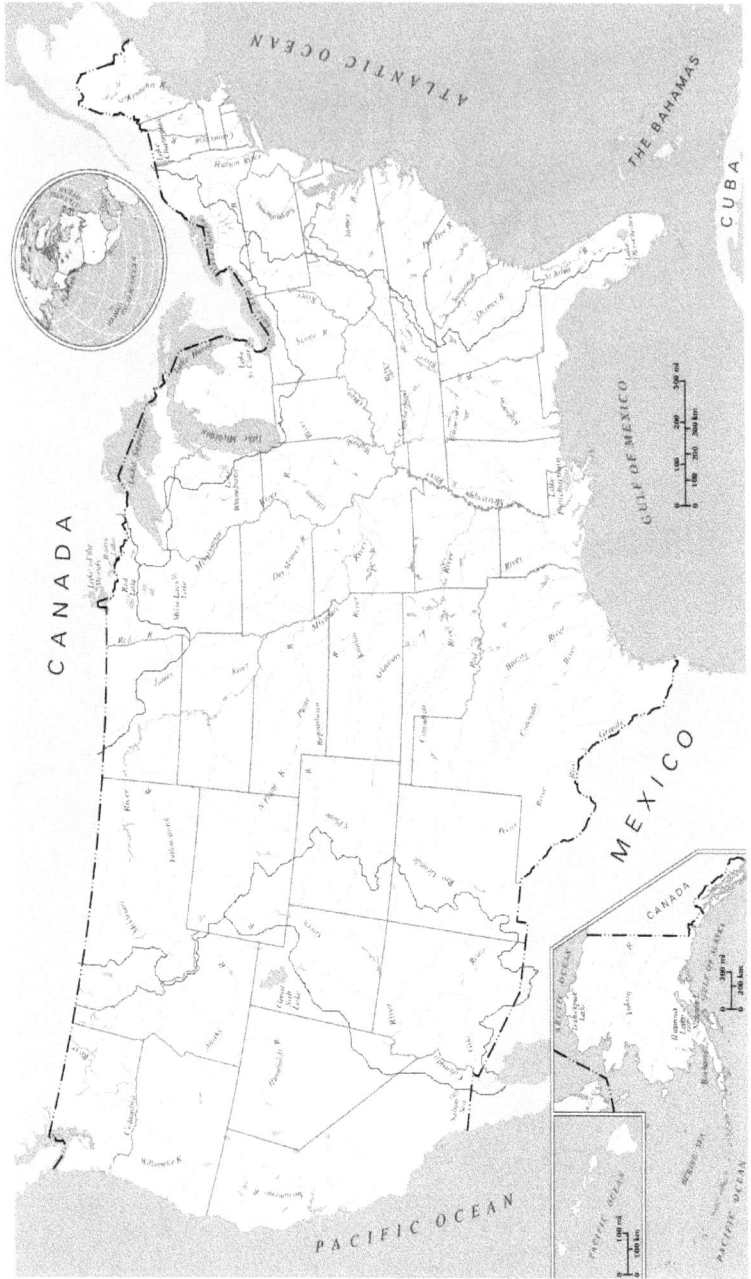

THE
NORTH
AMERICA
DIVE
GUIDE

A Scuba Handbook

Mike Hughes

Copyright © 2013 Mike Hughes
Photographs copyright the photographers

All rights reserved. No parts of this book may be reproduced, store in a retrieval system, or transmitted by any means or in any form without prior permission of the Author.

Caution: Scuba Diving can be dangerous if you dive past your level of training, experience, or expertise. Even with the right training and equipment, your own safety is ultimately up to you. The author takes no responsibility for loss or injury incurred by anyone using this book.

ISBN 0-9664130-3-2

This Book is dedicated to my brother
Patrick V. Hughes

CONTENTS

POTPOURI OF DIVE STUFF

INTRODUCTION

This scuba dive handbook is based on countless interviews done in person, by phone, and by internet web site sources. Personally, I have not gone diving in every state or dived every site in every state. That's not the main goal of this book. Instead, I have gathered information as provided by experienced locals who dive the local sites on a regular basis, and if perhaps any information is in error, please fill free to contact me and I will see that if indeed true, any error will be edited in the next edition. If I failed to mention a dive site in your state or province and you feel that it should be included in the next edition, then contact me for said reason too. The information in this book is as complete as humanly possible, but in keeping with the 1200word article format to make each article eligible for acceptance in Dive News Network's *North America Dive News, Northwest Dive News, Southwest Dive News, Southeast Dive News, Northeast Dive News, and Mid-west Dive News,* some detail information was omitted. For instructors and dive shops that don't have web sites, you may not seem to exist to potential divers under the age of 50. Having said that, your information was not omitted; like many other divers and would be divers, I just didn't know you existed.

Always check the altitude, currents, depth, and other dive conditions out for yourself and use local diver knowledge and unique custom experience just like you would check your own air pressure gauge on your tank before every dive; as redundancy is what makes diving safe and enjoyable.

The World Wide Hot Spot Section I plan to expand over time as I have already traveled around the world diving on layovers with the airlines, but haven't had a chance to write up those dive sites yet. Many potpourri style articles related especially to cold water diving and training can be found in my book, *The Northwest Dive Guide.*

Also, new dive sites will be included with later revisions. California and New York are barely touched in this first edition, but it was agreed on that it was better to publish now, than wait another year before adding more material on a few states. It's not that the diving here is any less great than any other state, it is just that the last few years while a writer for DNN, my publisher Rick Stratton had me assigned to the new up starts: Southeast and Southwest Dive News regional magazines. So there may appear to be a heavier concentration of topics in these regions than others places, but that will be corrected with time. Not all dive sites in the northwest are mentioned in this book, as I have already written *The Northwest Dive Guide* by Harbour Publishing, and many of the dive sites on British Columbia and Washington State I've already covered in depth in this book.

Lastly, if you know about any local diving that seems to be unique to a certain region, such as gold mine diving in Alaska, freshwater pearl diving in Texas, or catfish noodling dives in the Mississippi river, please give me as many details as possible and I'll follow up on it for Dive News Network as well as for the next edition of this book. What amazes me most I guess, is that so few dive related web sites mention the great dive sites in their own county or state, but these sites may have extensive reviews of the Caribbean. Divers may have little access to local dive site information for the weekly or monthly dives, but are overwhelmed with information for that once a year or less overseas dive.
Mike Hughes

divec2c@yahoo.com

Web site   mikehughesscuba.com

Finally, as the writer of dive gear for DNN for some number of years, I have amassed over 475 videos on dive sites and gear reviews that you may find interesting if not comical in nature on **Youtube** under **mike hughes scuba**. For those that enjoy Dungeness crab, as a scuba dive instructor I have made a complete serious video on how to catch Dungeness crabs while scuba diving. For those that just desire comedy, check out my comedy videos such as *how to play chess* (complete with foreign accents) on Youtube under **home groan news**. You don't even need to know the game of chess to find this video funny. Enjoy!

ACKNOWLEDGEMENTS

I would like to thank countless dive instructors and dive shop owners that supplied me with so many hours and pages worth of integral information. They say that to make a million in the diving business you have to start with two million, and this only affirms their love and support of a bizarre sport which uses self contained underwater breathing apparatus that lends access to explore the other 75% of this planet erroneously or ironically known as Earth even though it's mostly a water planet with a few patches of exposed lava beds, accumulated sand, and precious outcrops of soil.

I'd also like to thank my brother for making me get off the couch in while living in Hawaii some thirty years ago and taking our first scuba dive course, which lead to a degree in Marine Biology, a PADI Master Instructor certification, entrance into the realm of technical diving, ten years as a writer for Dive News Network, my first cartoon scuba dive book *Whoops Divers Guide*, and my first serious scuba dive book, *The Northwest Dive Guide*. I BLAME IT ALL ON MY BROTHER. Never again have I been able to enjoy down time on a comfortable couch. There are hundreds of thousands of islands with beaches and reefs to explore, and so little time. Mahalo brah.

UNITED STATES OF AMERICA

Alabama
Sweet Home Diving

Alabama is home to 77,000 navigate able miles of water which makes it second only to Alaska when it comes to looking for a site wet enough to dive in. If that isn't enough, Alabama has 35miles of white sand beaches and while the water may dip to 55° in the winter, it rises in the summer up in the 80's. Finally, Alabama was one of the first states to start an artificial reef program as early as 1953. From the 250 automobiles then to the 100 M60 battle tanks in 1987, to the recent sinking of culverts, demolished bridge rubble, and liberty ships, there is a plethora of dive sites to explore.

Rick Stratton and I asked some of the locals what their favorite sites were, and here are some of the answers we got:

Forrest Phelps from *Southern Skin Divers Supply* in Birmingham, which started in 1953, said that it wasn't so much his favorite sites, but his favorite types of diving. On the one hand he enjoys artifact diving and to him, he doesn't care how murky the river gets, he is more interested in what the water holds. Forrest and his dive buddies have found 6inch Megalodon shark teeth, Cobb spear points, coins, ceramic pot, jugs, and vintage bottles. The Selma area in particular has Civil War artifacts from 1865.

On the other hand, Forrest is a big spearfishing enthusiast. Red snapper are huge in Alabama waters. It 's common to catch 15 to 25lbs fish. Forrest once caught a 29 and a 23pounder in less than a minute on a dive. The limit is two fish, and that's almost 53lbs of fish total for just that one dive. A catch like this is not surprising considering all the local artificial reefs. Statistically, 30 to 40percent of all recreational red snapper are caught off Alabama, and Alabama comprises only 5% of the northern Gulf of Mexico waters.

Lawren McCaghren of *Gulf Coast Divers* in Mobile, which has been in business since 1972, also enjoys spearfishing, especially around the gas and oil rigs. Gulf Coast Divers also has 6-pack charter boats that routinely go out around **Dolphin Island** and **Perdido Pass** where you can dive pier pilings on the east side, and the jetty on the west side. One of Lawren's favorite dives it to hunt for lobster in a large natural limestone reef area named **Trysler Grounds**. It's about 20miles south of Perdido Bay. You'll find lots of soft corals here as well as spotted moray eels and lionfish. **Dutch Banks** is another local natural reef, but much smaller in size.

Gary Emerson of *Gary's Gulf Divers* in Orange Beach goes out to the Trysler Grounds on a 6-pack 30' Hydrocat. Two other popular sites that he goes to include the **Oriskany** which is, that is 911ft long, 150ft wide, and 150ft tall aircraft carrier sunk in 2006 in Florida's waters, but You can get there from Orange Beach by boat in about 1 ½ hours or less. Along the way don't be surprised to see turtles including leatherbacks leisurely floating on the surface. It's 80ft to the smoke stacks of the Oriskany, 120ft to the bridge, and 145ft to the flight deck. If you are a tech diver, the hangar bay is at 175ft. If you are truly lucky, you may even see a whale shark while on this dive.

The other popular dive is the **Navy Tug**. It's only 85ft deep and 80-100ft long. The top of it was blown off during a hurricane, but with vis running 40-50ft even when other sites are having a bad day of vis, this site still has lots of critters to view. Some suspects include grouper, amberjacks, angelfish, and more.

Jim Mahan an instructor at *Down Under Dive Shop* in Gulf Shores has been diving since 1973. He says that there are over 300 local dive sites, and it only takes two to three weeks after something is sunk before it is full life. He and the folks from Down Under Dive Shop have a 46' Newton Dive Special that you can charter out to the local dive sites. The boat can take a max of 20 divers, can hold 72tanks, and has two camera tables as well as two dive ladders, just to name a few of the amenities.

Some of the wrecks and artificial sites that I won't have room to mention include: Diving around the **Tenslaw River Bridge**, the **I-10 Black River Bridge Rubble**, The **Hopper Barge**, the 387ft long wreck of the **Antares**, the **Hugh Swingle General Permit Area** and **Don Kelly North General Permit Area** where most of the battle tanks are located. There is also the **105 tug**, the **151 tug**, the **Mobil Oil Platform**, the **buffalo barges**, the **dry dock**, **UNOCAL #254**, and last but not least there are three 441.6ft long and 57ft wide liberty ships nearby; the **Allen**, the **Sparkman**, and the **Wallace**. Did I name them all? Not even close.

Before I forget, *Gary Emerson* also wanted me to mention one of the best shore dives and that would be the **Alabama Point Jetties**. The area is only 15-35ft deep, but if you go on a high tide to hold off the fresh river water, you can see 5ft stingrays, Octos in the rocks, and mantis shrimp. On a night dive expect to find plenty of flounder resting on the sand and rock substratum. The **Whiskey Wreck** is 150yards off shore in front of Bahama Bobs Restaurant on west beach in Gulf Shores. The wreck is 200ft long and scattered in 300 square feet. **Alabama Point Bridge** and the **Alabama Point Sea Wall** are two other well-known shore dive locations.

Lastly, there are a few lakes and water filled quarries that locals like to frequent and hang out with trout, sunfish, bluegill, carp, bass, and turtles. Quarries run seasonal hours so check availability and current fees before you go. The **Madison Quarry** is 55ft deep max on 7acres of water and contains a mock up wing from Skylab, a F4 Phantom jet, a Minuteman Missile, a Titan Missile Nose Cone, a fire truck, boats, etc. If all this isn't enough, Britt Clark tells me that they have a Greek Restaurant run by Demetrius Dedes that brings non-divers up here just for the food; typically open from May to September. **Alabama Blue Water Adventures** has a max depth of 150ft and a 26acre water field. Below water you'll find a school bus, two 1940's fire trucks, steel boxes, cars, and boats. **Dive Land Park** is a picturesque quarry that dips down to 150ft of depth and offers a navigation course and buoyancy rings. **Lake Martin** offers dime size jellyfish in the summer and 80lb catfish, but most of all, after the parties and concerts near

Kowaliga Marina, divers go out in search of keys, rings, and cell phones . . .and I've run out of space.

As for a sumptuous summery summary, just read the article over a couple of more times, then the first chance you get go enjoy some sweet home Alabama diving. Great Dives!

Alaska
The Pinnacle Of Cold Water Diving

Alaska is one of the most beautiful States I have ever had the pleasure to visit. It has more shore line, more lakes, and basically more out door wilderness and wildlife above and below the waterline to view and enjoy than just about any other state in the Union. So what type of diving and where you can dive in this incredibly diverse land of the midnight sun?

To start with, let's go west of Anchorage to the city with the ever-familiar name of The North Pole. Here, Kate and Mitch own and operate *Test The Waters Dive Center*. Mitch is, literally in more ways than one, one of the top ice diving instructors in the world. Up here, at Summit Lake, altitude diving and ice diving go hand in hand and Kate says that they train year round. They have a 6-pack boat 6 & 1/2 hrs drive south at Valdez that they used even while Valdez was blanketed by 400inches of snow. They also occasionally dive the Artic Ocean, the upper Kenai River, Prince William Sound, and other quite cool destinations. At the dive shop they sell wetsuits to dredges. This is gold mining country, and there is more than one way to find gold in these waters. You can dig and vacuum local substrates, or you can look for gold laden wrecks that carried miners on their way back from the Yukon claims when on more than one occasion disaster suddenly struck. One interesting note about training with Test The Waters is that your Certification "C" Card will have the location North Pole printed on it. It's easy to be impressed by a diver who clearly has an in with Santa Claus and the Elves.

Over at Anchorage we find ourselves at *Dive Alaska* where a spokesman told me that they also dive year round and at least once a month have a scheduled drysuit training class, or an unscheduled class with the three weeks notice. From May to September they take a 46ft long 12pack boat out to Resurrection Bay to such sights as **Mary's Pinnacle**, which descends down to 200ft feet and rises to 9ft below the surface. **Hidden Treasure** is another notable site as it is a crack in the wall that extends back until you can look up to surrounding 200ft tall cliffs walls. Before I forget, waters temps up here are between 36 to 60° and vis is between 30 to 80ft depending on time of year. On this dive you'll also see tons of invertebrate life. During the winter, Dive Alaska teams go to **Smitty's Cove** in the nearby town of Whittier where starting at a cement boat ramp you will pass WWII debris, shrimp beds, and a barge on your way out to a crane; all within 20-70ft of depth. Don't forget the $10 parking fee and dive flag.

Ron Akeson, one of the top tech dive instructors in Washington State and owner of *Adventures Down Under* in Bellingham, WA, formerly resided in Alaska. I asked him what are some of his favorite dives in Alaska and he said, the 1918 **Princes Sophia** wreck because of its historic significance and the fact that it has lots of life including anemones and wolf eels. The ship rests on a slope from 80-150ft deep. 350 people lost their life when it went down. Ron also likes the **Princes Kathleen**, which rests relatively shallow on a slope in 60-145ft deep. For shore dives Ron likes traveling from Homer by ferry or plane over to Seldovia where you'll find juvenile king crabs, and not so common rock greenling covered with bright orange patches.

There are over a thousand wrecks in Alaska's waters. Besides the two wrecks Ron mentioned, there is the **Kad'yak**; a 132ft long Russian Bark than sank in Monk's Lagoon on Spruce Island in 1860. The **Torrent** struck rocks in 1868 by Cook Inlet while carrying Army troops and supplies to build a fort in the land the USA recently purchased. The 300ft long **SS State of California** sank in Gambia Bay in 1913 between 85-220ft with the metal frame still looming large. A small group of Japanese warships rest off Kiska Island including a submarine, troop transport, and a supply destroyer. Lastly, there are numerous fishing vessels, tugs, and trawlers scattered about the seafloor; this after all, is the homeland of the deadliest catch.

Locals know the southeastern region and the Inland Passage as tropical Alaska. It seems that half my family at one time or another has lived in the Juneau area. To get a birds eye view of the waters surrounding Juneau, I recommend hiking to the top of Mt. Jumbo. Climbing the Mendenhall Glacier with pickaxe and crampons is awesome too, but what I liked best was looking over the side of a zodiac boat at all the sea life, especially around Sitka the water was clear as glass and you saw everything 35ft below; it was like wearing a giant mask. Sitka is home to **Halibut Point State Recreation Site** and just north of here is **Magic Island Underwater Trail** in 40-60ft of depth.

Down at Ketchikan there are two dive sites at the 13acre Refuge Cove State park and shore diving to Mountain Point Underwater Trail in 26-30ft of depth, but only dive down here when the tides are right because large tidal exchanges, especially through narrow channels, are fast moving, indiscriminately dangerous, and notoriously unforgiving.

Now, to have you tides calculated for you, and to enhance your ease of entry and exit in the Southeastern Alaskan waters, I recommend a trip onboard the 90ft long *Nautilus Swell*. The Nautilus offers 11-15 day tours of Sitka Juneau and Port Hardy, BC. From here you can dive the Princes Kathleen and the Princes Sophia, do a sea lion dive near **Barinoff Island**, or just float on some ice, or whale watch. The number of dives you can do a day are really only determined by the tides and currents. The Nautilus Swell uses a 38ft skiff named *Indie* to take you out to the dive sites. You set your gear up when you first arrive aboard the main vessel, and you leave it ready to go on the skiff for the remainder of your stay. I personally loved this set up and no doubt you will too.

As you can see, Alaska has tons of dive sites and many types of training and different diving conditions. I didn't even get to mention diving near the **Sea Life Center** in Seward, the barge at 85ft off **Fox Island**, exploring **Kayaker's Cove**, diving for King Crab in **Barlow Cove**, or looking for artifacts at 80ft from the great tsunami of 1964 around the docks of Anchorage. The only way to dive all these sites is if you have plenty of daylight in the summer and you ignore the rain in the winter. If you are looking for great biological diversity in innumerable quantities, above and below water, then you don't have to look any further than the most northern State of Alaska. Great Dives.

—

Arizona
Delightful Desert Diving

Most tourists come to the Grand Canyon State to snap a few photos, do a little golfing, or hike up and down narrow sandstone trails, but they would be utterly shocked if you told them that Arizona also has some of the best dam diving in the entire southwest. It turns out that some of the largest dam dive destinations are right on the western edges of the state and Arizona has many miles of shoreline that double as a state line.

Near the northwestern edge of the state at 3700ft of elevation the Glen Canyon Dam backs up the water to form Lake Powell. At 186miles long and with over 2000 miles of seemingly endless shoreline to dive and explore a week long vacation here will leave you with little free time to shop in Scottsdale or even visit the Phoenix zoo. The main channel may be too swift or deep to dive, but countless bays and small inlets make this the ideal spot to find stripped bass, trout, catfish, squawfish, and crawfish. Above the surface don't be surprised to find big horn sheep, wild burrows, roadrunners, and wile coyotes. One of the best ways to visit this area is to drive north past Page Arizona to **Wahweap marina** and rent a pontoon houseboat to explore the isolated waterways.

Just down the river at currently 1094ft of elevation and held back by Hoover dam is Lake Mead. This lake is more accessible from the Nevada side, but dive highlighted sites include: the boat dive to the old **Batch Plant**, shore diving around the remnants of the old Nevada side scuba dive park, or around the foundations of the submerged towns.

Flowing down river and held back by Davis dam at 647ft in elevation is Lake Mojave. This 67mile long lake is flanked by several canyons and in places is around 200ft deep. The endangered Razorback Sucker fish is readily found in this man made lake. Lake Mojave, depending on time of season, may have better visibility than **Lake Mead** and because it's less than 2 hours from Las Vegas, it's a popular lake with both divers and boaters; on the Nevada side of the lake there is **Cottonwood Cove Marina** where locals we usually do clean up dives, and on the Arizona side some 8miles north of Bullhead City is the very popular marina called Katherine's Landing. One or two miles north of Katherine's Landing is **Campsite Cove** where you will find a van and a school bull down at less than 50ft on the south side of the cove, and a few boats on the northwest side of the cove. During the summer the vis gets real low here, but as I am writing this, the vis is 25ft near the bus, and over 40ft in the main channel. Jerry Portwood and his well known dive shop *"Dive Shack USA"* is only about 10miles south of Campsite Cove in Bullhead City. Divers drive here from as far away as San Diego on a regular basis. You can camp in Bullhead City at Davis Camp which is a great place to ride on inner tubes and jet ski, or you can drive across the bridge and spend some time at one of the many casinos in Laughlin Nevada and go from casino to casino by way of river boat.

Finally, at 450ft of elevation and penned in by Parker dam is Lake Havasu. The lake is 45miles long and is wedged along the California Arizona border. Above the water line is the old London Bridge brought over from Great Briton in 1997 by, (the name escapes me), the gentleman that invented the McCulloch chain saw. Below the waterline no one is quite sure what lurks deep down. It seems that in 1967-68 white sturgeons (the Columbia River species) were intentionally released into the lake. Fish and Wildlife officials haven't seen any signs of reproductive activity, but with a species that grows up to 20ft in length during a life span of 100years, there could be some 40year old 12ft plus prehistoric toothless bottom feeders still waiting to make a break for the Pacific Ocean.

Now if you're looking for a dam dive site that you don't have to share with any other state, then your best bet, and just over an hour north of Phoenix, is Lake Pleasant. The lake elevation is just under 1700ft above sea level and the water 260ft deep in selected areas when full. Some of the more popular dive sites here include **Scorpion Bay**, **Desert Tortoise Road**, and the **Old Waddell Dam**, which after the construction of the new Waddell Dam, rests 100ft below the lake's present surface level.

Just for the record, Arizona has the most traveling divers per capita than any other state, and according to the perspective of some local divers, the Arizona beach front extends south past **Puerto Peñasco** "Rocky Point" down to San Carlos Mexico, (both in the Mexican State of Sonora), and then the beach front continues right over to San Diego.

Rocky Point, adjacent to the Sea of Cortez, is 63 miles south of the border and the closest location for saltwater checkout dives for most southern Arizona dive shops. With a passport in hand and Mexican car insurance you are not far from sea lions at **Bird Island** "San Jorge", multiple dive boat operations, liveaboard vessels, and dive shops that see United States based scuba dive instructors on a regular basis.

San Carlos is host to **San Pedro Nolasco Island** and too many dive sites to mention in this article. There are two nearby artificial reefs: there is the 180ft tuna boat *"Albatun"*, and the 330ft long ferry boat *"Presidente Diaz Ordaz"*. The visibility here can extend over 100ft and since this area is 4hours or more south of the Arizona border, expect to see bigger and more abundant sea life; from small marine creatures right up to dolphins and whale sharks.

Don't be surprised to find excursions posted in local Arizona dive shops for "Wreck Alley" in San Diego which hosts 6 wrecks including the 366ft *HMS. Yukon*: a Mckenzie class Canadian destroyer that rests on her port side. You also see flyers for liveaboard boats to the kelp forests of the California Channel Islands, or dive shop brochures and web posts to join on countless numbers of the international dive destinations Arizonans frequent each year.

Arizona might have the deepest canyon, some of the driest deserts, and more golf courses than coyotes and road runners, but it also has some of the best dam diving in the entire southwest, and a few fairly frequented marvelous Margarita Ville style scuba dive locations thrown in for good measure with a touch of tropical marine salt; it all adds up to good tides, good times, and great dives.

Arkansas
Ozark Diving At Its Best

When someone mentions the fact that the geology of a region is so unique that over 70,000 diamonds have been collected from the area, you tend to perk up and take notice. If I mentioned the ancient rock formations that produced such conditions also helped make Arkansas attain great diving visibility conditions, then as a scuba diver, you have no choice but to read on with heavy interest. Arkansas divers have some of the best fresh water visibility in the entire southeastern states save for a few well-known springs in Florida. Diving in Arkansas is mostly relegated to reservoir lakes and rivers, like **Norfork Lake** where the vis can reach 40 to 60ft in the spring. I talked with Patten Traver of *Scuba Doo Dive Shop* in Mountain Home, and he told me that at Norfork Lake you can pick a spot to dive based on the topography of the land above the dive site, so if you use a boat and go to a spot that has a gentle slope, that's what you can expect to find underwater too. Dan Weber of the *Jordan Marina* says that one of the most non-natural attractions under the lake is the **school bus** at 25ft. It is actually welded on to a barge and the interior has been cleaned out to accommodate a schooling busload of big bad bass. There's some whimsical welded statues of people waiting to board the bus, but I digress . . . Another interesting site is the two room **dynamite shack** built in 1940 out of big oak timbers and now makes a nice 20x30ft swim thru for crappie and catfish. Now for something really big there is the old sunken Henderson Bridge where there may still be a parked Harley. There is also a 1939 **bulldozer** at 25ft and a 1955 *Snap On* **tool truck** at 70ft. Other sites to see include the stone slab called **Rock of Gibraltar**, **Arches**, a fireplace with a chimney, and assorted house foundations, and oh, don't forget about the Indian arrow heads found around **Indian Island** from 5 to 50ft. Basically, Norfork Lake is an entire article all by itself. I have to add that the depth goes down to 195ft and as Patten Traver explained, "I gets cold and dark past 60ft and there is lots of boat traffic, so bring a dive flag, and it you get a chance, dive the 722mile long **White River** too, because sections are just like a drift dive in Cozumel"; only colder at 54 degrees, and don't forget to have a chase boat follow after you.

Next in line in the White River Valley, in the Ozark Mountains, we have the picturesque dam of **Bull Shoals**, which has 1,050 miles of shoreline and provides electric power to a 6 state region. The max depth is 180ft. There are many objects placed underwater here including: the **SS. Minnow** on the south side of **Gilligans Island** at 20ft, a **troop transport** and **escort destroyer**, the **Bermuda triangle**, **Spanish wrecks**, an alien space ship, and a pirate long boat all the way down at 85ft. Although the sizes may appear diminutive, the will loom large when you note them in your logbook. Bull Shoals is more than just a dive destination; you can also stay at the *Black Oak Resort*, rent a houseboat, see an authentic *1890-mountain village*, or explore the *Bull Shoal Caverns*.

Beaver Lake, the birthplace of the white river, near Rogers, AR has 487miles of shoreline. An anonymous spokesperson from *Lost Bridge Marina* told me that they see lots of divers especially from Oklahoma come here to get certified and dive the sunken banks. A small **helicopter** at 50ft also makes a nice attraction even if you have to wipe off some silt to see the original colors. In 2006 when the water level fell dramatically, you could walk through the remnants of the **Monte Ne Resort** and follow the staircase down to the water's edge. Currently, you will be swimming over the ruins. The vis is 5 to 20ft and expect to see lots of flat slab rocks with fish hiding under the ledges and around long ago cut tree stumps. Recently, someone placed a **winged angel** with cool looking painted eyes, near the dam at around 25ft, which is 5ft before you hit the thermo cline of 50°.

Greers Ferry Lake is home to *Heber Springs Marina*. This lake is over 160ft deep in places. Vis is 5 to 35ft. There are walls and caves to explore, plus diving spots around **Goat Island**. Big fish dart from one rock ledge to the next. A nearby fish hatchery lets you unobtrusively view the local inhabitants.

Lake Degray in the hot springs region and part of *Degray Resort State Park* has 207miles of shoreline and is home to *Ocean Extreme Dive Shop* next to *Iron Mountain Marina*. Vis ranges from 8 to 25ft and there are ledges, boulders, submerged trees. While the surface maybe 80°, at 45ft it can be 62°.

Lake Ouachita is the biggest lake in the state with 60 square miles of surface water and 6 RV parks. There are deeper thermo clines next to the dam and the lake is the stripped bass capital of the world. The lake is also the 2nd cleanest lake in the world according to the EPA. There are underwater **limestone caves** several **sunken boats**, a **golf cart with clubs** for use on a fairway that can reach 200ft deep, diving around **Crawdad Island**, and diving over the quarts crystal rocks that run parallel to layers of sandstone forming what looks like zebra stripe rock formations. **Checkerboard Point** also has some interesting rock formations. In all, there are over 30 dive sites at Lake Ouachita plus a 16-mile long **Geo float trail**.

Lake Greeson in *Daisy State Park* is not far from Diamond State Park and has 7,000 acres of surface water and 418 campsites.

Between the white River and the other lakes there are over 120 species of fish including: bass, catfish, crappie, walleye, perch, and gar. Other favorite creatures include turtles and fresh water, no stinging, jellyfish. Spear fishing for game fish is a popular sport in Arkansas, but verify current regulations for annual times and allowed spearfishing locations. Keep in mine, that Bass spearfishing is closed during spawning season.

So to wrap it up: Arkansas has clean waters with visibility so good that divers flock from over 6 surrounding states. There is plenty of fish to see and a plethora dive sites to explore. Locals get to explore the waters year round, but dress warmly in the winter months when thermo clines are at their coldest and shallowest. In the summer, your options for summer dive fashion are practically limitless and so are the Arkansas fresh water diving destinations, as well as the location types and sites. Great Dives.

California
Channel Islands

The Channel Islands are comprised of 8 islands off the coast of California. These islands are swept by the warm southern waves then swept by the cold currents from the north in a never-ending procession of seasons that concentrate nutrients for kelp and plankton alike. The zooplankton feed on the plankton. Slightly larger creatures feed on the zooplankton, and the food chain keeps going right up to elephant seals and several species of whales. In the middle of this abundant food chain you'll find the California seals, garibaldi, and the ubiquitous California spiny lobster. They all reside on these islands in various mix and match concentrations. Four of these islands, San Miguel, Santa Cruz, Santa Rosa, and Anacapa Island, make up what is known as the Northern Channel Islands. They are all closer to Santa Barbara than to Los Angeles.

The other four islands are south and of little significance. No, not really. In fact Santa Catalina Island may be the most famous of all the islands for both its boat and shore dives. San Nicolas Island, San Clemente, and Santa Barbara Island, I will mention in an order that can only be considered random from a diver who has possibly endured too much nitrogen narcosis and in no way reflects the overall level of adventure or diver satisfaction with any particular island. So here we go:

Santa Catalina Island is 21 miles long by 8 miles wide. Mt. Crizaba rises to 2,047ft. Below the peak are eagles, mountain goats, and transplanted buffalos. The cruise ships love to stop here so some days are busier than others. Avalon Harbor is on the right side of the point. On the left side of Casino Point on the leeward or sheltered side, divers go right in the water at **Garibaldi State Park**. For boat dives there is the nearby **Sue Jack**, a 54ft long schooner, the 162ft long **Valliant**

30

Yacht, the deep reef, or the **Glass bottom boat** at 65ft of depth just to name a few. Up north there is the 69ft yacht called the **Diosa Del Mar**. Several movies as well as TV shows have been made in the surrounding waters because of the clarity and natural beauty. *Coustou* filmed *Night of the Squid* in these waters. Off of **Ship Rock**, a pinnacle, it dips down to 300ft fairly quickly and is a great spot for those of us not quite so famous to get our practice in by filming 6ft long Angle sharks.

On the backside or windward side of Catalina, the **Farnsworth Banks** are quite famous for their purple hydrocoral if you prefer a pinnacle at 100ft. One thing to keep in mind about Santa Catalina is that lobster season is usually between October and March.

Santa Cruz is the largest and most diverse of any of the islands.

There are multiple caves and caverns for divers to explore. **Diablo Point Cave** is the one used most often for cavern dive training. On the north side of the island is the wreck of the **USS Peacock**. This is a wooden hull WWII minesweeper similar to the *Calipso* and down at 60ft. Other dive sites include **Yellow Banks, Potato Rock, Valdez, Frazer Cove, Forney's Cove, Gull Island**, and the **Guardian plane** wreck at Laguna Harbor on the south side. The Yellow Banks are on the south side of Santa Cruz and have large kelp beds and parallel reefs. The Guardian plane wreck is a WWII Navy Grumman 2f-2w near Gull Island at fifty plus feet on the sandy bottom. Gull Island is a small rock where you can see purple hydras at 15-40ft of depth. I should mention that in this part of the Channel Islands National Park you might see dolphins, porpoises, or assorted species of whales.

Santa Rosa Island has a couple of interesting sites including the four-masted 268ft long **Golden Horn**, the 439ft long freighter the **Chickasaw**, the **Talcott Shoals** for lobster hunting and spear fishing, and **Bee Rock** which is a remote pinnacle. The 1894 3-masted 265ft long **Aggi** is just north of the island.

San Miguel is the farthest west island and is typically 5degrees colder than the southern Channel Islands. Expect to see wolf eels and halibut out here. **Wilson Rock** is a well-

31

known remote pinnacle. The **Ex-sachem** passenger vessel is out here along with the 307ft long **Cuba**.

Anacapa Island is the closest island to the mainland and particularly close to Ventura. Anacapa is really made up of three small islets. The third islet is the 40ft high Arch Rock. Anacapa is comprised of kelp forests and walls where kelp bass and sheephead wrasse are encountered along with sea lions, horn sharks, torpedo rays, bat rays, and morays. There is a lot of sea life in the marine protected areas. Some of the dive sites include: **Coral Reef, Landing Cove, Cathedral Cove, Underwater Arch, Aquarium, Guana Banks, Rat Rock, West End, and Barracuda Rock.** There is a WWII **TBM Avenger** torpedo bomber at 120ft in the sand. You may also see remnants of the 225ft long **Winfield Scott** side-wheel passenger ferry, which sunk in 1853 in shallow waters.

Santa Barbara is a small island not much bigger than an islet. It is home to California Sea lions, and harbor seals, abalone, and rock scallops. **Arch Reef** and **Brittle Star Reef** are two hot dive sites here. As far as wrecks go, the **Gaviote**, a SM1 landing ship sits in 75ft of water and the 281ft long **Gosford** also rests nearby. The **Coho** is another wreck a mere 10 miles from the SM-1.

San Clemente Island, which is shaped like a tie and 25 miles south of Catalina Island, is home to many dive sites including the **USS John C, Butler** in Northwest Harbor at 80ft in the sand. This is a 306ft long destroyer escort. Not far from it rests the 157ft long tugboat named the **Koka**. On the backside of the island you will find the destroyer the **USS Gregory** along with lobster and pink and green abalone. Other dive sites include: **Window Pane, Fish Hoot, Outside Boiler, Second Boilers. China Point, Nine Fathoms, Little Flower, Northwest Harbor, Octopus Gardens, LCI Reef, Ordinance Reef, The Caverns, and Castle Rock**.

Last but not least, there is **San Nicolas Island** way out southeast by itself. The Navy separates the local waters here into three zones. The eastern side is mostly off limits and the SEALS here may carry guns. The north and west side have sea lions, harbor seals, and elephant seals all packing lots of blubber, fast flippers, and playful dispositions. You'll find scallops, sea fans and the biggest bull lobsters in these waters. **Begg Rock** is a remote small dive site 8miles northwest of here. Closer by we have: **The Boiler, Three Mile Reef, The Alpha Area, and Dutch Harbor**.

Charter boats visit all these dive sites usually in one to five day charter trips. Most Catalina trips run daily from various embarkation points. To all the islands, you can book either by desired destination or by how many days you want to explore particular islands. Either way, you'll enjoy some great dives.

COLORADO
Getting High While Diving!

Colorado is by far the land of scuba divers with altitude. The highest dive sites break surface records at just around 12 thousand feet above sea level. The lowest water level point is down along the Arickaree River at 3,315ft above sea level. Almost any of the local dive shops will be glad to tell you that the water visibility level increases as you gain altitude. Unfortunately, the temperature of the water decreases as you ascend to higher lake elevations. Local divers have learned to adjust to the various water temperatures by wearing next to nothing in low lying reservoirs during the summer months and donning drysuits up in the highland lakes where ice melting next to the adjacent shore line is known to really make an impact on warming up pristine clear water columns.

At 11,950ft and first on our list where the water is cold filtered and clear is George Town Lake. The lake is situated near an old Victorian mining town. You'll find trout in the water columns. But the big plus to diving here is showing off your dive gear and seasonal ice diving skills to passing groups of big horn sheep or an occasional wandering moose. There are a lot of lakes that fit this highland profile. At Cameron pass down around 9000ft you have lakes such as Chambers, Laramie, Twins, Barns Meadow Reservoir that can reach 100ft of visibility. Down at 8100ft you can achieve 50ft of visibility at such lakes as Dowdy, Lone Pine, Lady Moon, and Nokomis. Aurora Lake at 5750ft elevation, has easy walk in access as well as a sunken Cessna twin engine plane to explore. The visibility can drop down quite low at times, but still try to keep an eye out for crawdads and enjoy a day at the beach for a slight fee. I always like low vis days because they help me hone in my basic skills and especially my navigation skills. Also, I keep remembering the phrase when the vis is low, that "a bad day of diving is better than any good day at the office," and so the search continues for crabs, crawdads, and crayfish.

Farther down at 5430ft and 6.5 miles long is Horsetooth Lake. The visibility may not exceed 20ft but there are plenty of fish to see here and the foundations of the old town of Stout, which rest down at the bottom of the substrate, were covered over in 1946 by the reservoir and give this popular lake a sense of mystery and intrigue. The water depth goes down to close to 200ft and some of the more popular dive site entry points include Dixon Cove, Quarry Cove, Orchard Cove, and Sunrise.

The last lake I'll mention here I held in reserve on purpose. Blue Mesa Reservoir is the largest lake in Colorado. At 7,519ft in elevation, 338 ft of depth in some locations, and over 36miles long this lake has something to offer everyone. This lake is also the largest fishery for Kokanee Salmon (land locked Pacific Sockeye salmon) in the entire USA". So there is a good chance you will see fish in this less than 20ft vis water, but you may also find the foundations of three towns, roads, and railroad bridges all deep underwater with little or no traffic issues.

There are many well-known lakes, but not all of them are easily accessible to divers. Each of the 64 counties that together form the state of Colorado may have their own department of resource rules. Some counties require divers to carry dive flags, to dive with buddies, dive designated locations only, or require prior permission for diving some potential dive sites. Some lakes such as Dillon Lake at 9, 017ft may only allow surface activities such as motor boating, kayaking, fishing, and wind surfing. Water contaminating contact sports such as swimming and scuba diving you may find are prohibited. I guess one would conclude that if you fell off a wind sail board and plunged down below an ever so slight motorboat oil slicked section of water, you might have to swim up and back over to your board, and thus, you could be in violation of lake contamination rules. The bottom line: if in doubt about the rules concerning a possible dive location, ask local officials for advice and permission well in advance.

Lakes such as Turquoise Lake at 10,000ft and named after the locally mined semi-precious stone are surrounded by privately owned land. In this case to dive here you need permission from a local sports club or private owners to cross over their land to reach the lake. This lake in the past has been home and host of scuba dive treasure hunts and local dive shops will be glad to let you let you know when the next one will take place.

As far as diving out of state fresh water locations goes, Blue Hole in Santa Rosa New Mexico has to be the most popular spot. At an elevation of 4,762ft, 81ft deep and at a constant 63degrees in water temp it's the ideal diver get away location. The warmest out of state site, fins down, has to be Homestead Crater near Midway Utah at an elevation of 7050ft. The water depth inside this beehive like natural structure is a mere 65ft of depth before reaching silt and mud. This natural hot springs keeps the water bubbling up between 90-96F. The dome's open roof brings in natural light and helps even those feeling close to phobic, feel more comfortable with these waters. For those local divers living near the New Mexico border, Navajo Reservoir is the place to go. Actually one third of this lake is in Colorado, and the other two thirds are in New Mexico. The elevation is 6,200ft and lots of dive activities take place at Navajo Lake State Park. If you like crossing borders, then you need to dive Lake McConaughy in Nebraska. At 6,200ft in elevation, the "Big Mac" it's called gives you 22miles of lake to kick around in. It's 142ft deep and also 4miles wide.

As for saltwater activities local divers either drive out of state to Bonneville Sea base 40miles west of Salt Lake City. Elevation 4,293ft. You may only get 2-3ft of visibility in this salty environment, but where else can you find a nurse shark and tuna roaming the southwest outdoors?

Keep in mind that if you desire real good visibility, but don't want to pay for air fare then you can sign up for a fee for a scuba diving tour at the Downtown Denver Aquarium. While in Denver be sure to also see the 280,000 marine invertebrate fossils at the Museum of Natural History.

Although the aforementioned lakes and reservoirs are great for getting your dive gear wet and your dive skills fresh, what local Colorado divers are really well known for is their self-sacrificing willingness to travel thousands of miles just to visit tropical fish in their natural native environment. By sheer volume alone, Colorado divers travel more than divers from any other state. Colorado is historically known as a great state for outdoor sports, and the highland lakes and mile high reservoirs just add credence this to this well deserved claim. Great dives.

Connecticut Diving
"Beside The Long Tidal River"

Connecticut sits boxed in between New York, Massachusetts, and Rhode Island yet it still encompasses some 600-mile of shoreline. It was first explored by a Dutch captain in the early 1600's and by 1635, 80% of the local Native American Indian population had perished due to small pox. During the revolutionary war, Connecticut became the arsenal of the nation. Today, Connecticut produces helicopters and nuclear submarines. The unofficial state slogan should be "Silent But Deadly," but perhaps this might scare off would be tourists. Anyway, what all this means to divers is that a long legacy of history equals a long list of shipwrecks, long lost and discarded items, and a chance to connect with moments of past history?

As for the shoreline of Connecticut, much of this area is privately owned, and recently, rules have been made to prohibit shore diving from state boat ramps, or public areas and parks supervised by lifeguards while on active duty. Also, near shore there is a bank of sand that keeps the inshore depths relegated between a mere 10 to 20ft deep. Farther out from shore though, it's a whole different ball game. I talked to Captain Saam of the charter boat *Silver Dolphin*, and he told me a few interesting things about diving off shore in Connecticut. First, 10 miles from his dock slip, there are over a dozen wrecks. Captain Saam and volunteers regularly clear fishing lines from the **Celtic** tug and barge that sit in 68ft of water. The barge split in two bringing down the tug with it. Each time they recover derelict hooks, and anchors, they also find up to 20lbs of lead. It's a popular spot to fish for black sea bass. Every spring they set a buoy here to kick off the start of the annual dive season and you can find the spot marked on coast guard charts. David Mendoza, one of Capt. Saam's Scuba School employees, likes to dive the **Green's Ledge Lighthouse** because at less than 30ft of depth there is so much life between the rocks. Before I forget, Capt. Saam also recommends diving "**Great Reef**". Previous to the 1940's when the old Sheffield lighthouse was in use, ships entering the western edge of Norwalk Harbor would occasionally run aground. Snuff bottles, rum bottles, and even spikes from wooden keels from the 1800's can still be found here wedged in between giant slab rocks. This dive is best done at slack tide or as a drift dive. Expect to see lobsters, blackfish, crabs, and even an occasional seahorse. Capt. Saam says that a couple of other interesting things about diving in Connecticut are the trenches in the Long Island Sound that have rock walls down at 100-120ft deep. Here you can find fluke, flounder, clams, and oysters. A lesser-known fact is that you can find certain types of corals and red beard sponges in the sound.

I spoke with Paul and his daughter Jill Kobrin at *New England Dive Center* in Wellingford, CT. They like to dive anywhere around Fisher Island where there are lots of fish and a few seals. They like diving the 275ft long steamship **Onondaga** that sank in 1918 at 55ft and the 250ft freighter **Olinda** that sank in 1887 down to 30ft. They use the 6 pack *Thunder Fish* operated by Capt. William Palmer. For shore dives they recommend diving at **Stonington Point.** Across this wedge of land and up a bit is the rocky entrance of the **Wall Street** dive site. At **Bigelow Hollow State Park** in Union New England Dive Center has big socials that include hot dogs, and you can bring the sides. They sponsor night dives in the summer at **Fort Wetherill State Park** where you may just encounter a squid, torpedo ray, or a wary lobster. Jill also wanted me to make a shout out for Jerry Shine's "*Shore Diving Guide To New England*". Also check out the book: "*Shipwrecks Of Connecticut and Rhode Island*," by Gary Gentile.

Off shore, Ed Rosacker of *Diver's Cove* in Essex, likes the 231ft long bulk ore carrier **Volund**. The Volund was built in 1899 and rests at 100ft some 30 minutes away by boat. Ed also likes diving off **Fisher's Island**, **Sugar Reef**, and anywhere off Rhode Island. Besides the usual shore dives like **Eastern Point Beach** at the mouth of the Thames River, Ed mentioned that if you have a wheel barrel handy, there is a decent site in front of the defunct seaside psychiatric hospital, but it's a long walk to the water. He also said that conditions at local sites might change in a minute so it's best to come prepared.

Jack La Penta of *Jack's Dive Center*, Inc in Plainville mentioned two very interesting fresh water dives. The first is at **West Hills Lake** in New Hartford between 25-30ft you may get 25ft of vis. At 50ft there is mud. Expect to find fishing equipment from people trying to catch kokanee salmon, bass, and sunfish. This is the lake where an intact Pequot Indian chestnut wooden canoe dating back 350-500years was discovered. There's no telling what else you could find in this lake. Jack also said that if you follow the **Connecticut River** into Vermont the River can reach 100ft deep and you can get up to 35ft of vis. Hundreds of years ago this area was a dump site, now it is a treasure site for old bottles and concretion slate/clay deposits of prehistoric fossils.

The Dive Shop in Brookfield mentions several local dive sites including: 85ft deep Brownstone Exploration and Discovery Park, AKA, **Brownstone Quarry**; a 27 acre former quarry known for bass, carp bluegills, perch and American eel. Also mentioned are Dykes Point, Lyn Deming Park, and Squantz Pond. New London Sub Base might be interesting to explore since it has been used for subs since 1915, but at 40-50ft there is lots of clay and muck. Caution, getting close to nuclear subs could be hazardous to your health and even perceived as a threat to National Security.

One last thing you have to check out before diving off shore near Connecticut is the Atlantis Dive Charters' website, as Capt. Gary Chellis has put together a list of both recreational and technical dive sites. The **Larchmont** for example, is a 1907 paddle wheel steamer at 130ft of depth and an hour out from shore. The German U-Boat, **U-853**, is 2hrs out and rests at 125ft. The **Vineyard Lightship** is 4hrs out and rests at 70ft. These are just a few of the many wrecks the 41ft *Atlantis* charters out to.

Now, I really never got to cover **Avery Point**, the **Waterford Boat launch**, or **Pleasure Beach**, but if you keep off the boat ramps, you just might like these shallow dive areas. Also you might like to volunteer at the Mystic Aquarium, be a trainer for a day, or have a beluga or penguin encounter. As you can see, Connecticut has too many places to dive to list in one article, and since I'd rather be diving than writing, I'll just end this here. Great Dives.

Delaware
Offshore Diving's Gateway

Delaware is the second smallest state in the union. It is only 13ft above sea level in the middle of the state and has only 28miles of shoreline, which makes it barely 3times longer than the shoreline of Lincoln City Oregon, but what makes this little State bigger than a single city on the opposite side of the country is its proximity to so many great Atlantic dive sites. One representative with 23years of diving experience at *Scuba World Inc.* in Dover, told me that part of the reason why diving is so good here is that once you go 13-23miles off shore, the visibility can average 20-100ft. He said that currently, the most popular wreck is the **USS Bradford:** DD-968. This artificial reef was sunk August 10, 2011. The destroyer Bradford is 26 miles off shore, 563ft long, the top deck is at 70ft of depth, and the bottom rests on the substrate at 140ft of depth.

The second favorite wreck has to be the 360ft long **Washingtonian**. This American-Hawaiian Steamship Company vessel was a steam-powered freighter built in 1914. She was carrying 10,000 tons of raw sugar when she collided with the **Elizabeth Palmer** January 26, 1915. She now rests at 100ft of depth. She left Honolulu December 30th, passed the Panama canal January 19th only to sink in 10minutes off the east coast. One man was lost, and two 11ft long Ivory tusks with silver end caps were never officially recovered from the wreck site. She is currently a great place to spear big fish and hunt for lobster. The 300ft long five-mast schooner, Elizabeth Palmer, sank two days later at 90ft. This was the second and last time she sank another ship.

Other collisions making for great wreck dives include: the 184ft long **Cleopatra** passenger freighter that rests at 100ft after a collision on October 29, 1889 with the **Crystal Wave**. The 228ft long passenger freighter **Manhattan** built in 1879 also sank in 1889 after colliding with the schooner **Agnes**

Manning. Her anchor, hull plates, boiler, and engine parts are still on display at 90ft of depth. The 309ft long **City of Athens** passenger freighter built in 1911 collided with the French cruiser **La Galoire** May 1, 1918 and now rests at 110ft. She is called the Ammo wreck because of the cases of 8mm La Belle cartridges she carried near the bow. She also carried pharmaceutical bottles some are still recovered corked with the original contents. One sterling silver pocket watch was also recovered. The 295ft long freighter **Poseidon** built in 1914 sank to 100ft after colliding with the **Somerset** on July 31st, 1918. The 171ft long patrol craft **Moonstone** built in 1929 was given a fatal gash in the engine room by the **USS Greer** in 1943 and essentially still sits upright at 130ft of depth. Tech divers from *Salty Dog Dive Center* in Wilmington like to go here for training purposes.

Besides collisions, there are several submarine related wrecks: The 322ft long steam powered freighter **Satia**, also known as the "Colorado", was struck by a mine on November 9th, 1918 by U-boat 117 and now rests at 90ft. The 325ft long freighter **San Gil** was carrying a deadly cargo of bananas when she was hit by a torpedo from U-103 She now rests between 130-140ft and lists to starboard. The 255ft long **Hvoslef** built in 1925 was carrying a critical cargo of sugar when she was sunk March 10, 1942 by two torpedoes from U-94. She now rests at 142ft deep. The 315ft long destroyer **USS Jacob Jones** (DD-130) was sunk by two torpedoes from U-578 and now rests at 120ft. The 231ft long **SS Five** submarine pretty much sunk itself to 140ft of depth when the crew forgot to close the induction valves and flooded the bow end torpedo room. The 311ft long **USS Blenny** (SS 324) was a WWII Balao-Class submarine and sank on purpose June 1989 as an artificial reef project (ARP). She has four large holes for penetration and sits on her side at 70ft of depth.

Speaking of artificial reefs, we have the 90ft long tugboat **Delilah** that sank January 15, 1999 and sits at 100ft. A US Navy surplus barge, **YC 1479**, rests at 70-90ft after sinking October 10, 2000. The 180ft long "Yogi Bear" **Yog-93** is a sunken navy tanker. The **Gregory Poole** is a 175ft long mine sweeper formerly known as the **USS Cruise** that rests 120-

130ft deep. **The Dry Docks** are five different sites Donated by Bethlehem Steel in Baltimore and rest between 100-130ft. But the grand daddy of all the ARP's has to be **The Subway Stop** or also known as **Red Bird Reef**. Over 100 New York Red Bird Transit Subway cars were sunk in August 2001. More cars have been added to this 1.3plus square mile area along with over 8 tugboats, barges, 86 retired tanks and armored personnel carriers, and thousands of tons of tires.

Near the *Delaware Seashore State Park* after a storm you may find some of the British pennies and halfpennies washed up from the 1785 wreck **Faithful Steward,** which carried 400 barrels of coins. For occasional finds of china plates and cups at 50ft, try the 160ft long **China Wreck** that sank in March 1891. If you are into remodeling, no wreck can match the marble slabs found on the iron-hulled barkentine **Clythia**. If you are in to spearfishing, then you might prefer the **Independence Day Wreck,** also called the "**Bimbo Wreck**", where at 110ft lobster, tautog, and sea bass like to hang out. If you like smaller tropical fish, then dive the **Fenwick Shoals Wrecks**. Swimming in strong currents and surge around 25-35ft deep remnants of tugs, freighters, and boiler wrecks, you may see triggerfish, butterfly fish, yellow encrusting sponges, stingrays, and sea turtles. If you are just out for the view, the 120ft long US Navy tugboat **Cherokee**, nicknamed "**The Gun Boat**", has a deck gun mounted to the bow and sank in 1918 to 100ft.

Other wrecks to visit include: **the Northern Pacific, Patty's Pitcher Wreck, Wendy's Wreck, the King Cobra, John's Wreck,** the **African Queen,** the **Joseph Hooper, H. Buoy, Sandy's Wreck, SI Wreck, Jake's Wreck, Jennifer's Wreck, Arthur T Hall**, and the 1789 British **De Braak** Wreck.

Now you may have noticed that all these wrecks are not directly off the coast of Delaware, but as *Captain Robert Stichter* of *Poseidon Adventures* at www.ladygodiver.org explained to me, there are many wrecks within a thirty-minute radius boat ride from the Indian River South Shore Marina and this includes sites off Maryland and New Jersey too. Captain Robert's 30ft long Seahawk goes out to selected sites every weekend; weather permitting, and twice a week during the summer months. One fun triple wreck trip includes the **Manhattan**, the **Washington**, and the **Elizabeth Palmer** all-in-one mile adventure. You can swim adjacent to the structural outlines of the wrecks or use a wheel and line to plot your own course to discover what no one else has discovered before. Either way, hundreds of years of wrecks are waiting for you to explore. Great Dives.

Florida Caves and Springs
Clearly Awesome Dives

If you are looking for dives with 150ft of visibility, the ability to see fossils from whales to mastodons, or the chance to encounter small shrimps and 12ft long 1500lb manatees, then the Florida Springs and underwater caves are your next diving destination. There are over 100 known and mapped springs and caves in the state of Florida. Most of these sites are off limits to open water or recreational divers. Many sites are on private land or surrounded by private land and only have access by paddling up stream by kayak or canoe. Many sites are only available to divers that have cave or cavern diving certified credentials. I won't go into cavern and cave diving training particulars; suffice it to say that the training is fun and challenging. Almost any time you enter a large cave like opening and the light is visible you are cavern diving, but when the light fades or you are a certain specified distance inside the cave you have now entered the world of cave divers. Besides cave diver training, cave divers use specific gear and specific harness setups, and specific redundant gear to keep then safe and ready for unforeseeable situations. I'm not mentioning all this to scare you, I'm just telling you all this so that if you go to a spring site and they tell you that you can't use a dive light on your dive because you're only an open water diver, there is a reason. Lastly, some places such as the largest and deepest spring in the state, *Wakulla Springs* at 180ft deep, will only let you view the animal life and artifacts below through a glass bottom boat.

So what's left for a recreational diver to explore you ask? Plenty. I have made a list of some of the top places to dive, but this list does not include every dive site. Each of these sites could form an entire article by themselves. So here are some top sites you have to put on your bucket list of fresh water dives:

46

Gennie Springs Outdoors. Two hours from Orlando. This private site consists of seven springs, a camping area, and 200 wooded acres. *Gennie Springs* dips down to 15ft where you will find the entrance to the ballroom that bottoms out at 50ft. The water is extremely clear and all other Florida dive sites have great visibility if they are said to be Gennie-clear. The *Santa Fe River* is a short channel away and you can drift dive the river and look for fossils. Devils Springs is a short distance away too with access to *Devils Ear, Devil's Eye, and Little Devil*. Gennie Springs Outdoors has a fulltime dive shop on site where you can purchase gear and train to become cavern or cave diver certified.

Devil's Den is a prehistoric cave turned into a 2acre dive pond and spring site located east of Williston. Misty steam rises up through a twenty-foot opening in the domed roof structure giving it its name by early settlers. You have to walk down 60ft of stairs to get to the waterline area set up area. The water inside the cathedral like chamber descends 65ft deep. Divers can see fossils of saber tooth tigers and giant ground sloths.

Blue Grotto is privately owned and near Devil's Den. It is a sinkhole that descends down to 100ft. There are three dive instruction platforms and a fresh air dive bell down at 33ft that can be used by up to six divers. The cavern is lit up so that all divers can enjoy the large cavern area. Caution, Turtles may follow you on your dive if they believe you're packing treats.

Morrison Springs in northwest Florida and south of Ponce De Leon. This 161acre park was acquired by the state in 2004. The blue clear pool is about 250ft in diameter and surrounded by picturesque cypress trees. There is a sand entry, a sandy bottom, and a dive platform down at around 18ft. The water is between 67-70° and ideal for freshwater eels, catfish, and bass. There is a vent opening at 30ft with a cypress tree lying across it. A second chamber opening is at 50ft descends down to 90ft.

Crystal River and Springs is foremost the place to go and snorkel with manatees. It is also home to several springs. The most famous is *Kings Springs* with a 75ft diameter cavern bowl at a depth of 25-35ft that goes back 55ft. This gives you plenty of light to view a cavern filled with a saltwater habitat home to tarpon, snapper, and blue crabs. Many charter agencies do guided tours of both the river with the manatees, and scuba diving at Kings Springs.

Wes Skiles Peacock Springs State Park near Luraville has 3 caves, two springs, and numerous tunnels and sinkholes. *Orange Grove Sink* is topped with algae in the warmer months and at 52ft of depth a large cave is visible. The cave opening and park setting make great photo settings. Tunnels and passages cover 28,000ft. Rare amphipods and cave crayfish can be spotted here.

Paradise Springs just south of Ocala is a privately owned sinkhole. Walk down the stairs an you will find fossil whalebone in the cavern wall a few feet underwater. The cavern opens up to 45ft wide and constricts at 66ft of depth then opens into a side cave at around 99ft. The tunnel continues down to 140ft of depth.

Merrits Mill Pond in the panhandle of Florida is home to at least 4 cave systems and 4miles of crystal clear water. There is a dam on the south end and *Jackson Blue Spring* on the north end. A rental pontoon boat makes it easy to get to *Hole in the Wall, Twin Caves, and Shangri-La*. The Georgia blind salamander can be seen in cavers.

Rainbow River Springs near Dunnellon is a drift dive where a guided dive charter boat can drift with you. With over 150ft of visibility you may see fossil shark teeth, otters, fish, shrimp, and turtles. Assorted springs bubble up beneath the river. Start up river of *KP Hole County Park* for the best vis, or drift down to Dunellion.

Manatee Springs is 6miles west of Chiefland. Swimming and 82 camping sites make this a great recreational area. From November to April manatees call this area home. There is a cavern down at 35ft. 200yards away is *Catfish Hotel Sink*.

Weeki Wachee Springs State Park is last on my list. This site is 45miles north of Tampa or 2hours west of Orlando. You can only dive here on a guided dive through a registered agency. This is possibly the only place in the world where you can dive with real live mermaids and take photos by backdrops of an underwater castle.

Caution, any one of these dive sites could turn you into an avid spring and sink hole diver, but repetitive dives and some interesting training could lead to certification as a cavern or cave diver which could lead to further exploration of some 100 other fresh water Florida dive sites. Great Dives.

Florida
Fort Lauderdale

Fort Lauderdale is so close to Miami that some considerate one of Miami's bedroom communities. I guess you notice this trend the most when you are sitting at the Fort Lauder International Airport first thing in the morning and you see a contingent of flight attendants and pilots from various airlines dressed in full uniforms trying to hitch a ride on the first flight going northbound. Most of them will be frank and tell you that they live closer to Miami than Fort Lauderdale, but getting on, "standby", on a quick one hour flight out of Miami, can be a whole day experience; if even possible at all.

For those lucky enough to live in the near vicinity of Fort Lauderdale they have to put up with over 22 miles of sandy beaches, over 75 artificial reefs, and the reputation as the drift dive capital of Florida. Early in the morning it is as if you own a few miles of beach to yourself. The water may be shallow for what seems like a mile or so, so the shore dives almost become snorkel dives at most locations. Still, expect to see plenty of creatures in near shore clear waters.

Now as for the diving in Fort Lauderdale, there are plenty of wrecks, reefs, and wrecks on their way to becoming artificial reefs. One of the oldest archaeological wreck sites is the **SS Copenhagen** resting in less than 30ft off of second reef at Pompano Beach. The twin-hulled steamship was 425ft long before she hit the reef going full speed in 1900. You can float above the metal ribbed remnants or take a photo near the state memorial plaque. A laminated underwater guide from a nearby dive shop can quickly point out the plaque's location.

Another famous Fort Lauderdale wreck is the **Mercedes I**. This 197ft long German freighter, which was nationally televised drifting to shore and specifically coming to rest next to a local well to do residence on Thanksgiving Day in 1984 during the *Hurricane Andrew* blowout extravaganza, now rests at the easy diveable depth of 100ft.

As for artificial wrecks go; it's hard to beat **Tenneco Towers**. Originally five structures were sunk in 1985, but one was turned to rubble after a hurricane. Currently, two towers are at 110ft and rise up 60ft, and two towers rise from 190ft of depth up to 80ft. Like most other oilrigs and towering objects, each level of depth has its own set of local inhabitants, with small fish next to the tower in shallower zones subjected to the whims of waves and currents, and bigger fish in the milder middle zones, and bottom fish where you would naturally come to expect them. Add to this wandering pelagics and schools of swim-by opportunistic feeders, and you have plenty of animal life to discover on every dive.

So how much animal life is in the Fort Lauderdale area? One estimate puts the species diversity at **Datura Avenue Beach** area at 300 species, which makes it the best shore dive in the State of Florida. It also makes it fifth in species diversity for the entire Tropical Western Atlantic. You know when the first four spots in this ranking sequence all belong to world famous Bonaire in the Dutch Antilles; you really can't complain that a dive site all the way across the ocean next to Fort Lauderdale came in fifth place.

So how many other dive sites are there in the Fort Lauderdale area where endless creature encounters are a diver's daily dreams come true? Well, according to some web sites there are 17 natural reefs, 17 wrecks, 17 deep wrecks where only tech divers with mixed gasses, such as *Fill Express Technical Diving* in Pompano, regularly venture out to. Personally, I think the number of actual dive sites is greater in each existing category, but why fill up a logbook with just one geographical region? Save some logbook space for *Bonaire* too!

For boat dives and large amounts of big fish and lobsters, one anonymous person working for *Sea Experience Scuba Diving*, owned by Bill Cole, told be her favorite location was **Third Reef** at 65ft of depth. I should mention that the Pompano Beach area gets less boat traffic, and clearer water too. Also expect to freeze in 72-degree waters in January, and barely stay warm in 82-degree waters in July. It almost makes you feel sorry for the locals who have to put up with warm clear waters year round. Sure, they have to put up with hurricanes from time to time too, but without hurricanes, the local artificial reef program wouldn't be so prolific.

Before I forget, I should mention that *Sea Experience Scuba Diving* (SeaXP) has been in business for 25 years and at the current location for the last 10 years. They are based right on the grounds of the *Bahia Mar Beach Resort*. The Bahia Mar is located 10 minutes from the airport, so divers staying here, really don't need a rental car as it is just a short walk from your room to the dive shop, to the restaurants, the bar, etc. Sea Experience uses one boat for snorkelers, and a separate 45ft long glass bottom catamaran boat for divers. It's best to call ahead to see if they have any current packages that include the Bahia Hotel for a bundled diver/hotel rate. The dive boat operates 7days a week: weather permitting.

On a side note, the Pro-Dive dive and training operation lost its lease across from the Marriott Courtyard and is currently not in operation. Their web sites, which is one of the first sites that pops up when trying to google Fort Lauderdale, suggests that all is well, but down on the bottom of the page mentions that they have joined forces with SeaXP. This is simply not true. One of the instructors did go to work for SeaXP, but that is as far as it goes. If you had air cards, or other arrangements with Pro-Dive, then all the other dive shops in the local Fort Lauderdale area feel for you, but as a rule, can't afford to accept all the coupons, tickets, or vouchers from Pro-Dive that are now worthless on the general market. Hopefully the defunct Pro-Dive website will fade away with time, but I have seen some defunct information stay on the web for years and years. I'll post this info on my own web site in a few months, and take it down sometime before the year 2050. It's just another reason to call the local dive shops for current information and not believe everything you read on the web.

On a positive note, visit the web site of *Force E* who have been at Pompano Beach for the last 25years. They list of plethora of dive sites including reefs, barges, tugs, freighters, etc and also visit the Fort Lauderdale web cams on local beaches. The bottom line, whether you are into sea fans or a fan of the sea, Fort Lauderdale has a boat or shore dive that's just waiting to make you a fan of local Florida diving. Great Dives.

Florida
Gennie Springs Outdoors

Gennie Springs Outdoors is one of those timeless destinations that 10,000 years ago was a natural springs for Pleistocene animals such as local giant ground sloths and roaming ancestral cousins of elephants. For the last thousand years it has been a watering and hunting ground of Timuqua and other native tribes. Before the Spanish marched up north and the monks brought with them their new religion, there were 200,000 native Timuqua and 510 chiefdoms. A mere 67 years later, their numbers had been reduced to 50,000 and only 13 collections of former chiefdoms remained.

The 72 degree year round springs are shaded by 500 year old cypress trees and remained unpolluted despite the fact that at one point a woman named Gennie used to wash her laundry right in the sparkling clear waters. Divers have been enjoying these springs for more than 35 years. The current privately owned outdoor park and camping grounds occupies 200 wooded acres and encompasses 7 natural springs. 4 of these springs are diveable. Gennie Springs and the Devil's Springs System are open to recreational divers while Devil's Eye and Ear System have over 30,000ft of passageways to explore exclusively for cavern and cave certified divers. The temptation to explore these last two sites is so great, that they have had to make it a rule that only certified cave or cavern divers may carry dive lights in the Devil's Spring System. Recreational divers can use or carry dive lights only at Gennie Springs. It makes sense since one is not so inclined to investigate a place that can't be seen within, and where natural light from clear skies above does not penetrate that far.

Gennie Springs is a 100ft wide bowl about 15ft deep until you pass through a 20x4ft cheese wedge opening in the limestone side wall and follow a sturdy rope past the boulders and descend into a 50+ foot deep ballroom. Here you can go up 35ft and touch the ceiling where there maybe several pockets of air left by former divers and listen to strange aquatic sounds, or you can move back into the cave around 50ft and pose for pictures next to the welded gate that prohibits divers from wandering into the Gennie Spring maze that has claimed many lives over the years. You will fill a rush of some 30 million gallons of water passing through here each day. In total, the springs produce over 100 million gallons of water each day. All this water goes out to the Santa Fe River where you can use a third tank of air drifting and looking for shark teeth from prehistoric times. The river is a thick brown color from tannin most of the year, but a couple of months in the summer, the vis in the river can get better than 30ft. A 150ft long run connects Gennie Springs to the Santa Fe River, but don't expect to see any manatees up here especially in the summer. What you will see besides the limestone formations, are a few varieties of fish and big turtles that some people cant resist to hold on to and see for themselves that turtles are in deed, a poor choice to use as underwater propulsion device. However, if you like looking up at over hanging trees, and passing bikinis on inner tubes, then you will definitely like the scenic view.

As for the Devil's Spring System, **Little Devil** is a fissure in the substrate that you can enter and descend down to 42ft. As with all dives here, be careful of excessive kicking with your fins, and you can get some great images of the mouth of the crack and the trees suspended in the overhead sky. You can find vids on You-tube that show divers swimming down a narrow run into a somewhat round well that descends down to 20ft; this is **Devils Eye**. At the bottom is a warning sign near the entrance of **Devil's Dungeon;** this area is off limits to recreational dives. The low overhead and need for lights are life saving indicators that more training is required before entering this area.

Just down from Devil's Eye you will come to Devil's you will come to **Devil's Ear**. Just past the log at 15ft is the entrance to the main labyrinth. The water shoots out of here fast, so be careful and watch out for divers shooting back out of the narrow entrance at the end of their dive. Past the restriction there is a cave warning sign at 45ft and non-cave divers must not proceed past this point. Now it is your turn to shoot out of the opening with vortex speed. Be careful, and hold on so that you don't run into another diver coming in or hurt the log with the indent of your facemask.

The gift store/rental store/air fill and dive store is top notch with T-shirts to make any diver happy and quality state of the art gear for even the most devoted recreational and cave diver alike. One of my good friends from Seattle and fellow PADI Master Instructor, Fred Doner, comes here a few times each year and says the training staff is excellent. This is where he became cavern diver certified. The staff is all NSS-CDS Certified instructors, (National Speleological Society-Cave Diving Section). Many are NACD, (National Association of Cave Diving), instructors too. The main difference between Cavern and cave diving, is mostly the fact that cavern divers are still theoretically able to make a controlled emergency ascent back up to the surface; cave divers may lack this option depending how far they have traversed through an overhead environment. Cave divers also use specific gear such as side-mounted tanks; where cavern divers may only have brief modifications to their existing equipment, cave divers gear and setup is specific, and different from other tech divers too. Cave divers may have stage bottles while open water tech divers may not have that option due to ocean currents. Equipment and training are critical in overhead environments so cave diver courses are usually split up a few weeks apart so you can ingest the knowledge and practice essential skills before moving on. Jacques Cousteau said that Gennie Springs Outdoors has the clearest water in the world. I can't think of any other sufficiently safe place where I'd rather learn to become a certified cavern diver.

Ginnie Springs Outdoors is approximately 2hrs north of Orlando or 40minutes from Gainsville airport. I didn't even get a chance to mention the 55 campsites, or the fact that you can swim, canoe, and kayak, play volleyball, or tube float in the springs or down the Santa Fe River. Gennie Springs Outdoors has just too much to do to include in one article. So if you'll excuse me, I need to do a few more dives, and at least a week of camping before I mention anything else about this great outdoor dive destination. Great Dives!

Jacksonville, Florida
Where diving and fishing go hand in hand

On my first visit to Jacksonville, all I knew was that the city had one of the best zoos that I have ever been to in the nation. The raised platform walkways make it easy to view rare species or get your hand licked by a browsing giraffe. Looking at the pool of crocodiles I had little inkling that I was also standing so close to the land of fish. Groups like the Jackson Offshore Sport Fishing Club and with the help of organizations such as the Jacksonville Scubanauts Reef Research Team, some 60 artificial wrecks have come to rest between 9-45miles offshore. The wrecks are home to baitfish, grouper, and barracuda. Kingfish fishing tournaments take place around these hollowed grounds as well as fishing for other large pelagics such as marlin, amberjacks, and anything else that cooks well like shrimp on a barbi. Although the vis may vary from spot to spot with vis from 40-100ft, you may not see a wreck until you are very close, as the site may be covered fish and obscuring the structure overgrown with gorgonian coral, barnacles, and other resident invertebrates such as spiny lobsters, shrimp, and cryptic teardrop crabs. And just for the record, while oyster toadfish and sheephead wrasse are cool at these sites, lionfish are not, so take and eat these invasive predators anytime you get a chance.

As for the type of diving in the Jacksonville area, one person told me no one goes shore diving because of currents, and low vis. On Jacksonville Beach down to Mickler Landing, old tiger shark teeth, and bones from prehistoric bison, horse and giant ground sloth have been exposed in the sand, so there, is no telling what you could find in the water near shore, if near shore water conditions were slightly better. Dive schools avoid the shore diving dilemma by training new divers at alternate locations. The oldest local dive shop, *Atlantic Pro Dive,* trains divers using a lake in nearby Georgia, where as *First Coast Divers* trains new divers in nearby springs. Springs in this part of Florida rightly deserve their own article, but once the divers in training are certified, they can obtain advanced and boat water status by going out with dive instructors on one of the many existing dive charter operations.

Now before I mention a few dive sites that have given Jacksonville the name of *"The Sea of Fish"*, it is important to give you some background information. Through countless efforts and costs, Jackson Offshore Sportfishing Club has brought about the placements of artificial reefs that are so productive that fishing tournaments and fishing are charters a like have become successful, if not down right famous. With this homage in mind, when a dive boat does part from shore, the first dive site may already be covered with fishing boats, so the secondary dive site may become the first dive site that divers get to descend upon that particular day and since the Captain has the final decision, you more or less sign up to go diving and not to visit a particular site. Second, the weather picks up in the afternoon, so the boat will leave early at 7am to get back before the afternoon weather maturates. On a side note it amazes me how many people sign up for a 7am departure on a plane and arrive at the gate exactly at 7am to see a plane pulled back from the gate and waiting for a last clearance check before the plane heads down the runway. I recommend showing up earlier than this for a boat dive, just to store gear and do a last minute check on dive and camera equipment. Once having left the dock, the local operators will usually try to squeeze three dives in before returning to shore. You may visit two wrecks and a reef in any order followed by arriving back at port around 1-3pm. If you are trying to dive something far from shore like the 615ft long **Dry Dock**, then the time or number of dives may have to be altered. Most dives are between 9-23miles from shore. Some are just as close to dive boats from southern Georgia as they are from Jacksonville itself.

So what are some of these interesting dive sites? Here is a short list that could keep you busy a very long time and not just to see all the dive sites, but to count all the different types of fish you saw too:

To the west, the closest offshore dive site is **Nine Mile Reef**. The site is almost nine miles from shore, but I'm not sure where the site name came from. It's an easy 75ft deep dive where you can encounter a couple of barges, a steamer tug, and a fishing boat sunk in 1988. Keep an eye out here for 15lb plus grouper. The farthest north dive site, before crossing the invisible Florida State border and only 13miles from shore has to be **Rabbit's Lair** at 60-70ft of depth. Several long ledges run here with the eastern ledge vaulting up 10 feet. A steel barge, a minesweeper, and a wooden tug gives this area lots of intrinsic *dive*rsity. A southern boundary wreck and at 85ft max depth should be **Middle Ground**. This is a series of small reefs and home to a tug, but what makes this place so unique is a section called the **Japanese Reef** where the Japanese government set up a pyramid made out of fiberglass tubes. I have no idea what the *porpoise* of this experiment was so don't ask; let's say it's just unique.

Now in between all this area boundaries are dive sites such as **Clayton's Hollar**. At a depth of 85-95ft, this is a very popular dive site. It is almost 17 miles off shore and consists of three reefs. The northern ledge has a swim through, the middle section is a wide mile long reef hosting two tug boats and a barge. The southern section stretches up with a ledge 15ft tall and is home to many lobsters. **Blackmar's Reef**, 95-110ft, has a total of 5 wrecks: the *Warwick*, the *Super*, the *Ocean Going Tug*, a banshee jet fighter, and a WWII Cosair. **East** Fourteen, 65-85ft, has the old Gator Bowl press boxes, red rock reef, and the Y-ledge. The 225ft long freighter **Anna** was sunk as an artificial reef , "reefed", in 1986. The 150ft long **Huggins** was reefed in1987. The 103ft long **Coppedge Tug**, 50-80ft, was reefed in 1988. The **Acosta Bridge Rubble**, 75ft max, **Amber Jack Hole** at 85ft, **Paul Main's Reef** at 75-90ft, and **Montgomery's Reef** at 50-65ft, round out the list of the most popular dive sites.

So there you have it, Jacksonville has a cool zoo, but also lots of older sunken ships, planes, reefs, culverts, cement artifacts, fiberglass oddities, and tons of fish. The dive boat leaves sharply at 7am. The fun and adventure starts the minute you plunge beneath the waves. Great dives!

South Beach Scuba Diving
The Ultimate Miami Vice

You've heard about the Miami Heat and the Miami Dolphins, but did you know that the best way to avoid one and get closer to the other is just a short plunge away from the South Beach/Miami shores? Depending on you charter boat radius, there are close to 80 some wrecks and reef dive sites to visit. Three reasons make the South Beach area such a great place to dive: the hurricanes, the artificial reef program, and the South Beach area itself.

Hurricanes and storms definitely add more vessels and boats to the potential list of wreckreational dive sites. The winds and waves have been known to pummel and destroy older wrecks too. Sometimes wave action will move, turn, or right one of the existing wrecks. And perhaps while the hurricanes don't expose the wrecks as much as the tourists expose themselves along the southern warm sandy beaches, a little removed sand can expose divers to all kinds of formerly buried under water treasures and limestone laden artifacts.

As far as artificial reef programs go, large freighters tug boats, barges, oil rigs, cement bars and blocks, and other man made objects make great homes for all types of local reef and transient pelagic sea creatures.

The boundaries for most South Beach dive charter operations extend northward up to the **Tenneco Oil Platforms** near Fort Lauderdale and southward to the **Blue Fire** at 110ft. This 175ft long passenger freighter was sunk in 1983. The **Doc de Mille** rests at 140ft, but is so far out that it is not often dove on except for long weekends. In between these boundaries there are dive sites of every nature. Some that are unique dive sites include: **The Spirit of Miami** a 727 whose tail section rests in 82ft of depth and the forward fuselage and wings are at 100ft. Tropical storm Gordon in 1995 ripped the aluminum shell apart like breaking potato chips in a wind tunnel. If you're not into planes, how about a pair of 40 ton Vietnam era **M-60**

army tanks at 50ft of depth. The two turreted war wagons are separated by tons of living wall boulders. If you're not into fin kicking, then it's always fun to drift over **Brewster Reef** at 50ft south of Fowry lighthouse. Nearby **Car Reef** is a good spot to find lobsters peaking out of tire wells. For night diving you can't beat **Deep Trench** at 60ft. This 15-20ft wide dug out access for an effluent pipeline used in the 1920's is now an express corridor for topical fish. For archeology purists there is the **Half Moon**, a 154ft long German racing sailboat built in 1908 and sunk in 1930, just east of Bear Cut off the tip of Key Biscayne. A plaque is set up at the preserve site. A laminated guide may be obtained from a local participating dive shop. **Key Biscayne National Underwater Park** is just minutes south of South Beach. Here there are four distinct ecosystems to dive for including: mangrove, Biscayne Bay, Florida Keys, and coral reefs. And if all this isn't enough, just down the road and south across a few waves is the **John Pennekamp Coral Reef State Park**; America's first underwater park which just celebrated its fiftieth year anniversary. If you don't get a chance to dive here, at least take a ride on a glass bottom boat and see what so many years of preserve have accomplished.

Some other more noted dive sites include: **Emerald Reef**, Miami's largest reef. Don't forget to visit the home of a large green moray eel named *Elvis* hanging out in the crevices of collapsed plate coral ledges at **Graceland Reef**. As for boats and ships, the 165ft long **DEMA Trader**, was taken into custody and sunk in 2003 after the ship was discovered to have a slight drug problem. The first artificial reef around here was the 120ft steel hulled **Orion** at 95ft of depth in 1981, and this is the place to visit if you like schools of fish and gorgonian corals. Other sunken treasures include the 215ft long **Belzona Barge**, the three **Belzona tug boats. Wrek Trek** includes the 85ft long **Miss Patricia** tugboat, the **Miss Karkene, Ben's Antennae Reef**, and **Billy's Barge**; all in one convenient location and al between 40-60ft of depth. For those that like plane wrecks there are the **F-4 fighter wrecks** south of Elliot Key. Old bottles can be located near Soldiers Key. And the resting place for many a diver, through a selected mixture of cement, ashes, and sculpture for all eternity, is 45ft deep at the

Neptune Memorial Reef in Key Biscayne. Recently the 165ft long **Princess Britney** was found to have a drug addiction and she is now recovering at 90ft as an artificial reef. Another popular wreck is the 230ft freighter **Sheri-Lyn** that rests at 97ft and is split in two sections. Some other natural attractions include a series of deep reefs called the **Cascades**, the 52ft deep **Fish Hole** north of Miami, and the 45ft deep **Aquarium**. For those that like to dive deep, there is the **Star Trek** at 210ft deep, but because it is out of the recreational dive guide limits I will refrain from mentioning it in this article. Lastly, many dive charters from the South Beach area head down the way to Key Largo to dive sites such as the 510ft long **Spiegel Grove**, which I don't want to mention until after I've spent some serious research time around the Key Largo area. As you can see, the tough demanding world of a writer isn't for everyone, but personally trying to dive everywhere on this water planet is a very rewarding first step...but I digress.

As for the third ingredient that makes the South Beach area such a great place to start your dives, is having the ability to spend time between dives in South Beach itself. In this short space of sand and surf there are numerous restaurants, nightclubs, and beach vendors of every manor, size, and description. Now according to my own personal South Beach diet, it's hard to beat a hot Cuban breakfast before going out on a dive. You may have to settle for a light snack between dives, but that's ok, especially if you are planning a festive night of Greek cuisine at *Taverna Opa* in South Beach on 8th street. Local grocery stores also tend to cater to international clientele with fresh foods and dishes from around the world that you just have to try between active or intentionally inactive beach sessions. Ok, at this point I might have to admit that around this section of Florida I have spent more time on land than in the actual water. It's not intentional; it's just that South Beach is so unique, that you can spend a week here before you even remember that the waves are just a few yards past the bottle of sun tan lotion, and great diving is just beyond edge of your painstakingly adjusted and smoothed out to perfection beach towel. Great dives!

Tampa and St. Petersburg
Two Cities, One Great Place To Dive

It's no big mystery or clandestine secret why there's not a lot of shore diving near Tampa Bay or St. Petersburg. Tampa Bay can on occasion look like a Mocha Grande next to shore, and from the main Gulf water shoreline the vis may be clear, but you may have to go out 25 miles before the water gets 70ft deep. For 130ft of depth, plan to sail or motor out 80 to 100 miles. But before you get on a boat and travel out to the local dive sites let me just mention a few more things. First, the waters can change temperature and be 82 in the summer and 52 January to February, so dress or undress accordingly. As far as vis goes, the vis can range from 25ft to 100ft. From June to August the vis is comparable to Caribbean islands such as St. Croix. I asked around what are the best dive sites to explore and hands down the most popular site was the wreck of the **Sheridan** on **Pinellas County Artificial Reef #2**. This wreck is full of baitfish and large grouper cruising in and out of the wreck. A large rectangular encased raised letter "S" mounted on a wall makes a great backdrop for taking pictures of fellow divers. The DT Sheridan was an ocean going 180ft long tugboat. She now rests 75-80ft deep and about 100yrds from 180ft long **USCG Blackthorn**. This Iris Class Buoy tender was struck by the 605ft tanker SS Capricorn and was caught by an anchor and capsized with loss of crew. The badly damaged ship was towed out to Reef #2 and sunk on Jan 28th 1980. **Tanks-A-Lot Dive Charters** has many vids on youtube that you can view of this site. One spokesperson from Tanks-a lot told me that the site is so popular because the water conditions here make it feel like swimming pool diving. Anyone new or advanced will like diving here. Easy diving conditions, and thirty plus years of wreck to reef growth.

For second place, the Tanks-a-lot spokesperson liked **Veterans Reef**. The reef sits at 42ft of depth and consists of 3 steel barges in a rectangular shape of about 300ft by 600ft. A *Lockheed Neptune P2V-3* plane rests in the center. A tall yellow buoy with a U.S. flag on top marks the surface spot commemorating past veterans. Lots of soft corals dot the structures. Expect to see tiny sardines, small grunts, and huge Goliath Groupers.

For third place he mentioned the ledges. There are limestone ledges running everywhere along the west coast of Florida. Ledges where the reef stands now, and ledges that follow the shoreline millions of years ago, when waters were lower, and rivers were more abundant. Chances are that a quick dive overboard and you may find one of these a ledged prehistoric reefs. There are so many of them that they are constantly being re-found and renamed. This may explain why bouts of reefer madness have given names to local dive sites such as **Dire Straits** and **One-eyed Willy**.

On the serious side though, some dive sites have more respectable names such as **Madeira Beach Reef** or **Tarpon Spring Reef**. Some reefs are known for the artificial structures that are sunk on them such as **Indian Shore Reef** with 2 WWII LSM landing ships, a silt hopper, and 125 pillboxes at 46ft of depth. **Treasure Island Reef #2** at 35ft of depth has a shrimp boat and pieces of concrete. **St Pete Beach Reef** has rubble from the old Corey Causeway sunk in 1976, pieces of the Skyway Bridge, and in 1984 they sunk a 200ft barge and 10 army vehicles out here.

Some dive sites are known for one item in particular, such as the **Tug Orange** at 45ft, which is 100yrs old and is home to nurse sharks. The **Gunsmoke,** an old shrimping boat had a run in with bundles of invasive weed named after of Mary Jane and local officials took such offense to this, that they sunk the boat down at 80ft in 1977. Besides being a popular wreck for fish and soft coral, she has had a sorted past history of association with alleged turn of the century pirates and supposedly other bone breaking encounters. Also I should mention that **South County Artificial Reef** at 45ft of depth has two reef systems and is known for nurse sharks activity and whale sharks have recently been found near **The Tug and Barge** at 105ft of depth. The limestone reef ledges themselves have been recently shown to have an increase in frogfish sightings.

One spokesperson from ***Jim's Dive Shop*** in St. Petersburg told me that their two other top dive spots besides the Sheridan were the **Army Tanks** and **The Rube Allyn**. While 8-10 tanks and an artificial reef at 50ft and stacked like a pyramid out of cement bridge pieces, culverts, and other material are interesting, what I liked most about talking to Jim's impromptu representative, was the fact that Jim's Dive Shop has started a local geocaching movement to give divers one additional compelling reason to dive the local waters.

Oh, and sure, everyone boasts of waters filled with bonito, cobia, hogfish, kingfish, mackerel, snapper, and wahoo, but not quite like Tampa and St. Petersburg. The St. Petersburg Open is claimed to be the world's largest spearfishing tournament. Members of the *St. Petersburg Underwater Club*, established in 1952, have been holding the tournament since 1966 with approximately 300 participants and thousands of spectators each year. And how can you go wrong with a 90lb amberjack, 90lb grouper, or a 9lb lobster? Some of the tournament size creatures were even bigger depending on the year, but I just liked rounding off with the 9's. For a 123lb Grouper, or a 50lb wahoo, one of the fastest fish around, you'll just have to enter the tournament yourself.

The other thing I like about diving in St. Petersburg and Tampa, is that both cities are not far from many spring diving sites, so you can try a little fresh diving too on the same trip. If you are in Orlando on vacation, it's not that far away to add on a day or two of diving off the west coast of Florida. I mean, after all, Orlando is a town where the biggest company is operated by a mouse, and everyone can use a break from a small world after all, or is it once in a while? Or better yet, Come to Tampa, and take a Minnie two-day break in Orlando to see some Goofey sights between dives. You win either way

Now, I'm not trying to say that Tampa and St. Petersburg are like Ying and Yang when it comes to diving, but while you might frequent a dive shop in Tampa, the charter boat you go out on may depart from a dock in St. Petersburg. Or it might be vise versa. Either way, both cities are a boat ride away from internationally famous spearfishing grounds and sites where you can easily enjoy great dives.

Vandenberg

It was May 2009, when the former missile range instrumentation ship called the USAF General Hoyt D. Vandenberg was intentionally sunk off Key West Florida. She is the largest ship sunk as an artificial reef in the Florida Keys National Marine Sanctuary and the second largest ship in the world sunk for recreational purposes. Her former surface missions included bringing troops home from Europe at the end of WWII, spying on the Russians, and hosting the cast and set of the movie "Virus". Now her mission is to create a marine habitat, relieve pressure off nearby reefs, and boost the local economy.

Before I mention how she has done on these three last areas let me just reiterate some background information. "Vandy", as some locals call her was first acquired by the artificial reef society in 1999. She remained docked with the rest of the ghost fleet in Norfolk, Virginia until March of 2007. She was purchased for 1.3 million dollars and by the time all was said and done, she cost 8.6 million to sink, but that included some 75 thousand hours of clean up work so she wouldn't be toxic to fish or dangerous to divers. The cost at first seems high, but when you consider that Florida expects to earn 7.5 million a year in added tourist dollars and the life span of the wreck in over a hundred years, then you can see that the long-term cost is somewhere closer to a penny spent for every dollar they earn. I can't think of one other tourist attraction that has even half that much lifetime earning potential. So for the state and especially Monroe County, it's an economic no brainer, a much-needed local job creator, and a great dive site for aquatic spectators.

When they built the Vandy in 1943 in Richmond California they had no idea that the ship would play so many roles over so many years, but as you dive along the ship you will see Cyrillic Russian letters left over from Vandy's duty as a vessel invaded by an alien force from outer space. I know what you are thinking, it's hard to believe that an alien race would attack scientists of any nationality when aliens are so often portrayed in the real world as visiting rural American farmlands and diabolically annoying uneducated locals who typically consume elevated levels of adult beverages. Well anyway, the Russian signs look impressive and real even if the movie doesn't.

Now the Vandy is just passing the one-year mark in its role as creating a marine habitat. To illustrate this point I'm reminded of the Mahi, a 135ft minesweeper sunk in 1983 off of Oahu. At first it was barren and few fish could be found on the wreck, and one lone sandbar shark swam around it. Now, 25 years later. The Mahi has rusted through and cracked in places. It looks more like a reef with thousands of creatures living on it as well as swimming over it. Algae have given way to coral heads and the ship looks like a coral island surrounded by a sea of sand. It could be said that the same transformation is taking place on the Vandy, only that the algae on the Vandy is currently being consumed by formerly rare sightings of longed spined sea urchins. It could take another 10 years or so before the growth of the coral is noticeable. What is noticeable however are the huge schools of fish that have already taken over the decks of the Vandy and the barracuda just waiting for one of the fish to make a wrong move or dart in the wrong direction. Spiny lobster usually found five miles closer to shore in shallower waters are also being spotted here.

The Vandy is 7 miles from Key West. The area is frequented by water currents flowing from the Gulf of Mexico, the Everglades, and also by that little pool of water commonly known as the Atlantic Ocean. It all adds up to an area rich in biodiversity flowing from multiple regions on a seasonal basis. What does this mean to you? On one dive on the Vandy you may encounter a giant loggerhead turtle. The next dive you might encounter a school of tuna, a family of dolphins, or southern stingrays. Big pelagics will move in and out with the currents, but the usual suspects such as parrotfish, wrasse, and small invertebrates have already moved in on a permanent basis. The one thing constant about this artificial reef is the unending change in creature encounters making no two dives exactly the same.

Ok, to be honest with you, even without the sea life no two dives could be the same on the Vandy. At 522ft long and 100ft tall, there is too much space to explore on a single dive, let alone several dives. The top of the ship is at a depth of 40ft and the ship rests on a sandy bottom down at 140ft. You can quickly see from a diagram that the wreck can be penetrated on several levels and only trained divers should enter certain levels and only trained tech divers should descend down to the sandy substrate and check out the four 8 ton anchors or the bottom of the rudder.

For most divers it is best to plan a dive and concentrate on visiting one surface section of the ship. You might want to float above the radar dishes to take a few snapshots to show your friends back home. You might want to explore the telemetry antenna, elevator holes, or the atmospheric balloon deployment area. The only way you can possible travel along the entire length of the Vandy is to coordinate the dive with the charter boat captain to pick you up at the other end of the ship at the end of the dive, but this can only be done if the currents are working for you. The problem with this type of dive is that it may not give you much time to stop if something really catches your interest.

Besides the recreational diving the Vandy gives tech and wreck divers ample opportunity to penetrate the interior of the ship. Holes cut along the length and at different levels ensure multiple safe emergency egress options. The Vandy is state of the art when it comes to artificial reefs and as you can see it makes a great habitat for sea life.

Just by being such a spectacular dive site, local dive charters and dive shops are busy booking trips to the Vandy instead of sending divers to the Dry Tortugas and other reef areas. This gives the local reefs a big break from ever present the tourist activities. You can still book a day to dive the Vandy then move over to do a shallow dive at the reefs, but you can also spend a day on the Vandy and put off diving the reefs for another visit altogether; this option definitely takes pressure off the local reefs.

As for what to wear while diving, in the summer you can get by with a 3ml shorty or a farmer john. During the winter months when the currents dip down to 65 degrees, it's recommended to wear at least a full 5ml wet suit.

From this writing you can see that it's been a great first year underwater for the Vandy. Moving in and calling a place home is a difficult undertaking for anyone above or below the waterline, especially if you're an invertebrate. The human volunteers did a great job making the ship diver friendly. The sea creatures are colonizing as quickly as possible. Large pelagics are swimming by on a periodical guest appearance format. Now all the Vandenburg needs is some outgoing divers to stop by for a look, adventurous divers who look a lot like you and me. Great dives.

Georgia Diving On My Mind

When I think of diving in Georgia, my first thought is of a prehistoric landscape where the Atlantic was shallow and 80miles east of the current shoreline. Mammoths foraged along this coastline and when they died, left their bones and tusks resting on sandstone that was formed by bits of seashell, sand, and mud, 2million years before their time in another sea that once existed in another time. When the glaciers melted and the seas rose, this area once again became a sandstone reef where Pleistocene gray whales and currently rare Atlantic right whales calved and called home. **Gray's Reef** is now a national marine sanctuary and besides 36,000yr old jawbones of whales and mammoth fossils this 22sq mile area is also home to over 150species of fish, sponges, soft corals, and even loggerhead turtles. At around 65ft deep, some 17nautical miles off shore, and with water temps in the 80's during the summer months, you can see why thoughts of diving here are hard to set aside.

You might want to come to Georgia just to dive this one site, but then you would miss out on the 441ft *A.B Daniels* liberty ship sunk in 1975 or the nearby *R/V Jane Yarn* research vessel sunk in 2007. South and East of St Marys Inlet there are at least seven artificial reef sites some with rubble from bridges, wharf rubble, and others composed of pallet balls. Site **KBY** is 10miles off the coastline and good to dive year round. Besides the basic ARF components, site **F** has M-60 tanks. Site **SFC** has the landing crafts *Optimist* and *Scalper*. Site **HLHA** (old G) has the workboat *Striker*, the *Nettleton* liberty ship, and a 152ft long research vessel. Site **CDH** has the *Esparta* wreck and an 85ft steel trawler. These sites were all off of Georgia, but the charters out of St Marys also routinely go across the invisible state line to 16 additional sites off the coast of Jacksonville, Florida for some coral reef diving as well.

As far as fresh water diving goes, Georgia has several lakes and rivers to try out for size. **Lake Lanier** has a few popular dive sites including **West Bank Park** and **Two Mile Creek Park**. One of these sites offers almost two miles of shoreline entry, but it escapes me which one it is. You can also dive the pilings around **Brown's Bridge**, or search for a camera that was lost at **Mask Cove** in 40ft of dark water with 5-20ft of vis. Lake Lanier offers 692miles of shoreline and is over 160ft deep. The lake is only 40minutes north of Atlanta. There is silt and mud on the bottom, so careful with the fin kicks and carry a light, a compass, and a knife for cutting fishing line.

     Carters Lake is 11miles long and has 62miles of shoreline. Going well beyond 450ft deep in places this lake has a level diving for everyone. 3lb channel catfish, 7lb flathead catfish, bass, bream, walleye, and crappie will judge your diving skills here.

     For a body of water strictly dedicated to divers try **White Stone Diving** formerly known as *Dive Haven* in White, Georgia. This 19acre quarry filled in with water to a depth of 165ft. It is currently privately owned and open on the weekends from the end of April until November when winter sets in. So check for current park fees and open dates. There is a crane down at 40ft. You'll also find several boats and a school bus. A 2ft long catfish likes to hang out around the van. Bass and turtles are also found here, but the main attraction from Mid-September to November is the cute little fresh water jellyfish. The vis can be 40ft. The surface water can reach 82° degrees, 70° at 20ft, but 46° at the bottom. So plan on using a 3ml wet suit and a hood if you like a little depth.

     Last and not least are the local rivers, like the **Chattahoochee** or the **Etowah**, where the vis might not be as good as the lakes, but where you can still get your gear wet and have a chance to feed some local resident fish or film a catfish who really thinks you are some kind of crazed paparazzi.

     Another lucky break for Georgia divers is the close proximity to so many other state dive sites. Divers from Georgia can zip over to **Lake Jocassee** in South Carolina in about 2 1/2hours. **J Strom Thurmon Lake** shares the border too. Florida springs are about 4hours away and Jacksonville dive sites are available by charters for the day or by car for the weekend or longer. For a guy that used to drive from Seattle to Port Hardy, Canada in about 11hours, these distances from Georgia to elsewhere seem to be refreshingly easy drives.

Finally, Atlanta is home to **The Georgia Aquarium**; the largest aquarium in the known galaxy or this world according to the Guinness Book. Bernie Marcus, co-founder of The Home Depot, gave $250million to build this ultimate best of the best aquariums. Where else can you go diving with whale sharks, manta rays, cownose rays, leopard rays, saw fish, zebra sharks, tarpons, pompano, and bowmouth guitarfish? The *"Journey With Gentile Giants"* tank temp holds 6.3million gallons of salt water at 75-78°, and is 284ft x 126ftx 30ft deep making it one of the best dive experiences on this planet. Check online for current dive conditions, fees, and available event times; it's a three-hour program including a half hour dive.

AT&T donated $110million to make the ultimate dolphin show and habitat. If this isn't enough, then visit the four beluga whales in *Cold Water Quest*. Their buddies include harbor seals, and African Penguins. At *River Scout* watch the endless play of short-clawed Asian otters. Albino alligators, assorted turtles, milk frogs, poison dart frogs, archer fish, red piranha, black crappie, bowfin, electric catfish, long nose gar, and pacu make up some of the 500 species found on the premises: some 120,000 individual members strong. And I didn't even mention the *Tropical Diver* area where coral reefs have come alive and are perhaps the next best thing to actually filming for Animal Planet off the coast of Indonesia.

The Georgia Aquarium also offers behind the scene tours. You can have a birthday party here, sleepovers, school events, or arrange for a special event. If you want catering, no problem, but I recommend not ordering calamari in front of the sharks. Although it may taste good, it's just in bad taste. For those of you who haven't seen the movie Nemo, I'll explain the shark twelve-step program some other time.
So there you go, prehistoric artifacts at dives sites within a national marine sanctuary, precipitous lake diving, and preeminent Aquarium diving. Add dozens of wrecks, artificial reefs, and hundreds of species of fish and it's no wonder that

Georgia diving is on my mind. Now, It just might be on your mind too. Great dives.

Hawaii

I was just seventeen when I first snorkeled around Kauai, but that's all it took to fall in love with the Islands. I eventually moved to Oahu and attended the University of Hawaii while working for Pan American World Airlines. At the time 80% of the local kama'aina population lived on Oahu, so traveling over to Maui, the big island of Hawaii, or Kauai was an exotic yet relaxing vacation. On Kauai we always stayed at the Poipu Beach Hotel until hurricane Eva wiped it off the map in 1983. My brother and I did a shore dive here before the hurricane and the undertow was so rough, that we spent most our dive just trying to make it back to shore. Had I known then that about **Turtle Bluffs**, or that we were just a few hundred yards from the **Sheraton Caverns**, our initial dive on Kauai could have ended up way better, but in those days, dive sites were mostly word, sketchy maps, word of mouth, or trial and error. Some of the 14 shore dives currently on Kuaii include: **Koloa Landing**, **Anini Beach**, and **Tunnels Beach**. *Seasport Divers* has more info on their website on these as well as other dives off Kauai.

Bubbles Below started trips out to **Ni'ihau**, **Lehua Crater,** and the west side **Barrier Reef** in 1984. Not only do you dive pristine reefs out here, but also on the way across the channel, you may see sperm whales, pilot whales, killer whales, false killer whales, bottlenose dolphins, and rough toothed dolphins. Several miles out on the west side of Kauai is the almost 11mile long barrier reef where you can see Acropora corals with their associated chevron butterfly fish and the rare Hawaiian Monk seals. Along the trip to the west side you may see rare seabirds that are too skittish to go near the populated areas of the islands, and all this in my book makes Kauai the most exotic Hawaiian Island; with or without the Waimea Canyon, the Grand Canyon of the Pacific.

At Lahaina on Maui they had already begun to map many dive sites. Our favorite was the USS Blue Gill submarine, max depth 140ft. You could stick your head in a torpedo tube next to some black coral and end up with a stunning photograph two weeks later after the film developed. The Navy has moved the sub to deeper water to keep narced or unscrupulous divers from breaking into the sub. Since then, divers have turned to **Molokini Crater** as the number one dive destination off Maui. Actually, Maui has over 80 dive sites including some 22shore dives. You see, in Lahaina, you turn the boat in a southerly direction and you end up diving at **Molikini Marine Preserve**, go straight across the bath tub like water way and you end up diving the lava tubes off the island of Lanai where some of my favorite dive sites include: **Menpachi Cave**, **Shark Fin Rock**, and **Three Fingers**, turn northwards and you end up diving off the coast of Molokai at **Fish Bowl**, **Fish Rain**, or **Hole in the Wall**. You can literally do three dives in one day and include three different Islands in one boat trip. That gives you over 20 shore dives, and close to a hundred boat dive sites to choose from when you dive off Maui. Being able to watch a sunrise from 10,023ft up on Haleakala or viewing the sights on the road to Hana make the visit to Maui even more spectacular.

Our next stop is the big island of Hawaii, namely the Kona side. This is where everyone goes to go night diving with the Mantas. Big Bertha is a manta with a wingspan of just over 13ft. Dive charters here also do night dives over deep waters where they place divers in the water next to the boat and while holding on to a rope you just sit and wait for sea life to swim by. You can see squids, silky sharks, dolphins, or iridescent comb jellies, and if you are really lucky, you might see 6inch pelagic sea horses. *Jack's Diving Locker* calls this the **Pelagic Magic Dive**, while *Kona Honu Divers* call this the **Black Water Dive**.

Some of the other dive sites on Hawaii include: **Henry's cave**, **Garden Eels**, **Pyramid Pinnacles**, **Turtle Heaven**, **Kaiwi Point**, and **Long Lava Tube**. On the Hilo side of the big island shore dives include: **Kehena**, **Isaac Hale Beach Park**, **Richardson Beach Park** and **Leleiwi Beach Park**. The Hilo side is the rainy side of the island, but you have to come to this side to see the magnificent black sand beaches.

Separating Hilo from Kona are Moana Kea and Moana Loa. Moana Kea is 13,803ft high and has enough snow for skiing on during the winter months. It is also home of the highest alpine lake in the U.S.A.; 10ft deep 1.8acre Lake Wai'au.

Oahu is the last stop on our quick tour of the Hawaiian Islands. There are less fish to see on the reefs of Oahu compared to the outer islands, and the dense population has taken a toll on some of the reefs and that's why **Hanauma Bay,** which used to be easy to dive in is now a tough place to dive. You've to get here early as 6am as the parking lot may be full by mid morning, and you have to view a park rules and ecology video before you can lug your gear down to the beach. Best entrance from the beach is straight down the telephone line, and no feeding the fish! If you are diving with a dive guide from a local dive shop, the logistics process is way easier. All this effort makes the other 30 some shore dive sites look and feel comparatively easier to dive. Some of my favorite shore dives include: **Magic Island** where we caught slipper lobsters, found big eels, and discovered big shells after storms. **Pupu Kea, Sharks Cove**, and **Makaha Caves**, all have caves and caverns with white tip sharks, big eye fish (oveoweo), and slate urchins. Sharks Cove is a great night shore dive for seeing bioluminescent organisms, and there is a blowhole type entrance in the middle of the old lava field on the right side of the beach. You jump in the hole slightly after the wave comes in then swim through the two people wide lava tube the short distance to the open ocean.

Boat diving adds another dimension to diving off Oahu. Boat diving makes the reefs off **Toilet Bowl**, **Sandy Beach**, **Pokai Bay**, **Waimea**, **Kaneohe Bay Islands**, and **Rabbit Island** accessible. The 135ft minesweeper, the **Mahi** is my favorite artificial reef on the islands. I took photos of it when it first sank in 1982 and went back out with *Aaron's Dive Shop* 25yrs later to take digital images of the changes; it is one of the most dynamic and active reefs in all the Islands and it represents what local Hawaiian divers and shop owners truly can achieve when they work together in the Spirit of Aloha. Great Dives

The Hawaiian Mahi

Aloha, half a mile off the western shore of Oahu rests one of the best examples of when a wreck truly becomes a reef. The *Mahi* was a 165ft long Navy minesweeper converted into a cable laying vessel. It was sunk in 1982 as an artificial reef. At the time, the decks were void of marine life except for a few Damselfish and occasional larger fish passing by. A six-foot sandbar shark swam near the wreck, and an eight-foot wide manta ray circled above the site. That was the extent of the marine animal life. On that first dive we swam through the main bridge and then down to the sandy bottom at ninety-two feet of depth.

Thirty years later, the Mahi is home to thousands of resident and transient sea creatures. Schools of eagle rays and spiny puffer fish take turns floating in the currents above what is left of the main bridge and radio antennas. Coral outcrops adorn the main deck and exposed sides of the ship. There is almost too much diversity of various sea creatures and countless numbers of fish to take images and capture them all in frames this time around.

A local captain insists that it wasn't hurricane Eva that turned the 800-ton Mahi around so that the stern now faces shore. He claims it happened after just a small storm, which could be true considering the powerful waves, winds, and currents generated by even a minute gale. Previous storms have helped cave in the main bridge section of the Mahi as well as the starboard midsection. While the port side is relatively intact, the starboard side looks like a fringing reef sculptured out of soft pliable clay. Hundreds if not thousands of fish pass through this area on a daily basis on their never-ending quest for safety in numbers and their simultaneous search for their next meal. The view of the colorful fish schools passing through this coral encrusted region is spectacular.

Swimming along towards the bow, you'll come right up to the large reel that once lowered cable down below the waves. It's covered with coral and now appears to be a cleaning station for bigger fish to get worked over by small rainbow colored wrasse.

The entire wreck is just the right length for swimming completely around and then across the main deck on a single tank of air. There's enough of the ship left to cause a wreck diver's imagination to run wild, and the build up of coral and other marine life is guaranteed to impress dive buddies, photographers, and especially budding reef ecologists. After thirty years the Mahi is still one of the best dives off the island of Oahu, Hawaii and I recommend that it's a "must see" for anyone visiting within a few thousand-mile radius of this tropical island paradise. Mahalo.

Idaho At Altitude
Deep Lakes And So Much More

Idaho may be a quiet state, nestled in and surrounded by six other states plus British Columbia, Canada, but a state as long as Oregon and Washington combined, and covered with rivers, reservoirs, lakes, and pure mountain water springs, is literally bound to have some great dive sites, so I asked a few local divers what some of the best dive sites were called, and where you could find them too.

I asked one diver at *Dive Magic* in Boise what her top local places to dive were and she said **Payette Lake** in McCall, Idaho and next to Ponderosa State Park. Payette Lake is 5,000ft in elevation, covers 5,330acres, and is 392ft deep. At 30ft of depth, it was 68° a few days before writing this article, and the vis was over 30ft. She likes **Fishers Pond** in Hagerman because even though the depth may only reach a max of 13ft, the vis can be more than 50ft. She also likes **Redfish Lake** in Stanley, which is deep, has good vis to view bull trout, but the temp can be 45 to 55degrees.

Mary Branchflower from *Boise Water Sports* also likes Payette Lake. She says the students like the fool's gold and the glittery pyrite covered substrate. Mary was down doing a deep dive the other weekend; 85ft here equals 108ft at sea level, so you can see how easy it is to go deep at this site. Mary likes **Dierkes Lake** east of Twin Falls. This site was a 5acre orchard farm, but it was sitting on top of lave tubes, and when they collapsed, the site became a 25ft deep lake with vis between 25-30ft except on weekends, and is now home to blue gills and trout who seem to like the Orchard's tree stumps. One of Mary's bucket list dives is **Red Fish Lake**. It's called red fish because of the number of sockeye coming back to spawn, literally would change the color of the water. The elevation near the local lodge is 6,547ft. The lake is 4.5 miles long and 387ft deep. There was an avalanche on the north end of the lake making it a pretty interesting tumble trees dive site. Mary also want me to mention that Idaho divers may be inland land locked, but they are just a few hours from dive sites in Oregon, Washington, and Utah too.

Tammy Browning from *Island Scuba Emporium* in Idaho Falls, told me that for away dives and collecting rings and sunglasses, you can't beat the diving next to where everyone cliff dives at Fire Hole, Wyoming. Locally, Tammy likes **Ririe Reservoir**. I heard the max depth was 120ft on a wall dive near the fishing dock and also a good spot for finding fishing lures. Tammy likes this spot because there are crawdads everywhere and as a group, they will usually collect and cook a whole mess of crawdads at a party following the dives. She also mentioned to me that even though the vis may be less than 10ft, divers go out in the river right in front of the dive shop just to view the rock formations.

James Flodin from *Divers West* in Coeur d'Alene has been diving for over 30years. He likes diving **Lake Coeur d'Alene** because of all the wrecks that have accumulated on the bottom of the lake over the past several hundred years. The lake itself is 220ft deep, 25miles long, and at 2,125ft in elevation. At 100ft there are three wrecks that include the **Seeweewana**, the **Spokane**, and the **Rutledg**e. Gamblers used these pleasure boats in the 1940's. If you go to Youtube you can see video of divers swimming through the Seeweewana. Paint is coming off the white washed interior walls, but other than that, the boat looks almost seaworthy. For shore dives, there is a tug and barge in 40ft of water near Eleventh Street Marina. For shallow dives, the **Harrison** steamer has its bow at 12ft and the stern at 40ft or dive the **Bonnie Doone** at 20ft near the bridge at the resort boardwalk. For technical dives there is the **Eagle** tug off Tubbs Hill at 120ft or try the **Flyer** at 140ft. Off of **Three Mile Point** was the dumping site or final resting site for many a boat and barge. Besides all this, it is rumored that there are old model T cars on the bottom of the lake as a by-product of driving across ice in the winter. A load of silver ore is said to have gone down in the lake back when silver mining ruled the area, and supposedly there is booty in the form of submerged slot machines near Tubbs Hill. You can clearly see why this is such a great lake to explore.

Now if you really want too go deep, then Idaho is one of the top five places to dive in the United States as only four other lakes in the nation are deeper than **Lake Pend Oreille**, pronounced "pondoray". This glacial lake sits at an elevation of 2,064ft, is 65miles long, 4miles wide, and 1,170ft deep. During World War II the second largest navel base in the United States was at the location we currently know as Ferragut State Park. Before the navy left structure remnants, like the brig, this area was the summer home of the Salish Indians. There are hundreds if not thousands of years worth of artifacts such as arrowheads in this area. A canoe that may date back 380yrs was found in 40ft of water here. Loggers accidentally left many now mineralized logs on the lake bottom. I don't know what the navy left underwater; submarines and torpedoes perhaps? At the Trestle Creek Recreational Area divers have followed old railroad tracks at 45ft and found two railroad cars known as the **Boxcars** down at 92ft and 102ft respectively. Divers on trimix at 150ft have discovered a railroad **Handcar**, also known as a pump trolley, similar to the one used in the movie *Blazing Saddles*. Keep in mind; while the surface may be 60° at depth it will be more like 40°.

Some other places to dive include: **Blue Heart Springs**, which is a boat dive up the river to a spot where 100ft clear spring water feeds into the 7ft vis **Snake River. Honey Suckle Beach** in Hayden has a depth of 20ft, there is **Clear Lake** in Buhl, Idaho, and **Anderson Ranch Reservoir** is 75ft deep and the vis is 15-20ft. Basically, where permitted, you can dive just about any other reservoir for that matter if you are not too particular about vis and more interested in seeing what people threw or dropped in the water.

So as you can see, Idaho has a plethora of places to dive and lots of diverse types of diving to try out. Many of the locations are at high altitude, so it's best to take an altitude diver course before exploring some of the following locations. And of course, for more specific information, ask for more details at the local dive shops that know these waters well. Great Dives.

3 Top Illinois Dives

It's hard to narrow a state's top dive sites down to just 3, but with a little help from my friends I thought I could do a fair and equitable job. To start with, I asked Scott W. Kurth a former dive instructor out of Chicago what he thought the top three dives in Illinois were and Scott told me the top dives for Chicagoans were the SS Wisconsin, The Straits of Mackinac, and The Prins Willem V. As you can tell from his choices, he prefers the more adventurous advanced dives. In fact he even told me that Lake Michigan should never have been named a lake, because it is more like a freshwater sea. I would have to agree with him there, because the moon can have subtle effects on the tides of the lake, this fresh water sea can go down to depths of 925ft, but averages around 279ft, it's over 118miles wide, and the storms of Lake Michigan have been too much of a match for many a ship in the past.

The SS Wisconsin, built in 1881, was 48years old when it sank 6.5miles SE of Kinosha, Wisconsin. It went down November 29th, 1929. The steamship was just over 200ft long and carried iron castings, boxed freight, and 1929 era automobiles. If you anchor mid-ship and descend down the line you will come to an open hatch. Inside the compartment are an Essex, a Hudson, and a Chevrolet touring car. It's a penetration dive to tour the car show, so it definitely requires wreck diver training. At 130ft of depth it's best left for deep water or tech divers too. And like any dive on the lake, you have to be prepared for stray fishing lines below the surface and wind and wave action by the time you return to the surface due to brief changes in weather. Also, the surface temperature may be 80 degrees in the summer, expect 55 degrees at depth. If the water dips in the 40's keep and eye out for Chinook and Coho salmon.

The Straits of Mackinac, not to be confused with the wrecks in the straits of Mackinac, was sunk April 11th, 2003.

At the time it was the 23rd wreck to be sunk for diving pleasure. It rests 10miles NE of the Chicago Navy Pier in 73ft of water. This 1928 steel hull steamship is 204ft long. "The Mack" was a car ferry before the bridge over the straits of Mackinac was built. It's only 50ft down to the top deck by the smoke stack, making it readily available to divers who don't like to dive too deep.

Prince Willem V, "The Willey", is a 250ft long Dutch freighter that sunk in 1954 at 93ft of depth resting on its starboard side. It's the most popular wreck dive off the coast of Milwaukee. However, because you have drive to Milwaukee for this wreck, which isn't all that far from Chicago, I'm not going to keep "The Willey" in my top three Illinois dive category. Besides, there is another cadent of Illinois divers that don't ever jump into the cold lake. They prefer to keep their skills current in flooded former rock quarries where the surface may be 84 degrees, at 20ft 78 degrees, and it only drops down to 50 degrees at the deepest part of the quarry. The Haigh Quarry is just such a former rock quarry. On the north end at 30ft or so of depth you will find some mining equipment. At the SE end it dips down to 85ft of depth. Along the way you will have visibility between 15 to 25ft and you may see sunfish, blue gill, catfish, bass and a pink flamingo perched on a lawn tractor; and yes you aren't suffering from nitrogen narcosis is you see a pink flamingo. However, you are if it winks at you.

Another quarry, Mermet Springs, comes to mind if you like steep walls going down to 100ft. Actually, you might not even care about this site being a good wall dive, because it has a Cessna 152, a Cherokee 150, and a sunken Boeing 727 jet used in the movie "US Marshals ". As far as sunken 727 jets go, you can either dive this one or you can upgrade to the saltwater version located near the city of Sydney on Victoria Island, British Columbia. If you don't have mileage plus points to go to western Canada, then you have to visit Mermet Springs.

So you can see that I would like to add a quarry or two to the top three list, but in 2010 the "Buccaneer" a 1925 ice breaker was sunk 10miles from Chicago in shallow waters making this possibly the best wreck for Illinois divers to explore. You can find images and video of the sinking of this wreck online and it has already been cleaned and ready to go including painted pirate decorum on top complete with black swords and a skull that may unfortunately soon be covered over with zebra mussels and obscured from sight.

There are also older wrecks for those that love antiquity such as the Wells Burt an 1873 3-mast schooner in 40ft of water, or the 147ft long Rotarian, a side-wheel steamer that sunk in 1937 in 85ft of depth. And of course I would be remiss if I didn't include the Material Surface Barge built in 1929 and sunk in 1936. This 239ft long 40ft wide barge was made to go under all the low-lying bridges of Chicago. The top of the barge was less than 3ft tall. You might say that the same openings that made it able to fill fast with grain, eventually made it fill fast with water. Now it's a great site to explore and a great place for crayfish to call home.

Besides these favorite dive spots, there are some wrecks that I just don't have time or room to mention, because after all, this article is only about the top three dive sites, and I'm not one to stray.

But if I did have enough room, I would certainly mention the planes that went down in Lake Michigan during training missions during World War II while trying to land on the aircraft carriers Essex and Sable. I would also mention the German Submarine UC-97 launched march 17, 1918, that was sunk as target practice on Jan 7th, 1921 in 300ft of water. We had to sink the sub after a war bond tour as part of the armistice agreement after World War I. Now the submarine is nothing more than a tech divers dream dive site. Cris Kohl's book, *The Great Lakes Diving Guide* is a good place to search for more wreck information.

Ok, now you can see why I had such a tough time deciding on the top 3 dives of Illinois. And even though your top 3 choices may be different from mine, the fact remains that we are all going to have some great dives in the Illinois area and plenty to talk about when we all meet back at the dive shop. Great dives.

Indiana
Diving Hoosier Style

If you see a dive boat out in Lake Michigan with divers jumping over the side to explore one of the hundreds of wrecks that met their fate in this freshwater ocean, your first guess might not be that the charter boat came from one of the marinas along Indiana's Great Lake coastline. It turns out that the only 5masted schooner to traverse Lake Michigan, the 365ft long *David Dows*, came to rest 7miles from Chicago, but only 5miles from Indiana's shoals in 40ft of water. The David Dows was built in 1881 and sunk in 1889. She was such a massive ship that when fully loaded, she road too low in the water to enter or leave most ports. Her masts stood up to 97ft tall and it took some 8hours to unfold the ships sails. Besides running aground in shallow areas, she was reported to have collided with and sunk two other schooners as well as taken out a port dock. Her masts were trimmed down in 1883 and she became a coal barge until she sank in a storm.

Right off Indiana Dunes State Park are the remains of the *Muskegon*, a sand pumper, that caught fire in 1910, and the 154ft long *J.D. Marshall* that sank to 35ft deep in 1911 during a squall while performing a salvage operation on the Muskegon less than a mile from Indiana's lake shoreline. Two popular dives off the coast include the 240ft long *Material Service Barge* at 30ft, and the 100ft long patrol boat *Buccaneer* at 75ft. For Deeper dives there is the Thomas Hume at 147ft, or the side wheel Rotarian at 84ft. Other notables include the *Wings of Wind*, the *Straits of Mackinac*, *Wells Burt*, *Louisville*, *Tacoma*, *Car Ferry #2*, *Flora M. Hill*, *George F. Williams*, and for those that get seasick on a boat, there is the shore dive at **Hammond Marina** by the Horseshoe Casino on the 280ft long *George F. Williams* that sank in 1915 some 300ft off shore with the bow at 7ft and the stern at the almost insurmountable ear equalizing depth of just under 12ft.

Traveling to inland Indiana there are several quarries where diving is either exclusive, or permitted in conjunction with other sports such as fishing, camping, cliff diving, swimming, and boating. Starting off with **Dream Lake**, which is a 15acre spring fed quarry, near St. Paul and next to Hidden Paradise Campground, you can dive down to 35ft and see 6ft long paddlefish that get up to 200lbs and have been around some 20-40million years. Paddlefish are not as skittish as most other fish, so you are likely to get a chance to see this prehistoric species up close and personal. You can also find lawn furniture, a mini-school bus, coal rail car, motorcycle, a sailboat, and a new 40x40ft dock. From July to September you can find harmless freshwater jellyfish.

Next we go to France, **France Park** that is, also known as the old Kenith Stone Quarry, and located 3miles west of Logansport. The park is open for divers on weekends and holiday Mondays from May thru October. Call *The Diving Den* in Kokomo for updates on times, reservations, and park diving rules. The substrate is filled with rock slabs, a Culver to swim through, a 1940's school bus, a pick up truck, and a max depth of 35ft. They did have big paddlefish here, but the dive area was not too long ago opened to fishing, so watch out for hooks.

Phillips Quarry in Muncie is open 365 and doesn't ice up for very long in January. The vis can be 20-75ft depending on time of year and max depth is 55ft. cars, boats, and an airplane fuselage are suspended just beneath the surface or rest on the algae and silt laden substrate. Turtles, bass, blue gill and some newly introduced paddlefish can be viewed. Contact *Tom Leairds Underwater Service* for reservations.

I called **Blue Spring Park** and was told that the dive park is currently closed. **White Rock** might be an option, but is busy with cliff divers, boats, and only 25ft deep.

I talked to John Sloan of *Lake City Scuba Center* in Warsaw about local lake diving because you never hear much about it except by one diver to another. John told me that in the Kosciusko County alone, there are over 100 lakes. **Lake Tippecanoe** is 122ft deep max and a vis of 15-20ft. The lake has carp, catfish, and 3ft long pike that tend to stay in the shallow areas in the weeds. Below 20ft, there is a lot of silt, but this is where you can find the old thick glass antique bottles. In the summer, the lake has a lot of boat traffic. **Lake Wawasee** is the largest natural lake but it is very shallow with one or two spots no wider than four cars parked together that max out at 75ft of depth. The middle of the lake is very shallow and this gives the contour of the lake a weeds and sand theme both on the shoreline, and in the middle of the lake like the shape of a "w". **Lake Syracuse** has a barge down at 30ft. **Lake Waubee** has low vis, but low boat traffic too, so this makes a good refresher dive lake. **Shriner Lake**, 10 minutes north of Columbia, has easy access, but is most notable because two divers went in here and because they didn't have a dive flag, they both received a $328 fine. So carry a dive flag with you in Indiana or anywhere else where boats are likely to be for that matter; protect your head, as well as your pocket book.

Some other lakes you might like from northern Indiana moving south include: **Clear Lake** in the NE corner of the state near Fremont. The max depth is 107ft and vis between 30-50ft; hence the name. Besides the regular cast of creatures, this lake is noted for crayfish and mud puppies. **Big Long Lake** is located near Wolcottville and has bass, perch and trapdoors snails, besides zebra mussels. Vis is about 15ft. Moving to the northern far left of the state you can dive **Lake Etta County Park** in Gary with a max depth of 25ft and vis of 5-10ft. **Lakewood Park** in Burns is 30-40ft deep and vis is 11-15ft. **Three Rivers County Park** near Lake Station is 50-60ft deep and the vis is 16-20ft. **Flint Lake** in Valparaiso if 60ft max and the vis is 5ft. **The Barbee Chain** in North Webster and east of Fort Wayne includes close to a dozen lakes by itself. Finally, down at Linton in the Southeastern Park of the State we have **Sunset Lake** with a depth of 30ft and vis from 8-25ft. The lake is in a city park and has bass, blue gill and a cabin cruiser.

So to wrap it up, Indiana has wrecks, sand dunes, and lakes; one big Great Lake, and tons of little ones, and as if this isn't enough, local divers also flock to dive sites in the surrounding states on a regular basis. Great Dives.

Iowa Dive Sites
Midwest Divers Delight

Iowa is a state full of pleasant surprises. In a land where one would think that the food served is all traditional Americana cuisine, you can order Vietnamese Pho noodles for lunch at the *China Garden*, authentic British Pub food at the *Royal Mile* such as Shepard's Pie made with lamb, instead of the American cowboy version made with beef, and then wash it all down with authentic German libations at the *Hessen Haus*. This is definitely not the Iowa you might have experienced 20years ago. Chances are that some of the local dive sites will surprise you too.

To start out, I talked with Dave and Pat Swanson from *Blue Water Diving* on **West Lake Okoboji** at **Arnolds Park**. This glacier carved lake has three deep holes and drops down to 140ft max. The vis reaches over 40ft in the winter, and the lake temp swings annually from 40 to 70°. Down below is a 1938 Ford icebox truck in **Smith Bay**. There are three pipelines to follow, a few boats to find, and a sunken **Milford Tower** to discover. Some 25 different species of fish call this lake home including: Muskies, Northern Pike, White Bass, Buffalo Carp, and Blue Gill. Dave says that in the spring they conduct Eco dives to monitor the egg sac development of the nesting fish. He also said that one of the cool finds in this lake are the fresh water sponges that come in different colors depending on what they feed on. You can find the sponges hanging out on rocks and clinging on pipelines.

Pat wanted to mention **Little Rock Wall**. This wall runs at a depth between 12 to 22ft deep, but the wall is the length of 6-7 football fields and runs from **Fort Dodge Point** to **Pillsbury Point**. Lots of fish inhabit the crevices along this wall. Also, in the winter when the lake freezes over, ice divers from Texas and Oklahoma come north to play. Nearby **Spirit Lake** is the biggest natural lake in Iowa, but at only 24ft deep, it gets green with algae in the summertime, and vis drops accordingly.

Moving on to *North Iowa Scuba* in Mason, owned and operated by Don and Carrie Brown, Carrie says that they like to go to **Turkey Ridge** and **Big Blue**. The Turkey Ridge Wildlife Area is used for hiking, bird watching, hunting, fishing, and was formerly known as the Yokum Rock Quarry before 2006. In 2010 it was opened to scuba diving. Carrie likes the site because of the easy shore entry and floating docks for practicing giant stride entries. You might see them there with short or tall students on Saturdays and Sundays, as they are both Boy Scout merit badge councilors too. The depth at this site is 35ft max, vis is 5-20ft, and the temp is 50 to 80°. Blue Gills, Crappie, and Catfish here, love to ignore new divers in training. Divers have to call *Scuba Too* in plenty of time in advance to get the weekly changing gate code in order to drive down a 7/10ths of a mile road to drop off gear next to the dive site; for latest phone numbers see turkeyridgedivesite.com. To dive Turkey Ridge you will need to show your dive "C" certification card, sign an annual liability release form, and register your vehicle. Scuba Too in Cedar Falls also has their own private quarry called **Glennies Pond**, but this little heart shaped quarry is only for private use by Scuba Too for such things as picnics and barbeques now that Turkey Ridge is open.

Scuba Adventures in Bettendorf also has a nonpublic private quarry for training purposes. The quarry is 25ft deep. For advanced training, they like to go to the Caribbean of the Midwest: **Haigh Quarry** on Kankakee, Illinois. This quarry has 12 acres of spring fed water and can accommodate some 300 divers on a single weekend, but chances are your group won't be that big.

Big Blue, also known as **Lester Milligan Park**, is in the southwest side of Mason City. The max depth is 35ft, and vis ranges from 5ft plus and it boasts a sunken cabin cruiser. Straight north from the tree stump at the southern entry point will take you to a platform, then the boat. One thing to mention here is that some small ponds and lakes may be closed off occasionally due to algae, nitrate levels, Ecoli levels and other chemical or bio substance levels deemed temporarily unsafe according to government standards. So ask a local dive shop before you go, if you're concerned about a certain local destination, as they may have already learned about such sites through other divers or local officials.

Now besides using all these dive sites, Randy Molnari who has been diving for 40years, and training for the last 36years, from *Adventure Diving* in West Des Moines, likes to take technical divers on a 5hr trip up to **Lake Wazee** in Wisconsin. The vis here is 30-50ft and the max depth is around 355ft. At 235ft there is the Hoffa skeleton complete with chains. Randy is also known for traveling up to **Lake Michigan** and diving on the *Lender* charter boat. Locally, he teaches recreational, technical, and Professional Public Safety diving for firefighters and SWAT teams. As a salvage diver, Randy replaces chewed up pipes and gnawed on tubes by muskrats and turtles, he removes river rocks from drain systems, and he also repairs pontoons. Even the day I visited his shop Randy was busy working on dive gear while I chatted with him.

Last but not least, we have **Pleasant Creek Recreation Area** in Palo, Iowa. At 60ft max and up to 5ft or more of vis near the spillway, this might be the best dam dive site in the state. Ok, well it at least might be the best place to find fishing gear, and boat items gone overboard. This "no wake" lake is also home to good fishing, 69 campsites, and two showers and restroom facilities, which makes it a full weekend dive destination even if it's just to camp and get wet.

So to round it up, Iowa has some great places to explore above and below water year round. In the summer, watch put for jet skis and use a dive flag. Locals also have the option of diving in some great close by out of state spots too. Most of all, during winter when the snow is falling, the streets are deserted, and the business people in Des Moines are bustling through the second story tubes that go from downtown building to the next downtown building as if moving through a giant gerbil maze, there are some happy folks from Texas and the surrounding southern states dressed in drysuits, cutting triangular holes in ice, living it up and enjoying a type of cool diving they just can't seem to get back home. Iowa waters have something to offer almost for everyone. Great Dives.

Kansas Flippers
And Ruby Red Slippers

Ok, so you may not need the magic generated from wearing Ruby Red Slippers to find a place to dive in Kansas, but you may need the help of the Great Wizard of Oz to find suitable diving visibility. You see, all the rich soil that makes Kansas such an ideal place to grow crops also blankets the substrate of most local streams, rivers, and lakes. Go online and many websites tout the diveability of **Wilson Lake**, but as one local diver told me, "I thought they put Wilson Lake in the magazine as a Joke." It turns out that the vis in Lake Wilson may be 1-5ft, but at 65ft deep, this lake may be one of the deepest dive sites in the state. Lake Wilson also is host to fish such as bass, crappie, perch, and catfish. **Tuttle Creek Lake** next to Tuttle Creek State Park is 50ft deep. **Clinton Lake**, which has four nearby state parks including Clinton State Park, is 55ft deep. Now I've flown over **Lake Waconda** and taken pictures of it from the air, but I would like to personally test out the visibility of this 55ft deep dive site as well as stay at the adjacent *Glen Elden State Park*.

In an never ending quest for deeper water, I know at least two instructors that will stop by every water filled private quarry and sand pit they see and ask the owners for permission to dive and explore the quarry. What they have found in most situations is a private place to dive that is less than 15ft deep and has low vis.

If you talk to some locals or scan the Internet you'll read or hear occasional stories that at one time there was diving available at one or more of the former intercontinental missile silos. The standard intercontinental ballistic missile silo is hollowed out and cement fortified straight down to 130ft making an ideal training site for divers once it is filled with clear water. Unfortunately, missile silos are hot commodities now days and are in demand for those seeking an alternative home life style or doomsday asylum. The days of buying an underground silo for 40grand, filling it with water, and calling it Joe's Dive Park are pretty much over. So where do the rumors of diving silos come from? Midland, Texas is where the real diving silo is located. All it takes is someone to say or write "We need a diving silo here," and the next thing you know is that someone else is repeating the story as if it is fact that a diveable missile silo already exists in Kansas.

So if all there is a few mud holes and shallow lakes in the state, how come there are so many dive shops in the state and what makes the employees, owners, and instructors so enthusiastic when talking about diving? Turns out, that divers in Kansas tend to think of the other surrounding states as an extended area of their back yard. Ask about last week's dive and there's a good chance it took place in Arkansas or Missouri. I asked an employee at *Topeka Dive Center* where he and others like to go diving, and he said "Any where in the Ozarks." *Beaver Lake* in Arkansas is especially popular because of its visibility that can extend more than 20ft and also because of its' depth. A spokesperson from *The Dive Shop in Merriam*, Kansas mentioned *Table Rock Lake* and *Stockton Lake* in Missouri. Stockton may have 5ft to 20plus feet of vis, 100ft of depth, the chance to see a perch, and the fact that it's only 2hrs from Kansas City help put it on the local places to dive list. Hey, you don't need a house to drop on you before you start following the yellow brick road down to better dive locations. The practice of crossing state borders is not as uncommon as one would think. Divers from my home state of Oregon have been crossing the Washington border for checkout dives in the Puget Sound and Hood Canal for decades. Those dive sites can be over 4hours away. Both Missouri and Arkansas have many other great places to dive, but I cover these over the state border locations in more detail in their own respective exclusive state articles.

So to wrap things up, there are many public and private places in the state of Kansas where you can put on your gear to get wet, but the locals don't mind going out of state to find depth and visibility. In the end, the other states may be fun to play in, but as I recall hearing in a movie once, "There's no place like home."

Kentucky Blues:
Music, Lakes, Quarries, & More

Kentucky is the home to Bluegrass music, Col Harland Sanders founder of Kentucky Fried Chicken, Johnny Depp, Mohammed Ali, Jim Bowie, and even Daniel Boone explored here, but the one person from this state that really sticks out in my mind is Ernie Brown Jr., AKA The Turtleman. From Lebanon, the heart of Kentucky, he has captured by hand, via "Live Action", more than 12,000 turtles from local ponds creeks, and waterholes. You can see him on Animal Planet under "Call Of The Wildman." Anyway,

Kentucky waters are rich in wildlife, and if trout, bass, bluegill, catfish, crawfish, jellyfish, and the possibility to see even more turtles sounds interesting, then here is a list of some large local lakes, quaint quality quarries, and other Kentucky diver quintessentially qualified aquatic destinations.

We start our exploration of Kentucky with **Lake Cumberland State Resort Park**. Wolf Creek Dam was completed in 1951 by the U.S. Army Corps of Engineers and has 1200miles of shoreline, and covers 63,000acres. At around 200ft deep, 101miles long, and at an elevation of 760ft, it is the longest Dam Lake in the state. As for divers, **Pig Pen Point**, AKA Government Point, is the place to go. Vis can vary between 0-30ft and is best in the spring. Besides lots of fish, there are a few small boats and one sunken houseboat. The flooded ruins of several small towns are sprinkled along the lake's substrate. Wreck and/or Cave diver ratings are suggested for some of the still barely standing intact structures that dot the underwater topography. Beaver Creek Marina is the nearest place to refill scuba tanks.

Laurel River Lake is next on the list with an elevation of 1015ft, a depth easily over 130ft, covering 5,600acres, and 206miles of shoreline. There are submerged rock formations, sunken boats, and a sunken 1975 Blazer. A spokesperson from

New Horizon Dive Center in Lexington said that diving locally really gets divers prepared for their Caribbean vacations. She also likes the fresh water jellyfish that are out and about in Laurel Lake around the month of September.

Dale Hallow Lake formed in 1943 when the Dale Hollow Reservoir dammed the Obey River. Towns like Lily Dale were submerged and most of the 27,200acres of water rest in the State of Tennessee, but a small portion of the 130ft deep lake crosses the Kentucky boarder and is part of Dale Hallow Lake State Resort. This means that with a few extra fin kicks, you can dive two states on one dive and all while using one tank of air. With vis as high as 25-30ft at times, it is easy to find the submerged remnants of the former **Willow Grove School**. Some foundation sections are still standing upright, while other sections of the school's brick walls lay in large and/or small groupings on the lakes substrate. Bluegills mostly guard the ruins, and it doesn't take much effort to find snagged lures along almost any course heading.

Moving on to quarries you've hit a home run when you come across a former quarry filled in with naturally clear spring fed water that now goes by the long name of **Pennyroyal Scuba Center/Blue Springs Resort** in Hopkinsville in western Kentucky. The quarry covers 22acres, is 120ft deep max, vis averages 30-40ft, the water temp is 80° on the surface in the summer, but 43-50° below 75ft of depth, and is owned and operated by Dennis and Kris Tapp. Several local dive shops have nothing but praise for the staff, and their safety and emergency plans. At the Resort there are a few cabins and primitive campsites. For a small fee, you can go below the surface where there are over 40 artifacts ranging from a 1941 Dodge Fire engine, a UH1 helicopter, a motor home, small boats, and a cabin cruiser. There are a few oddities such as a giant spider on top of a school bus, and a cement statue of a lion sitting on his haunches with a dive flag painted on his back. Yeah, you guessed it: a sea lion. Dennis told me that a twin-engine plane is coming soon. I wonder if the plane is coming from nearby Fort Campbell? Now the day I talked to Dennis, visibility was between 50-60ft. They don't have a 727 in the water yet, so their slogan is simple: "Where the difference is clear."

Dive Cerulean is in Cadiz, KY and is a 16acre spring fed former quarry. David and Cindy Westerfield own and operate this scuba and swimming site. Because no fishing is allowed, fish are plentiful. The water reaches a max depth of 35ft, and a pool filtration pump circulates surface water down to 30ft of depth almost eliminating the cold thermo cline syndrome. The surface temp may be 80°, but only 70° at depth. Vis can range from 10 to 50 feet. Besides easy access and several training platforms underwater, there is a cabin cruiser, rock crusher, conveyor belt, a Cadillac, a pickup truck, and quite possibly the largest lawn mower artificial reef collection in America. They have an air fill station and you can check online for seasons and times that Dive Cerulean is open.

Falling Rock Quarry is 50 to 55ft deep and vis is 20-40ft. On the bottom there are boats, and quarry cart that runs on rails. One local dive instructor told me that he likes this park because it is close by, inexpensive; it has easy entries, and port-a-potties, but no air fill station. Joe Clark is the sole owner.

In addition to frequenting the dive sites already mentioned, Kentucky dive shops travel out of state too. *The Scuba Shack* in Florence for instance is by far closer to Cincinnati than to Lexington. So for them it is just as easy to go to **Gilboa Quarry** in Ohio, as it is to visit the quarries down in southern Kentucky. *Island Dive Center* in Bowling Green, KY likes to visit **Mermet Springs** in Illinois. Ray Scott, and his team at *Louisville Dive Center* go farther than just about any other dive shop around. Besides all the in state locations Ray told me that they drive down to Pensacola, Fl to dive the 911ft long **USS Oriskany** as well as dive sites in the Panama City area, so often, that a couple of people from the shop have gotten their Captains' licenses just by helping out over the years.

Lastly, Ray told me that the **Ohio River** can get up to 8-10ft of vis after weeks of no rainfall, and sometimes you can find interesting wrecks and discarded artifacts on the sandy bottom.

Kentucky has several popular manmade dive sites to explore; mostly rivers turned lakes and hollowed out quarries. The sites are filled with plenty of fish and turtles. Divers from the surrounding states as well as Canada visit these locations both monthly and annually. You don't have to be famous, born in the state, or even purchase a well-known bucket of chicken to visit these dive sites, you just need the desire to have fun and explore the Bluegrass state from the bottom on up. Great Dives.

Louisiana Diving
Blackened, Brackish, & Salted

To tell you straight up, fresh water diving in Louisiana is fraught with low vis, but that doesn't detour local divers. Nancy Cohagan of *Seven Seas Dive Shop* in Baton Rouge, which has been in business since 1977, told me that local divers like to hold a weekend picnic called a "Lake Bash." The object here is to see how fast you can spear or catch 500lbs of catfish, then cook it up right then and there. You may only get less than 3ft of visibility during one of these get togethers, but lunch and leftovers make it all worthwhile. Meanwhile, other divers like to go hunting for sunken cypress tree logs that have recently become commercially worth the recovery effort.

Some lakes you might want to visit include: **Lake Charles**, **Lake D'Arbonne**, **Lake Maurepas**, **Lake Pontchartrain**, and **Toledo Bend**, among others. Toledo Bend lies on the Texas-Louisiana border. The lake is 70 miles long and 3-5miles wide with 80 access areas, and lots of water activities, beaches, and coves. Lake Pontchartrain is a 10,000 square mile brackish water shed. Here the vis may get past 8ft if the winds, waves, and weather permit. The water depth averages between 8 to 12ft, but Rick Sutton of *Coral Reef Dive Shop* has done salvage work near **Rigolets** and by **Lake Front Airport** that dip down to 90ft of depth. In the lake there are freshwater catfish, saltwater stingrays, bull sharks, and once, even a state record tarpon was caught here. If you want to dive Lake Pontchartrain it is best to first log on to www.saveourlake.org and check the fecal coliform count to make sure it is safe to go in.

River diving has similar vis limitations, but Mike Giles of *Mike's Dive Center* in Lake Chamber, which has been open since 1962, has 56years of diving experience and while under bridges searching for boat motors, he has found additional boat motors, fire arms, and other thrown out or intentionally discarded items. Mike also said that when the rivers alter/change course after a big rainstorm or flood, the sediment is moved and the surface striped down to the underlying sand substrate and old dug out canoes can be uncovered along with other historical artifacts. Probably one of the biggest artifacts that has been found, but can't be touched, is the Civil War Iron Clad that rests in a levee. It's the one I believe that a former manager of Seven Seas Dive Shop helped do research on for Clive Cussler before "Sahara" hit the book stands and big screen.

Now, salt water diving off the coastline is a complete different story. As Mike Giles told me, you can go out 25 miles and still be in waters only 60ft deep. The shrimp trawlers over the decades have run their nets over the bottom until it has turned smooth and flat as a pancake. You still might find derelict crab cages here though. After hurricane Katrina, Rick Sutton was busy recovering shrimp and crab boats off the bottom. A crab trap recovered may only fetch $30, but each boat that went down lost up to 200 traps and that adds up fast. Another reason you have to go out far to dive is the lack of visibility near shore is cause by the Mississippi River. For vis over 30 to 40 feet, you have to plan on going out 40 to 70 miles off shore, and at the oil rigs, vis can occasionally exceed 100ft. I should say that when locals talk about diving the rig, they are talking about diving around oil transfer platforms, and not where drilling by actual people are currently underway. These towers are vertical reefs that may reach down 400ft like the popular **High Island 389** in the protected **Flower Garden Banks** area. These oil and gas rigs are islands of life in a sea of sandy substrate. Each one has it's own ecosystem of invertebrates such as corals, sponges, and slipper and spiny lobsters. The fish may be one of 60species that year round live on the rigs, such as the damsels, black drum, or red snapper, or one of the seasonal pelagic visitors such as tuna, wahoo, large sharks, and whale sharks. High Island 389 also has a resident loggerhead turtle. Some other rig hot spots include the **Vermillion Block**, a five square mile block of ten rigs 40miles out, and the **Circle Rigs** that are 30miles off Port Fouchon. There are literally hundreds of rigs off shore and you can take a day trip out to a selected few sites, or do a long day of bounce diving and see 5-6 rig sites. For an over night trip, you can go out on the most popular local dive trip aboard the 100ft *MV Fling* and visit Flower Garden Banks. This over night trip out of Freeport Texas, allows you to visit natural coral gardens on caps as shallow as 60ft, as well as the rigs that dip past 350ft deep. There are over 21 species of corals out in the banks as well as over 200 species of fish and invertebrates to date.

Ok, so the saltwater diving is cool off Louisiana, but here is the sad part too. Just about anyone will tell you that it is hard to find a local charter that goes out to the rigs. After 9/11 in 2001, the dive business took a hit. In 2005 when Hurricane Katrina roared in, businesses all but faded away. As business recovered, Hurricane Gustov in 2008 disrupted things for a while, then the BP Deepwater Horizon oil spill catastrophe in 2010 wiped away just about any hope for dive charter survival. Now the waters have cleared up again, but the local state legal system has kept charter services from sprouting up again in Louisiana. Unlike Florida, Texas, or most other states, a dive charter operation in Louisiana can be held potentially liable for just about anything a customer does on a trip; just by supplying the transportation. So, what you currently find are private parties going out to dive the rig sites, but not too many commercial dive charter boats unless they are from another state.

I should mention that spear fishing is very popular around these rigs, but you better have plenty of experience spearing fish before you tangle with a 100lb lemon fish whose first inclination after being struck incorrectly is to dive 300ft straight down the side of an oil rig. *The Hell Divers Spearfishing Club* started in 1963 dives these rigs. They hold the annual Hell Diver Rodeo Tournament. Members once speared 90lb amberjack, but recent winning amberjack have been closer to 30-40lbs.

So there you go, blackened fresh waters good for lake bashes, recovering river items gone overboard, finding historical treasures, brackish waters where you can catch just about anything, and salt water rigs that form hundreds of artificial reef communities, all the way out to the Flower

Garden Banks. There is also a plethora of surrounding state dive sites. I can't imagine why some tourists never step foot off of Bourbon Street. Great Dives.

Maine

There are many dive sites along the coast of Maine that come up during a typical scuba related conversation. Actually, two dive sites always come up and one of two other dive sites come up depending on your starting point and how far you don't mind driving. On the south coast of Maine the top dive site has to be without doubt Nubble Light just south of Sohier Park. There is plenty of sea life here including crabs, lobster, and lots of fish.

There are two main dive loop routes to follow to make the most out of your day. Be sure and use a flashlight to peer between the rocks. Some of the rocks at low tide can be slippery. You can see almost everything on the second dive without ever getting deeper than 30ft. This site is extremely popular with out of state divers. I won't mention names, but "masses choose it" because of it's easy entrance and close proximity to Boston. It also has free parking, but with up to 150 divers on a single summer day, spaces could fill up early. Many of the dive sites in Maine have free parking, but even without other divers you have to compete with tourists coming to the coastline to take in the scenic beauty. Especially, here at Nubble Light with its lighthouse sitting so close on it's own picturesque island not far from the main shoreline.

Anonymously I was told that once upon a time Nubble Light was so popular that dive shops from afar would bus divers in training over to Nubble. They refilled their tanks on site with portable air compressors, and then rotated the divers out with a new busload of divers in training. For the local who lived nearby, it must have been like watching the US Marines landing with the noise of downtown construction inserted for good measure. Perhaps that's why air compressors are forbidden at Nubble Light and scuba diving is not be permitted on Sundays.

Moving up the coastline we come to the second most often mentioned dive site Kettle Cove that is part of Cressent Beach State Park. You can dive it any season, it has free parking, and an easy entrance. There is lots of sea life. Maine is fortunately infested with lobsters of every size, color and demeanor, but unfortunately, the lobster season is closed to scuba divers. Not to worry though, because lobster stew is already being served hot at a plethora of well-established Maine eateries. Kettle Cove has one of the highest amounts of juvenile lobsters of any of the twenty some juvenile lobster monitoring locations in the state. The lobsters are nocturnal by nature, though so you might have to peek between rocks or peer inside hollowed out areas to find the lobsters hiding out from flounder, cod, and seals.

Now usually I only carry my C-card for air fills or dive boat verification, but in Maine, state park officials may check your C-card, so have it readily available if asked.

For the third dive site I'm going to give you two sites for your consideration. First we have Rachel Carson Salt Pond not far from Portland. Rachel Carson was an environmentalist and marine biologist who wrote *The Edge of the Sea* in 1955 and *Silent Spring* in 1962. She wrote about and then set aside 40 acres next to Muscongus Bay. The local dive site is called Round Pond and you will understand the name as soon as you view the site. As for sea and land life, this site non-impartially and very openly has been approved for decades by the work of marine biologist Rachel Carson.

Julie Footnan an instructor out of Aqua Diving Acadamy in Portland likes this site because it can be shallow or a deep shore dive. With more than a hundred dives at this site she still has not been below 110ft of depth here, but when you are a good instructor and busy teaching student divers all the time, the students come first, and deep dives here will just have to wait.

The second dive site we have as a contender for the third top dive site in Maine is Acadia National Park. As Randy Cook from Aqua City Scuba in Waterville pointed out, it's all about the visibility. While the visibility may be 12-16ft at other dive sites in Maine, here the visibility can go up to 20ft. It's a rocky bottom with lots of marine life, but you'll have to go out quite a ways to get below 40ft of depth. The other side of this site Randy would like to point out is that this national park lends itself to multiple activities, so you may come here to dive, but you can camp, hike, or observe nature above sea level too. When it comes to outdoor activities Acadia National Park is a real Maine attraction.

Now I know that I'm only supposed to write about the three top dives in Maine, but everyone keeps mentioning Two Lights, Dyer Cove, which is close to Portland. Beside easy access and a rocky bottom filled with marine critters. There are lots of crevices to explore and two dive route loops to follow at 40ft of depth or less. One other thing about Maine I should mention is that there are probably more boats here than cars in Detroit and kayaks are stealth bombers waiting to separate snorkels from masks, so it's a good idea to carry a dive flag when venturing out and a close eye on the surface before raising out of the water. Also fishing line can be a problem, so always carry a knife and scissors to disconnect you from someone else's snagged lines and unsuccessful fishing expeditions.

Ok, so I couldn't keep the count down to just the top 3 dives in Maine. I apologize for the extra great dive sites to explore. There are many more dive sites that I didn't even get a chance to mention. Stop by your local Maine dive shop, or ask members of the *Maine-iacs Divers* dive club and I'm sure they can mention more. Great Dives.

MARYLAND
The Gateway To Mid-Atlantic Diving

Annapolis may be home to one of the best-known naval academies in the world, but a mere 14million years ago this area was 100ft underwater and teeming with over 30 different species of prehistoric sharks including mako, thresher, and the extinct 60ft long, great white on steroids, megalodon shark. Calvert Cliffs in Calvert County in our current historical age is above the water line and sporadically studded with shark teeth and other fossil remnants of the distant past inland sea world. If this isn't enough to define Maryland, the state is literally split in two by the Chesapeake Bay, which is more than 3 times the size of San Francisco Bay, and is also the site of a Meteor impact during the Eocene period some 35 million years ago. The Chesapeake Bay with a max depth of 208ft and an average depth of 46ft sounds like a natural place to dive, but with all the runoff from all the rivers and tributaries, the vis can get low. Still, several locations have become great spots for divers harvesting oysters in a mere 8 to 12ft of water. These areas are great for experienced divers to catch an oyster meal while getting in some bottom time, and for new divers to see all the sea creatures such as blue crabs, horseshoe crabs, sea stars, and the myriads of small fish.

For divers wanting to explore coastal Maryland and the Mid-Atlantic waters, Ocean City, is the local home of charter dive boats which go out to five different zones that together comprise over 20 well-known wrecks and natural reefs. I asked *Jeremiah Kogon* of **OC Dive Boat SCUBA Charters** what are some of the top dive destinations and he said **The African Queen** oil tanker bow section, which is south and in blue waters some 15miles offshore in zone 3. While the stern section was towed to dry dock after running aground, the bow section became a natural wreck with lots of life with reliefs 30 to 70ft deep. Lobster and big tog "tautog" are found here.

Fenwich Shoals is an easy 20-30ft dive with an upper thermo cline. From mid-June to September you can easily get by wearing a 3ml suit when you dive here. This last July the Vis was around 30-40ft. There are several wrecks out here covering more than an acre of substrate. Some of the wrecks on the outer Fenwick Shoals include the steamship *Brinkburn*, the Norwegian *Siam*, and on the inner Fenwick Shoals rests the 300ft long *BoilerWreck*. Lots of fish make this a popular site for spearfishing.

The Marine Electric has been described as one "Bad @ss Wreck". The former coal carrier sank in 1983, 32miles out in zone 5 to the sand at 130ft and the top is at 70ft of depth, but at 605ft long, it will take several dives to see it all. Capt. Kogon would like to mention that spear fishing and catching lobster is the number one sport in the Mid-Atlantic and at this site you can catch black bass, cobia, amberjacks, and jack crevalle, but in the summer months when the warmer waters slide up, you can spear mahi mahi, and blue fin tuna here.

George Carter from **Undersea Outfitters**, Says that the 563ft long **USS Arthur Radford** sunk as an artificial reef in 2011 in zone 5 is very popular with divers. Lots of mussels and lobsters at 70ft on the top deck are already calling the 140ft deep former destroyer home. George also likes the 165ft long buoy tender **Arthur Hall** sitting upright at 80ft on deck and down to 120ft touching sand, and the 120ft long merchant ship the **Sussex** at 85ft which recently had vis between35-45ft and was frequented by several angel sharks; both are in zone 4 and have swim thru sites for advanced divers. George says this last summer was unseasonably warm and water surface temperatures were around 85 degrees, but at 70ft of depth, the temp occasionally dropped down to 62 degrees, but If you got cold, all you had to do was ascend just a little bit to warm back up.

Since George has been diving for over 30years, I asked him about **U-boat 1105** near the mouth of the Potomac River near St. Mary's, MD. The U-boat was brought back to study the synthetic rubber called "Alberich" which was used to cover the hull and help make it less detectable by enemy warships. After the studies were complete the sub was used to test explosives. The subs compartments ruptured from the test explosions and it sank upright to 91ft in 1949 and wasn't rediscovered until 1985. You would think that thousands of divers would be flocking to this dive site, but the problem as George explained it, is that quite often it is hard to see your own hand in this low vis area. To see up to 8ft, you may have to look 4ft in front and 4ft behind you. It's an advanced diver only area, and you may, or may not get a chance to see the upper works and the conning tower rising above the substrate and camouflaged with marine growth.

Undersea Outfitters also operates **Hydes Quarry**, which is the only fresh water quarry open to divers in Maryland every Saturday and Sunday. There are small boats, a jeep, a school bus, and the other typical quarry attractions that make it interesting for divers preferring to concentrate on training, or just having fun underwater. From the air I have seen other quarries, but they are privately owned and you would have to ask the owners for permission to dive these sites.

Other local dive sites include: **Greenbrier Sate Park**, **Cunningham Falls**, **Deep Creek Lake**, **Rocky Gap State Park**, and sections of the **Potomac River** above the dams during the week when boat traffic is low. With any of these locations, consult a Park Ranger before you dive, and have a dive flag or boat with a dive flag trailing right with you during the dive. I've heard there are spots to dive in Baltimore around the marina, but seek a local dive shop consultant before tempting fate around so much local boat traffic.

Last, but not least, I know I'm a marine biologist, and I like seeing fish in their native environment, but I do get a kick out of diving aquariums. In this case, we are talking about **The National Aquarium in Baltimore**. You can see sharks, rays, and some 50 other species of fish close up and personal with unparalleled visibility, and no boat travel time whatsoever. After a little class time and conservation messages you are going to be tanked, converted, and hooked on aquarium diving. Check online in advance for scheduled experience times, openings, and prerequisites.

To wrap it up, there are plenty of outstanding Mid-Atlantic wrecks to explore right off of Ocean City. Freshwater sites include state parks, lakes, and Hyde's Quarry. You can also dive The National Aquarium in Baltimore. Maryland, the Mid-Atlantic, and the Chesapeake Bay have a long rich history of marine sites, aquatic life, and numerous dive adventures. Great Dives!

Massachusetts
Bring On The Boston Lobsters

When it comes to choices, Boston has a plethora of activities to choose from. You can visit the USS Constitution, the oldest commissioned warship afloat, and then historically dine at the Union Oyster House: America's oldest restaurant. You can visit Bunker Hill, then grab a bite and brew at the original *Cheers* on Beacon Street. You can mix and match by visiting Kings Chapel, the oldest continuously operating church in America across the street from the Parker Omni House Hotel and near the Boston Commons Park, then devour a foot long Subway Sandwich. Or, you can travel out to Fenway Park and have a ball, fly by you, as you enjoy an all American hot dog.

The underwater attractions around Boston have many similarities to the land attractions. You have tons of choices and unless you live in the Boston area, I recommend you call in sick for a few months to try and explore all the dive sites. My short list of dive sites around the Boston area includes over 20 dive sites. My expanded list, which includes the dives around Cape Ann, mounts up to over 40 dives, and neither of these two lists includes all the possible dive sites around the islands out in the Boston Harbor. What topographical substrate to expect at each site varies from pinnacles, boulders, rocks, gravel, sand, walls, wrecks, and kelp. So with so much to choose from, I asked local experts at a few dive shops, what their three most favorite dive sites are and here are the results of my enquiry.

Captain James Sulivan of *The Boston Harbor Diving Company* said **The Graves, Martins Ledge, and the wreck of the City of Salisbury** were his favorite three dives. He likes **The Graves** because, " the color of rocks, the swim throughs, the stripped bass and lobsters." **Martins Ledge** "has walls in some spots, a pinnacle starts at 25ft and drops down to 60ft. With Pollock, flounder, and lobster. The **Wreck of the City of**

Salisbury "has scattered debris. The wreckage dropped off into two sections. One section is against a 25ft deep pinnacle that goes down to 55ft at the base. The bow section rests at 90ft and there are still gadgets and bronze items down there." The city of Salisbury went down in 1938. It was a 415ft long freighter.

Nick Sazah from *East Coast Divers* likes **Magnolia Rocks**, **Cathedral Rocks, and Pickett's Ledge**. He likes **Magnolia Rock**s shore dive because "of its boulder formations and lots of sea life." He likes **Cathedral Rocks** because, "it's a nice easy deep shore dive: 70 to 80ft with big boulders and lobsters. At high tide you can do a giant stride entry." At low tide, not so much. For Boat dives he likes **Pickett's Ledge**. "Lobsters and soft corals such as anemones. From 20ft to 60-70ft. Wall of rocks, tons of crevices, and lots of marine life because it's offshore."

Mark Potter of *MASS Diving* recommends **Saturday Night Ledge** its between 80 to 130ft deep. "It has northern rays, spider crabs, sea anemones, starfish such as blood stars and sun bursts . . .it's like a coral reef." He likes **Halfway Rock** because "it's a big rock that looks like an upside down Ice cream cone. 50ft of pinnacle the bottoms at 120ft. Soft corals between 80 to 100ft. You just spiral around the rock. A pretty dive." It's Mark's favorite dive site, but he stresses that it is for more experienced divers due to drifting tendencies. To round it all up Mark likes **Dry Salvages**. "There are grooves, swim throughs, and crevices. It's only 45ft deep and it's fun to play with the seals." And of course there are the lobsters.

Besides these hot spots, other wreck dives include:

The **Romance**, which sank in 1936 in 70-80ft of depth. The **Kiowa**, which sank in 1903 at 30-40ft. The **Charles Haight** liberty ship sunk in 1946 in 45ft of depth. The wreck of the **Chester Poling**, an oil tanker, sunk 90ft in 1977. These are just a few of the wrecks most often named.
For drift diving there is Broad Sound. You can drift from **Nahant to Deer Island** with kelp and gravel at 30 to 70ft.

For shore diving most of it occurs on Cape Ann. Besides choosing between rock, gravel, or sand terrains, you have to also take parking into consideration. **Marblehead**

Light, aka (Chadley Hovey State Park) allows no diving on the weekends. **Norman's Woe** allows residents only to park nearby. So you have a long walk to get to the kelp beds in 10-35ft of depth. At **Stage Fort Park**, there is a fee in season, and no fee off-season. **Whale Cove** has no parking, so plan to have someone drop you off. As with all shore dives, keeping pets on leash, reducing levels of noise, and leaving the area litter free will build respect and friendship with the locals and keep these areas open to divers for years to come.

Now if you are new to the area and unsure of where or with whom to dive, one good method to meet and dive with other locals is to take a Losbster Hunter Specialty Course at a local dive shop. You might introduce yourself to your next dive buddy and have a chance fine dive and dine with lobsters. Of course if you catch a lobster over 22lbs, 3.5ft long and over 140years old, don't eat it, because you may have just won a world record. Whether or not you are in to lobsters, you can also join a local dive club such as the *Boston Sea Rovers, Decapod Divers*, or join the *MIT Scuba Club* to meet and buddy up with fellow divers.

Besides all these dive sites, Boston divers are known to go over to **Deer Island**, dive the coast of **Maine**, and explore the **St. Lawrence River** in Canada. Some Boston divers are known to frequent **Dutch Springs** in Pennsylvania as a yearly event. I've also met Boston divers out in the Grand Cayman Island. Sure, the spiny lobsters may have a historic background of over 110 million years in the fossil records, but they are slight of meat compared to Boston heavy clawed cousins.

So there you go, dozens and dozens of local dive sites. Great boat dives as well as shore dives. There are multiple substrates filled with diverse forms of sea life. Some shore dives will make you plan ahead to meet the parking times, fees, seasons, and other regulations, but they are all worth the effort. There are wreck dives sites still laden with wreckage. Pinnacles and wall dives seem to be everywhere. In all, there are many dive site choices to choose from and it will take time to explore them all. This is what makes the diving around Boston unique, and if you love diving, this is what will keep you coming back to dive the Boston area for years to come. Great Dives.

Michigan
Four Great Lakes And More

Michigan is like no other State in the Union when it comes to diving. The territory of Michigan might have become just another medium sized state had it not been for the Toledo War with the U.S. State of Ohio. In exchange for giving up its rights to a small strip of land not much bigger than a white borderline on a map along with the city of Toledo to Ohio, Michigan not only attained statehood, but also in the compromise was given an enormous strip of land right above present day Wisconsin. With the addition of this strip of land, Michigan became the largest state in total square foot area east of the Mississippi River, the only State consisting of two peninsulas, and the only State to share borders with four out of the five Great Lakes. It is said that Michigan contains close to 65,000 lakes and ponds and that you are never more than 6miles from one of these water sites, and 85 miles from a great lake. Driving from the airport into Grand Rapids is a good place to look for ducks in the ponds between the buildings and office centers. Grand Haven and the sandy shores of Lake Michigan are a mere 25minutes away from Grand Rapids.

Needless to say, Michigan has to be the number one King of freshwater dive destinations in the U.S.A. Over the last 200 years, hundreds of ships have come to rest off the shores of Michigan. Ships were lost in storms, torn open by ice, burnt to the waterline, sustained sudden death by colliding with other vessels, abruptly beached while trying to keep from sinking due to leaks, ran into rocks due to faulty rudders, faulty maps, faulty judgment, and a great repeated deal of tragic human error and exceptional bad luck.

Since the 1950"s divers have been collecting artifacts from some of these wrecks, but in 1980 the Michigan Underwater Preserve System was enacted by the legislature and the support of divers who wanted these wrecks to remain intact so that generations of divers to come could enjoy these historic monuments too. It is currently a felony to remove any item from the wrecks in some 13-preserve areas that include some 209wrecks and 2300 square miles of substrate. Anyone caught removing a porthole, lantern, or spoon, can receive up to two years of imprisonment and a large benthic fine. Because of this enactment, you can dive on a wreck and see tools still on a bench, artifacts resting where they went down with the ship, and cargo holds still full of coal, lumber, and other goods from a time long passed by. The water temperature of 40-60° has helped keep preserve these historic sites.

For a complete list of all the known preserve area wrecks check out *A Diver's Guide to Michigan Underwater Preserves* or go to www.michiganpreserves.org. Near Alpena, *Thunder Bay Underwater Preserve* has the highest density in any preserve with a total of 27 documented wrecks and close to another 80 wrecks still in the discovery process. The **Mackinaw** rests in 6ft of water and the **Pewabic** from 148ft-168ft. The south east side is also home of limestone walls and reefs. Recreational dive trips on charter boats out here may include 2-3dives per day and this area is only 4hours north of Ann Arbor.

Whitefish Point on Lake Superior has some of the deepest wrecks so when you dive with charters here, they may require you to be an advanced diver with at least an extra redundant 13cf pony bottle of air or double tanks. Whitefish is home to 28 documented wrecks of which four are in 10ft of depth, and the **Superior City** is 190-270ft deep. Intermediate and advanced divers have several wrecks to choose from, but seven of the wrecks are strictly for Technical divers.

The Straits of Mackinac Shipwreck Preserve has 13 wrecks, two of which have the bow region separate from the stern. The 600ft long freighter **Cedarville** resting in two pieces down at 105ft is the third largest wreck in the Great Lakes.

Isle Royale National Park is only 20miles from Minnesota and Silver Bay, so expect to see summer charters up here from multiple states. Isle Royal is 45 miles long and has 15 wrecks. Because this is a national park, divers need to register to dive here. The 182ft long freighter **America** rests in 2ft to80ft and the bow of the 250ft long **Kamloops** rests at 240 to 260ft.

Keweenaw Underwater Preserve is home to 12 wrecks and more artifacts on **Eagle River**, **Eagle Harbor**, and **Copper Harbor**. Near Houghton there are three breweries that are the most northern breweries in the state. Did I mention that there are over 90 breweries in the state? And that Michigan is the third largest producer of Riesling wine in the country?

Marquete and Alger Underwater Preserves have a combined 21wreck. *Manitou Passage, Grand Traverse Bay and Southwest Michigan Underwater Preserves* have over 33 wrecks, and *Detour Passage, Thumb Area Bottomland, and Sanilac Shores Underwater Preserves* have a total of over 46wrecks. The proposed *West Michigan Underwater Preserve* will soon be coming online with 12 additional wrecks. Two things are certain in Michigan and one is that more wrecks are increasingly being documented or discovered, and more preserves are certainly being created or increasing in area size.

For shore dives along Lake Huron, any harbor such as the abandoned **Rock Harbor**, **Thompson's Harbor**, or other landmarks such as **Presque Isle Point** and **Forty Mile Point Lighthouse** are good dive sites.

Now if you like collecting artifacts, then you might like a drift dive down the **St. Clair River** starting at the Blue Water Bridge with depths of 80ft, or near the **St. Joseph River** Bridge off Planger Park in Benton Harbor with a max depth of 8ft. What many divers are searching for at these sites are old onion flask bottles from the 1700's to blob top bottles from the 1800's.

As for lakes and ponds go, there are several quite popular dive sites including: **Lake Sixteen** at 85ft max in Allegan County, **Baptist Lake** at 65ft deep in Newaygo County, **Fisher Lake** in Three Rivers, **Pickerel Lake** near Lansing, **Orchard Lake** in Oakland County, **Clark Lake** near Jackson, **Big Portage Lake** in the Waterloo Recreation Area, **Spring Mill Pond** near Brighton, and **Paw Paw Lake** in Coloma.

Because there are so many dive sites in Michigan, there is no way to cover them all in one article. Fortunately for you, it easy to find out more about local diving through one of the 35 or more dive shops located throughout the state. Wolf's Diver Supply in Benton is one of the oldest dive shops in the country; starting in 1956. With so many dive shops, so much combined diving experience, and so many bodies of freshwater wrecks to explore, Michigan is a top dive destination; I hope you soon have a chance to dive and discover this fact for yourself too. Great Dives.

Minnesota
Superior & Unusual Dive Sites

Minnesota is a land full of diveable lakes including a big one called Lake Superior. This might have been enough dive sites for most divers, but not for the people of Minnesota, so they dug and mined the earth and removed huge loads of iron ore out of the way just so that they could later let the holes and mines fill in with fresh water to make even more colorful dive sites. Not completely satisfied yet, they slowly accumulated wrecks along Lake Superior's shoreline, a distance of at least wider than my index finger, according to my map. Finally, to out do the surrounding states, Minnesota diving enthusiasts added a saltwater habitat where finding shark teeth is as simple as running your hand through the sand, which I pleasantly found a lot less risky than running a hand along the mouth of a shark.

Starting out with Lake Superior, there are many shore dive locations such as the boulders at **Gooseberry** or the break wall of **Silver Bay**. Structures such as those around **Split Rock Light House**, **Silver Cliff Caves**, and **Knife Island Wall** may be neat, but these dive sites are all overshadowed by famous wrecks that rest some 5 to 360feet below Superior's surface. Some of the more popular wrecks in alphabetic order include:

The *A.C.Adams*, a 62ft long wooden tug boat built in 1881 that sank to 118ft of depth after a collision in 1892.

The *Hesper*, a 250ft long wooden steamer built in 1890 and sunk in 1905 and broke up on the Silver Bay Harbor breakwall. Some parts sunk in 42ft of water, while other parts drifted and sunk at various depths 5 miles away.

The *Madiera*, a 436ft long schooner barge built in 1900 and sank in 1905 after hitting Gold Rock north of current day Split Rock Lighthouse. Divers found it again in 1955. The non-salvaged parts rest between 15 to 100ft deep. Over a thousand divers find this wreck each year.

The *Mayflower*, a 147ft long wooden scow built in 1889 and sank in 1891 in 90ft of water. The bow and stern are still in good shape and make it seem like the wreck has only been below the surface a few years rather than over a hundred years.

The *Niagara*, a 130ft long rafting tug built in 1872 and lost in 1904 after running ashore and breaking up on Knife Island. The wreck rests on a slope between 65 to 95ft deep.

The *Samuel P. Ely*, a 200ft long schooner barge built in 1869 and sank in 1896 against the breakwaters in Two Harbors in 25ft of depth. Divers found the wreck in the 1950's and started removing many artifacts in 1958-1961. Since that time, divers helped keep the haul from breaking apart and from some of those divers, the Great Lakes Shipwreck Society was formed.

The *Thomas Wilson*, a 308ft long whale back freighter built in 1892 and sunk in 1902 in 70ft of water after being rammed by a steamer named *George Hadley* one mile from the entrance to the Duluth Harbor entrance. The Wilson along with its cargo of mesabi iron ore was dynamited, as it was a navigational hazard, but still there are a lot of remains to explore.

Check with local dive shops as well as local charter operators for departure dates to these great dive sites.

Now when it comes to other lakes, it is sometimes hard to tell natural lakes from the artificial lakes. Both are lined with trees and filled with fish such as walleye, crappie, bass, trout and northern pike, but the former mined areas turned lakes may also come with sunken foundations, roads, and mine shafts. Some former pits are deep too, such as the 352ft deep **Portsmouth Mine Pit** or the 530ft deep **Mahnomen Iron Mine/lake**. Some lakes like **Caribou Lake** at 152ft max depth are used for Ice diving in the winter and free diving in the summer. The **Cuyuna State Recreational Park** part of Crosby, Ironton and Deerwood comprises some 55 former open pit mine dive sites. The dive site that were formerly mines, were in operation so long that trees grew at all levels, so expect to see many trees still in place with branches at these sites; **Diamond Cove** would be a good example. Also plan to see cars underwater like the white car that needs some work and a new front hood such as the one in (Alstead) **Shangri La**, or the white van in **Ironston Lake**. By the way, if your van says "*City of Crosby*" on the side and has a license plate ending in 722, you might be a bad driver or have bad brakes. The sunken dump truck that reads "*L&L Const, Inc.*" was possibly stolen.

All the aforementioned dive sites sound and look normal, but these last two dive sites I'll mention are in a class of their own:

Square Lake in Stillwater, part of the twin cities area, is only 30-40ft deep, but it is used year round for diving. Underwater there is an eclectic collection of objects including: a tail section of a plane, a toilet, small boats, and pipes arranged to hang in the water in an artful way. There is also a chainsaw, which I presume someone dropped while trying to cut a triangle out of the 18inch winter ice to go ice diving. An annual treasure dive is held here when the ice has moved on and warmer waters prevail. There are also six other well-known diveable lakes in the twin cities area from the 113ft deep **Lake Minnetonka** to the 76ft deep **Little Long Lake**.

Eternal Bliss dive site, Louise Mine Pit, is like Halloween on every dive and includes: underwater fake tombstones, a large crayfish holing a skeleton head with a dive mask, "*Marrisa*" the mermaid with a funky algae infested hairdo at 50ft, a pirate skeleton on a small boat, a skeleton biker hauling a skeleton passenger in a cart, and the ever popular "*Sparkey*"; a skeleton working on an electrical box at 60ft. There are other objects like the lawn mower to keep the dive platform silt free (when it runs), and a small boat down at 100ft incase you care, but the real haunting nitrogen narcosis seems to kick in around 60ft or less at this particular spooky cool dive site.

Lastly, At the **Mall of America** in Minneapolis, and for less than the price of an American Girl Doll plus accessories, you can dive with sharks at ***Underwater Adventures Aquarium***. Here at *Sharks Cove* you can take pictures of sawtooth, zebra, stingrays, and wobbegong sharks. Also, if you look closely near the exit point you can find sand tiger shark teeth resting right on the sand. At *Fishing Hollow* you can swim with paddlefish, turtles, alligator gars, and sturgeon in spectacular high vis definition fresh water.

With mines, lakes, the wrecks of Lake Superior, and where diving at the Mall is on a floor of its own, Minnesota has a dive that is just right for any diver almost anytime of the year. Great Dives.

Underwater Adventures Aquarium
One Of A Kind Diving; Multiple Reasons

When it comes to the bucket list of places you have to dive, the Great Barrier Reef, Bonaire, and the Grand Caymans are near the top of the list, but so should a dive in Minnesota. Not just any dive in Minnesota, but two specific dives at, of all places, the Mall of America at Underwater Adventures Aquarium. At first you might think I'm crazy, but after you've discovered what goes on on these dives, you'll know why it stacks up chin to chin against a typical day of diving in some other rather exotic location.

What makes diving in an Aquarium of this caliber so unique? First of all the water clarity is a major plus. But the biggest single aspect to consider is that the aquarium animal life is accustomed to divers and don't see divers as a threat like they might in the wild. They are comfortable to glide and swim right beside you making this an ideal dive site to nuzzle up next to an enthusiastic sturgeon fish or a curious bow mouth guitarfish. You could also find yourself mere inches away from a large loggerhead turtle, something you could almost never do in the wild.

A typical adventure starts with a behind the scenes tour of the aquarium. What you may see are baby freshwater stingrays in a private tank with their mother; they won't go on exhibit until they are much larger, so this may be the only way to see them this small. You could also see fish not currently on exhibit, such as the juvenile paddlefish, or the piranha as they wait to be shipped to another aquarium. You'll also see the touring hand held creatures like the cowries and brittle stars. Finally, you'll see the fish in quarantine before they ever get to join the aquarium, and the wildlife recovering from health issues. As a marine biologist they had already hooked me, and if I lived nearby, I would probably be working here every free minute, but on this day, for everyone else, the best was yet to come.

We suited up, the aquarium supplied the tanks and weights, and we went for a dive in Fishing Hollow. On this dive the staff was Kelly Drews, Kathy Bonjie, and Katie Kirschbaum. Kelly was the lead guide. While Kathy and Katie came in the water behind us carrying a bucket of night crawlers to feed to the fish. Kelley and I made a slow pass around the tank and I took pictures of alligator gars, longnose gar, walleye, muskie, turtles, catfish, and sturgeon. I thought the exhibit tank was bigger than I first expected. The logs in the tank and sea grass are not anchored down so that every wave from every diver or fish can constantly change the overall look of the surrounding environment. After a swim around the exhibit photography session, I took images of Kathy and Katie feeding the sturgeon and turtles worms. Katie gave me some worms and I have to tell you that it feels weird as sturgeon suck the worms right off your hand like a low pressure cycling vacuum cleaner. The turtles hang down on the sand and just wait for the extra worms to fall their way. Life is good when you have clean water, no natural predators, and plenty of worms. We did some more leisurely diving around the fresh water exhibit then exited to have a snack.

Having warmed up, Kelly led a dive briefing for the salt-water exhibit, Sharks Cove. There are seven species of sharks in this exhibit along with stingrays, tuna, and sea turtles. We geared up and made our way into a little entrance pool; that is once we got the little white tip sharks to move out of the way for a few minutes. They prefer sitting in one place and having the currents blow oxygenated water through their gills. Outside the pool Kelly took the lead and I followed behind him. Kathy and Katie were right behind me. The three K's all had black and white striped pvc poles for moving the sharks away if they decided to get too close to us. Only the large sand tiger sharks were aggressive enough to ever warrant a slight touch by the poles. The sawtooth, wobbegongs, zebra, and reef sharks were indifferent to our being there. They just swam around in endless patterns giving us ample close up views of these beautiful cartilaginous creatures. The first corner of the tank we came to we saw the nurse sharks huddle together. We swam by them and up over the cement roof section of the underground tunnel system. Down below us on of the display only inches away from us.

Too soon, it was time to leave. We changed into street clothes and I thanked them for the dives. They give you a T-shirt that proclaims to the world that you swam with the sharks. You then get to tour the aquarium and walk through every tunnel you just swam over. It gives you a completely different perspective about the exhibits, and the animal life in those exhibits. I took more pictures from the dry side including some images of the tropical fish, the many varieties sea horses, and the ubiquitous jellyfish of every sort and size.

With all the fresh water animals and all the sea creatures you get to dive with in such close proximity you can't afford to pass up on an adventure like this. Sure, you should still go to the Caribbean, but add Adventures Underwater Aquarium to the top of your dive bucket list. This is a unique dive experience like no other you've ever experienced before. Great Dives.the over side was a group of southern stingrays. We swam past them over to a sandy area next to the see through glass tunnel. Human families were walking through the tunnels and we waved at them and the kids waved back at us. More wobbegongs were perched on the walls behind us. A big sawtooth shark, then a large sand tiger shark went by. I took some images, then we swam over the tunnel and over to a patch of sand where the sharks swam by as part of their regular exhibit tour route. More time for images, then over another section of the underground tunnel we glided. On the other side we stopped to look in the sand for shark teeth. This was actually harder than I thought it would be, because the sand they use in the tanks is high quality tropical sand complete with pieces or whole invertebrate shells that have the same white glossy finish as the shark teeth. Kelly showed me how to find them and soon we were putting the teeth on the ledge for the kids walking by to stop and see. While holding pointed teeth in my glove, I took out my regulator and pointed at my teeth with my free index finger. This was a big hit with the kids watching on the other side

Mississippi Dive Sites
Can you keep a Secret?

It's no secret that if you dip in a lake or pond in Mississippi, you may not see your hand in front of your face, let alone the sudden flash of a catfish as local divers catch giant catfish bare handed while in the midst of a sport called "Noodling". Eons of silt moving across the land has made it difficult to see anything, and as the Mississippi River flows into the Gulf, it can leave a layer of heavily silted brackish water that looks like chocolate milk, 20 to 30ft deep. Mississippi State has put in 67 artificial reefs near shore and next to fishing piers, but you may have to go out more than 2 miles before the depth reaches 15ft. This makes it almost impossible to descend near shore and have any visibility. Far from shore, the visibility is clearly better, but as of yet, the diving here is an untold story.

Jerry Atkinson of *The Dive Shop* in D'Iberville says that once you are out 30-40miles, the visibility may pick up to 40-100ft or more. So when you are diving an oilrig, the top may have a layer of suspended silt particles. The bottom may have silt sediment, but the middle column of water may be a horizontal artificial reef sweet spot with great visibility and with lots to look at. Out from shore, oilrigs are known as vertical reefs in an oasis of empty substrate. Keep in mind that when the shrimp boats are dragging their nets during shrimp season, the vis may go down, but the vis will eventually improve again, with July to September being the best time of year for visibility.

So why isn't everyone jumping onboard boats to go out for a dive? Well, it turns out that there are few charters that go out to the rigs and other dive sites. Also divers have to pay a little more for the trip and gas because the sites are so far out, and the journey could take the entire day from 8am until 4pm. So when divers look at the expense for diving out here in the gulf compared to traveling out of state to dive, at first glance the out of state trip looks like a better deal. I say at first glance, because most people don't count the gas, food, or time it takes to drive over to another state.

Teddy Craven from *Adventure Charters* at Moss Point has an even better reason to dive off Mississippi, and that's because the wrecks off Florida are dove at least twice a week, while some of the wrecks off Miss are dove only twice a year. So what you see on an Ole Miss dive are artificial reefs full of life in virtually pristine virgin condition. He thinks that the reefs are diamonds in the rough as well as the uninhabited islands that you pass by on your way out to the sites. Teddy has been diving since the eighties. He is a former SSI and Handicapped Association Diving Instructor and operates the boat "Sea Angel". On his web site you see a picture of a brightly painted yellow wheelchair facing the ocean. After a brief conversation with Teddy, I got the impression that the wheel chair displayed on the website is purely a device to get someone to the ocean, but not a device to hold anyone back from exploring the ocean.

So now you know that the dives sites in Miss are a diamond in the rough, but that's just part of the story. It turns out that the 67 inshore artificial reefs have much to do with why local fishing is so good, but little to do with why diving in old Miss is a diamond in the rough. Off shore, the Mississippi Gulf Fishing Banks, Inc " MGFB" has been working with the Mississippi Department of Marine Resources "MDMR" to form 14 numbered off shore fish habitats. The fish habitat "FH" sites cover thousands of acres of formerly barren underwater substrate and contain, tugboats, shrimp boats, barges cement culverts, and reef balls, among other objects. FH sites 8-10 are actually inshore of the outer islands while FH7 is miles and miles out by itself. So what actually is out at these sites? Here is a brief short list: FH-1 has reef balls, culverts, **Ole Faithful** shrimp boat at 68ft deep, the 50ft long **Elsie** landing craft at 58ft deep, and a 180ft long barge. FH-2 has culverts and the 70ft long **St. Elmo** shrimp boat at 58ft deep. FH-3 has the 48ft long **Chevron Vessel** down at 45ft. FH-6 has reef balls, FH-7 the **Rowan** oilrig crew quarters down at 128ft, and the nearby 400ft long **Jumbo Barge**. FH-8-10 have reef balls and culverts.

FH-12 has the 195ft long hopper barge **Mathews** at 42ft and the 45ft long shrimp boat **Frank Taylor** (Lucky Jimmy). FH-13 has the mother load of culverts, concrete catch basins and manholes, the "**BRT**" Big Round Thing, which is a hydrogen accumulator tank at 85ft deep, the 80ft long **Southern Star** shrimp boat, The **Tiger Shark** shrimp boat down at 88ft, the 175ft long **Great Wicomico** (Pogey Boat) at 88ft, the **St. Johns** shrimp boat down at 84ft, the **Linda Susan** (Gerald Corcoran) river tug, the 70ft long **Four Boys** at 66ft of depth, and the **Kay Eckstein** tub boat at 80ft. FH-14 has the **MyWifeII** shrimp boat. At these sites expect to see tons of fish and critters including red snapper, triggerfish, tomtate, drum, cigar minnows, cobia, tuna, butterfly fish, sheep head wrasse, spadefish, grouper, arrow crab, shrimps, and soft coral.

Now if all of this isn't enough, George Burton of *Dixie Marine* in Biloxi and with his boat the "Scuby Do", likes go to the east end of **Dauphin Island** to dive around the working **Rig 925** or the **Apache Rig**. A mile from these rigs, and for years before Hurricane Katrina, the wreck of the 65ft long **Blue Wing** at 70ft had a resident nurse shark and a sea turtle. George also likes the diving around the **Horse Shoe Rigs** 60miles out from shore. South of FH-13 you can also find the rig **VK68**, the **V-Rig Air Force Tower**, and the **Fox Tug**.

Weather, currents, river, and commercial shrimping activity can effect the visibility dramatically, but when you do dive Ole Miss, you'll see pronounced activity and unusual abundance of sea life in the fish habitats and around the wrecks and rigs where few have ever visited before. It may up front seem like it costs a little more and takes a little more time to travel out to some of these sights, but there are no long car rides and associated expenses as with diving out of state, and when you arrive at these dive sites you won't be waiting for your boat's turn like planes waiting to land in Las Vegas, you'll be able to gear up and dive in like your in charge of an Apollo moon mission. You may feel like you're the first to ever visit one of these remote dive destinations, but don't tell a soul; it's our little secret. Great Dives.

Missouri
Diving Mecca Of The Midwest

Missouri diving is in a class by itself for many reasons. Missouri is only one of two states that touches borders with, and is surrounded by, eight other states. Divers pour into Missouri from the surrounding states and perhaps that explains why there are more dive shops in Missouri than just about any other state except for Florida. I stopped counting dive shops and stores when the count was close to two dozen, and that doesn't include the dive shops that are just on the other side of the eight bordering state lines. So what brings all these divers to Missouri?

To start with lets talk about what brought Jacques Cousteau and his team to Missouri's **Bonne Terre Mine**. Bonne Terre, "Good Earth", mine started operating in 1870 and stopped in 1961. Almost one hundred years of digging tunnels, making scaffolds, staircases, pillars, and an elevator shaft mixed with slurry boxes, ore carts, gratings, lanterns, and natural cave mineral formations have given this mine the appearance of Disneyland themed movie set with four of the five levels of the mine left underwater. In short, if Indiana Jones had dive gear available, this is where he would have dove. You can only dive here on the weekends, but during the week they have walking and boat tours. On Saturdays, underwater trails 1,2, & 4 are typically dove. Once you have these dives stamped in your logbook, you can do other trails on Sunday. There are some 50 underwater trails in all. Average depth is 40-60ft; advanced dives 100ft. Vis is around 100ft and temp 58°, so bring a 7ml wetsuit or preferably a drysuit. At this current time, the dives are $65 each with a two-dive into the drink minimum and you need to sign up and pay in advance: your dive fee includes tanks and divers go out in escorted groups. Each group consists of up to 12divers max, plus a dive guide in the lead, and an additional safety diver. Other rules concerning no dive lights and flash photography apply. The busy season starts in November, when diving an indoor underground lake void of fish sounds way more appealing than diving outdoors in ice bound lakes and cold breezy reservoirs. At 60miles from St. Louis, Bonne Terre Mine is easy to get to.

Moving on to a lake above ground and encompassing 52,300 surface acres or 857 shoreline miles, we have **Table Rock Lake** next to Branson, MO. This is a big lake with the best dive sites reached by boat. Some of theses sites include: **Zebulon Pike** where down at 95ft you can find a 90ft long double-decker excursion boat. At **Enchanted Forest** you will find giant oak trees still standing and rising up towards the surface. At **Jakes Point Island** there is a cabin cruiser. Other sites of note include: **Dutch Island**, **The Saddle**, **Breezy Point**, and **Spoonbill Bluff**. Shore dives include **Dewey Short** with a staircase down to a gravel beach, or around the marinas, but watch out for the boats and carry a dive flag. Vis may be low until you pass around 30ft in depth then the vis opens up from 10-25ft. Expect 50° temps at depth too.

Bennett Spring State Park in Lebanon is a pool stocked full of trout and down at 20ft a corridor of 10x20 leads down to a max depth of 85ft where a bed of pebbles sound and are shot upward like popcorn. Only six divers per day are allowed to dive here, with four divers max on any given decent: two dive groups of 3 people each works best. The site is open to divers from November till February. Vis can reach over 40ft, but goes down dramatically after rainy days. Sculpin fish, minnows, and crayfish like the 56-58° temp. Reservations are necessary. There is no dive fee, but perhaps we should all give a small donation for Park upkeep and future improvements; check out the Bennett Spring trout web cam.

Stockton Lake has 300miles of shoreline and 24,000 acres of water filled with walleye, bluegills, flathead catfish, and several species of bass including white and Kentucky. Max depth is around 100ft. The vis averages 8-10ft and increases in the springtime, and activities such as camping and horseback riding make this a good place to get wet. Popular sites to enter the water include around the marinas and east of the 215 bridge.

Now when it comes to quarries, Missouri has some of the oldest in the nation. **Mine La Motte** in Madison County, had lead mined here in the 1600's by local Native American Indians, in the early 1700's, by French Colonials, and in 1861 by Confederate forces. It is now called "**The Off-Sets**". It is divided into two sections, one open recreational diver quarry side with a couple of cavern areas and one cave diver only side. Dive here before or after summer, as this spot is highly sought out for 50ft cliff diving, zip lining, and camping in the summer. With a max depth of 50ft, vis up to 30ft, and a temp at depth of 40 some degrees, dress warmly and bring your "C" card.

A couple of quarries have recently undergone changes, and **The Dive Stop** in New Melle, set next to a 5acre, 62ft max deep lake is now operated by *Trident Rescue* and used for Public Safety and Recreational Training and currently not available to the open public. **Captain John's Sports and Scuba** in Oronogo is currently set to be part of the Super Fund cleanup. This 14acre, 230ft max deep lake may have to be filled in to meet EPA requirements. There was a Budweiser style small boat at 85ft, a cabin cruiser at 100ft, an air cave, an old blacksmith shop, platforms, and various statues. The reason I mention these two sites, is because putting off a dive today may mean never getting a chance to make that dive at a later date and time.

Quail Run in Rolla, Mo is a former quarry, and has 35ft of depth, but vis is between 5-15ft. **Finger Lakes State Park** in Columbia is not your typical quarry, but is an actual open strip coal mine converted into an elongated lake. It is 1.5miles long, depth is 30-100ft deep, and it is stocked with bass and bluegill. There are several other dive sites such as **Rubidoux Spring Cave** that is open year round to certified cave divers. Some other Missouri State springs are restricted to scientific divers only.

As you can see, Missouri has several "one of a kind" dive sites to explore and you will have to compete with divers from many states for reservations and the chance to explore. Many Missouri dive sites are spring fed and the temperatures drop fast below thermo clines, but many of the sites have visibility better than the surrounding states, which help make these dive sites extremely popular. It's Ironic that French explorers first mined many of these quarries, only to be later dived by French divers such as Jacques Cousteau's team; no doubt you too will enjoy these sites. Great Dives.

Montana
Big Dive Country

No matter how many times I visit Montana it never ceases to amaze me how big and sparsely developed the landscape actually is, with blue skies, rolling plains, robust mountains, and tons of natural wildlife, but even more impressive than all this, are the streams, rivers, lakes . . . and of course, the dive sites.

Starting right in the northwest region of the state we have the Glacier National Park, which is home to more than 700 lakes and 200 waterfalls. Only 131 of the Lakes have been named and the smaller ones are locally known as glacial tarns. Some of them have milky white or opaque turquoise colored waters due to suspended particles; other lakes have over 50ft of visibility. **Lake McDonald** is the biggest of these lakes weighing in at 6,824 acres, 9.4miles long and 464ft deep. The lake is stocked with cutthroat, rainbow, bull, and lake trout. Divers come here to view and film the spawning of the Kokanee Salmon and to view woodstoves, and other artifacts thrown into the lake over the past 80years near the town of Apgar and known as the *Pitch Fork Forrest*.

Also near Apgar is **Sprague Creek** where a drought 100-200years ago then allowed trees to grow where there is now water flowing. You can view the trees and kokanee salmon on a swift paced dive.

Southwest of here and some 35 miles west of Kalispell is the 1,521acre **McGregor Lake**. The elevation is just under 4,000ft and the vis 25 to 65ft. Average depth is slightly over 100ft, and max depth is 220ft. Some of the popular sites include: Mac Point Fingers, Glacier Wall, and Wrecking Yard where you can find 2cars and a boat. McGregor Lake is a popular spot for catching crawdads by hand, or you can camp or spend the night in a cabin at the Resort, let the traps do all the work overnight and feast on crawdads the next day.

Flathead Lake is 6miles south of Kalispell, the lake covers 197sqr miles in surface area, is 227.3miles long, 15.5miles wide, it's slightly larger than Lake Tahoe, making it the largest fresh water lake east of the Mississippi River in the contiguous states. The Max depth is 370.7ft and the vis 40-100ft. This lake is actually a remnant of the once bigger Lake Missoula, which was an ancient inland sea. When it comes to fish, I can't think of anything you can't catch here, except for the legendary Flathead Monster. Mackinaw or lake trout over 25lbs and 42inches in length are caught here. Some of the dive sites include: *Wild Horse Island, Big Flat RockDeep Big Rock, Skidoo Bay, Big Arm Area, Wayfarers Recreation Area, and Blue Bay Campground.*

Seeley Lake is one of the few lakes where spearfishing is allowed. It's only 1,025 acres big and 125ft deep, but this stocked lake has produced 34inch long pike, and trout over 15lbs, but remember, any lake stocked with fish, is also stocked with lost lures, tackle boxes, and lost fishing poles.

Coopers Lake is another small lake at an altitude of 4500ft and has lots of hardwood logs at the north end where fish like to hang out.

Hardy Creek off HWY 15 is close to Tone Rock State Park and River's Bend Lodge Bed and Breakfast. Cliff divers like to jump here on weekends. It has medium size cliffs, a beach area, and the depth is 35ft max. Cliff divers are known to loose everything even their pants so its best to dive here when the jumping is minimal and you could be rewarded with kinds of prizes from watches, rings, sunglasses, and coins. The water can become swift at certain times of the year, so ask a local about conditions before you jump in over your head.

Canyon Ferry Dam is 20miles east of Helena. On the western side are picnic tables and a sandy shore entrance. As a boat dive you can dive Cemetery Island or near the flooded old dam and power plant where the depth is 24-80ft. Vis is lower here than some of the other sites, and a local guide is recommended.

A short distance west of Helena is **Spring Meadow Lake State Park** at 3,911ft. This 30acre non motorized boats only man made park was the site of a former gravel pit and is now home to trout, bass, sunfish, and turtles. At the dock, set a course for 190degrees and you will find a boat. Max depth is 35ft.

Hyalite Reservoir comprises 206acres and is 12 miles south if Bozeman at an elevation of 6,700ft. Here you will find nice diving in the summer and ice diving in the winter. Sites to see while underwater include the old forest service bridge and a small cave. Above water there are picnic tables and fire pits. The water is over 100ft deep and vis max is about 20ft.

Finally, we go 90miles south of Billings over to **Bighorn Lake** and the Bighorn Canyon National Recreation Area also known to locals as Yellow Tail Dam. The lake is 50miles long, has a surface area of 17,300acres, an elevation of around 3,660ft, and the vis can get up to 30ft in the summer and 50ft in the winter. The Dam is 525ft tall and the water depth is a few feet less. The Lake travels 71miles from Montana into Wyoming, and has 55miles of lake just in the Big Horn Canyon. *Barry's Landing* is the place to back a boat into the water or use the small beach to do a shore dive. There are 15 designated campsites here. If you need a marina for supplies or want to rent a boat, then you can go to *Ok-A-Beh Marina* near Hardin and Fort Smith. The marina is surrounded by majestic 2,000ft high cliffs and is closed in the winter. *Horseshoe Marina* in Lovell, Wyoming, is the southern alternate marina also has access to Bighorn Lake. Lake trout, burbot, and catfish are big draws here. Bighorn Canyon National Recreation Area visitor centers are found both in Lovell and Fort Smith. Keep in mind, when diving Montana the water temp can range from 30-70degrees depending on the time of year, and lately the winters have left less ice in the usual spots.

Before I wrote this article I took a 5mile stroll over to *Adventure Scuba* from downtown Billings. Things look deceivingly close on a map of Montana; yet end up miles apart in real life. Mandy Glover a PADI dive instructor at Adventure Scuba told me that it takes them about 7hrs to drive over and dive Flathead Lake, and a mere 12hours to drive and dive over at Seattle, where I had seen their group in years past. Montana divers also go south across the Wyoming border to dive

Yellowstone and **Lake Desmet**. It turns out that Montana is a big state with several big lakes to dive in and divers here don't mind traversing long distances to dive in other states as well, but what else would you expect from Big Dive Country? Great Dives.

Nebraska
Flat Waters, Record Size Fish

Some how Nebraska has been able to keep a low profile over the years and all the while the number of species and record sizes caught while spearfishing has been slowly over shadowing the surrounding states. This isn't the first time Nebraska has loomed large with wild life. The skeleton of the largest Mastodon ever found is now on display at The University of Nebraska State Museum in Lincoln. Nebraska was also the home to Eocene camels, horses, large bison, giant land tortoises, and huge lions. Nebraska was home to so many 35 million year old land dwelling species that one third of the Smithsonian collection from this time period were excavated right here in Nebraska. Back some 65million years ago during Cretaceous times, Nebraska was part of a vast sea, and that's why Lincoln has so many deposits of marine rock formations. Even 70million years ago, Mesozoic creatures of record size like the 40ft long plesiosaurs were swimming across the saltwater state.

So ok, Nebraska in the past had large creature species, but that doesn't explain the numbers of record size fish being found by divers in the flat waters today. Well, the record size fish turns out to be a combination of many factors. First, while making Interstate 80, road crews dug up the materials they needed to construct the roadway right next to the sites where they were directly building. Later, after the highway was completed, these abandoned sand and gravel pits filled in with water. Fish were then introduced on purpose or through floods. Speaking of floods, many reservoirs in the state were built to not only retain water for periods of drought, but to safe guard against periodic floods that had killed so many pioneer settlers in the past. The reservoirs are filled with numerous species of fish and are great places to dive and spearfish. Some of the record fish found locally include: 1lb sunfish, 67lb grass carp, 2lb white bass, almost 2lb yellow perch, 17lb drum, 1lb bluegill, 7lb long nose gar, and 26lb bigmouth buffalo fish. 3lb European rudd have also been caught in Nebraska, but this is an invasive species and local officials would like to see every single member of this species caught and cooked without much ceremony, seasoning and/or delay.

As far as places to go diving, spear fishing, or just looking at fish goes, **Lake McConaughy** near Ogallala, is the largest lake in the state with white sand beaches at an altitude of, 3,214ft. I should also add that it is 22miles long, 4 miles wide, 142ft deep by the dam, and attracts scuba divers and dive clubs from other states such as the *Rocky Mountain Scuba Divers*. Many divers like to go to **Martin Bay** on the NE side. The vis averages 12-15ft, but it can drop as low as 3ft or up to 40ft. You can search for the foundation remains of the old town of *Lemoyne* or try to find the old Model A Fords that rest at a max of 50ft. On the south side of the lake there is an old highway bridge down at 100ft of depth.

Now when it comes to personal favorites, Ron Johns who has been diving since 1966 of *Heartland Scuba Center* likes to dive at **Sandy Channel** State Recreational Area near Elm Creek. It's a multiple lake site in South Central Nebraska. The best-unnamed lake is the first one on the left when you pull off the highway. The lake has black crappie, green sunfish, yellow and painted perch, and snapping and leather back turtles. The lake also contains 6 boats, 4 platforms, 3 3ft tall metal dolphins, concrete coyotes, a turtle, an alligator, a statue of the Virgin Mary, and more, including the sightings of one homemade UFO. The surface temp may reach 78°, but it will still be 65° down at 25ft of depth. The vis can range 5 to 20ft, but visibility has been as high as 40ft during January when Ron has conducted ice diver training classes.

Dan Stalder of *Husker Diver Scuba & Snorkeling Center* in Lincoln uses a private sand pit for training purposes along I-80 and that it contains bass and bluegill, and a submarine made out of a large jet fuel canister and a little creativity. Dan is also looking forward to the opening of the

637acre lake and recreation area **Lake Wanahoo** near Wahoo this April. This site is 30miles from Omaha and has been under development for quite some time.

Jessica Wilkins of *DiVentures* in Omaha likes **War Axe** State Recreational Area near Shelton; it's a 16acre no wake lake with camping facilities and lots of bass. Instructor Mark Sidwell of *DiVentures* likes to do lake clean up/ecology dives around the Omaha area such as **Lake Zorinski** Park, which a couple of years ago was stocked with wide mouth bass and walleye. In **Standing Bear Lake** the clean up crew found a revolver and a laptop computer. In the lake at Benson Park they found a safe and a stuffed teddy bear.

Some other lakes you might want to explore include: **Lewis and Clark Lake** which is the second largest lake in Nebraska and sits right on the border with South Dakota near Crofton. The lake is 16miles long and 3 miles wide, with a max depth of 45ft. **Crystal Cove** in South Sioux City is 40ft max deep and the vis averages 5 to 13ft, but the big draw here is that twice a year the state pumps in 3500-4500 juvenile trout. **Harlan County Lake** is nine miles long, covers 13,250acres, and has two marinas. The lake is home to northern pike, channel catfish, walleye, wipers, and white bass. **Bridgestone Sand Pits** next to the North Platte River near Gering, have 78acres of water in several sand pit formations. **Johnson Lake**, **Lake Francis**, **Cotton Mill Lake**, **Rockford Lake** and the gravel pits around Beatrice are also known diving sites, but the biggest little lake of all has to be the **Box Butte Reservoir** in Nebraska's pan handle. This lake is only 7miles long, 1,600 water acres, and has 14 miles of shoreline, but many record-breaking fish are speared at this remote lake. The max depth is 40ft and the visibility is a mere 10-25ft, but the crappie, bluegill, perch, channel catfish, and assorted bass love this spot. Dustin Noble has speared many record fish at this site, and has even beaten his own records at times. He also spears many trophies at a private lake of which there are many in the state of Nebraska. It makes you wonder if the fish get so big in Nebraska just because they are in remote locations spread out around the state, or if it's because there are so many little lakes, that it's just a matter of time before one of them contains the next record setting species of fish.

So as you can see, from ancient giant swimming reptiles, the largest mastodon in North America, to the current record of several speared fish, you never know what you may find on your next underwater adventure in Nebraska. Great Dives.

Nevada

From the northern Wheeler Peak glacier to the southern end of the Mojave Desert there is no other State in the Union that has more extremes than the state of Nevada. Seas and inland oceans have swept across this landscape repeatedly over millions of years in the not too distant historical past. Chances are that if you go up into the mountains surrounding the Valley of Fire State Park, just fifty minutes north of Las Vegas, you will find fossil remnants of trilobites and other Cambrian creatures that lived in the local seas some 400-250 plus million years ago. Found 300 miles away in the outskirts of the town of Berlin and now housed at the Nevada State Museum in Las Vegas you can view and walk under the skeletal remains of a 48ft long ichthyosaur fossil, a dolphin shaped Triassic sea creature with giant eye sockets, three inch long coned teeth, and seven foot long front flippers that roamed the Nevada seas more than 225 million years ago. By 110 million years ago the land dried up and Iguanodons, Titanosaurs, and Tyrannosaurs, among others, roamed the rivers and wooded valleys. Petrified trees and skeletal fossils are all that remain of this era.

By 20,000 years ago Nevada was a land filled with thousands of fresh water lakes. Mastodons, horses, and camels, claimed this land as home. They all disappeared as the water dried up and early Indian settlers moved in to the area.

So much for the history lesson, today the most ubiquitous sea creature in Nevada has to be humans and their sub-species "the scuba diver". The dive locations are lakes filled with fresh water and no overly dangerous or prehistoric creatures. In northern Nevada Lake Tahoe is the most popular dive destination. The clear see through waters make it ideal for scuba diving, but at just under 7000ft above sea level this is definitely the grand home of altitude diving. Local dive shops teach altitude diving in as little as two dives. There are many parks, points, coves and bays to dive here. The lake is home to a wide variety of trout, fresh water Sculpin, fresh water shrimp, and crawdads (crawfish). The lake is 1645ft deep, but it's best to dive above the 80ft mark due to the altitude and cold temperatures at depth. Many of the local dive shops train here, but in addition; most of the dive shops hold monthly dives off the coast of California from kelp forest diving in Monterey to Abalone free diving in northern California.

Lake Mead at a max elevation of 1,229ft and currently down to 1,094ft is the southern most active dive area. Here the water visibility goes down in the summer time and up in the wintertime quite like the annual fluctuations in the water's level. This water boasts bass, blue gills, catfish, and fresh water sponge. Below the water's surface there lays the foundations of several towns covered up by the backwaters of the Hoover reservoir. To visit most of the dive sites of Lake Mead you really need a dive boat to navigate around the high cliffs and get in close against certain towering canyon walls. If you find a dive charter operation online, be sure to call them way in advance to book your dive; as businesses have come and gone, but web pages seem to linger forever. Below the waters of Lake Mead are sunken boats, old construction artifacts, and even a B29 Super fortress that's remained relatively salvage free and all this makes this the best Dam recreation dive area in the state.

A couple of things to keep in mind about the B29 bomber is that it is just below the recreational depth limits; meaning it's a tech dive and you should be trained as such and use tech gear on this dive. In order to curtail recreational diver use, limit the number of tech divers on the plane, and according to one diver source, "to reduce the amount of personal salvage operations that have allegedly taken place in the past", only a few charter operations have ever been given permission by the Parks Department to charter dives to this military plane's final resting location.

Now if you need an excuse to take an educational sea life trip around Nevada, but really don't want to pack more than a swim suit, then Las Vegas has to be a must see destination. At the **Silverton Casino** they have a circular 110,000gal salt-water aquarium filled with 5 species of stingrays as well as more than a 1000 other species of fish. The marine biologists are on hand to answer questions several times daily. In the Bass Pro shop a mere 15ft away, there are freshwater trout and other fish swimming in the tanks, plus stuffed and mounted sharks and pelagic fish hanging in various schooling formations from prominent ceiling locations.

Over at the **Golden Nugget** I recently watched at least four species of shark and assorted fish swimming in a 200,000gal mostly glass walled tank that has a clear tube running slightly diagonally right through the center of the shark and fish exhibit. Hotel guests zoom down a 3 story tall water slide and pass straight through the tube giving them a close and personal view of large teeth swimming all around the outside of the tube. Once through the tube the guests land with a small splash into a swimming pool that entirely surrounds the glass shark exhibit. This is one cool, yet safe, way to mix fresh water enthusiasts with salt-water inhabitants.

Next we move on to the **Mandalay Bay** Resort and Casino, which is the home of The Shark Reef. Aquarium. Here you can view Amazonian fish including piranhas, black tip reef sharks at the tropical reef, and in the big 1.3mil gallon aquarium you can watch countless species of fish and sharks including one big sawfish shark that circle endlessly around the tank perimeter. Glass enclosed tunnels let you look up and count the rows of teeth on passing sandbar sharks, and surface eddies give the sea turtles a little room to cruise and generally go with the flow.

If you are into marine mammals I suggest checking out the pod of dolphins living in the Dolphin Habitat at the Mirage Resort and Casino. The dolphins don't read cards, sing, or put on shows: they just swim around in the giant 2.5million gallons of water and are mesmerizing to watch. The daily buffet comes to them and their favorite entree seems to be fish.

So as you can see, Nevada has been home to saltwater creatures, both big and small, for many millions of years. Fortunately for us, the giant marine reptiles with voracious appetites have all gone extinct and cute lovable dolphins are the current intellectually dominant aquatic species in all of Nevada. Sharks, stingrays, and other tropical fish tend to congregate only around selected hotel and casino locations. Scuba divers generally tend to keep to the damned fresh water lakes or along the coastline of California. And all this possibly makes the landscape of Nevada one of the most historically ancient as well as eclectic water realms in the entire southwestern United States.

Lake Mead, Nevada
Dam Delightful Diving

       Lake Mead is not your typical reservoir. It's the largest man made lake in the United States. The water flows down from snow packed mountains from Colorado, Utah, and Wyoming. Each spring, Lake Mead's water surface elevation begins to rise as the heavy snow packs in Colorado begin to melt away. When Colorado has a bad year of snow on the ski slopes, the water surface level of Lake Mead drops accordingly. In the past, the lake elevation has been high as 1,225ft in July 1983. You don't have to even imagine how high this had to be, because the water is full of minerals that turn a grayish white color when exposed to the sun. It's like a giant washtub ring and it rings the entire lake over 100ft above the current waterline. From any point overlooking the lake you can view how expansive the lake once was, and how little the islands off shore were at one time. As for the lowest level, the lake was down to 1,083ft in October 2000. What this does to divers, it that it makes it hard to tell another diver how deep something is unless you specify the year dove or the actual current altitude above sea level. Right now, the water is back up to 1122ft, which means the spot we picnicked at last year is 20ft below the surface, but still looks like half a mile below the gradual slope from where the official camp grills and picnic tables are cemented. It makes it hard to shore dive too, because the scuba park from the 1990's is above water, and the entrances to other shore sites vary in degrees of difficulties. For instance, my feet went down and stuck in what was heavy mud when walking out past an old motorboat and two six foot round tires that had once been underwater and you need rock boots to cross some of the newer exposed rocks. The old beaches up the hill are better groomed and easier to traverse. Nearby Boulder Beach is easier to walk across, but it is designated as a swimming beach only. I'm only telling you this, because it is just easier to go out on a charter boat, than it is to follow big horn sheep trails with dive gear in tow.

Another thing about Lake Mead is the actual visibility. My youngest daughter and I like to go down to the marina, buy a bag of popcorn, and feed it to the fish on either side of the *Boat Haven Restaurant*. Carp and stripped bass swarm the water for the kernels, but the catfish tend to stay down lower at about 15-20ft and they are just barely in our view of sight. Away from shore near the small Islands and wall dive sites, the vis is more likely to be 40-60ft or greater, which is just another reason to boat dive instead of shore dive at Lake Mead.

The third and final thing about Lake Mead is it's historical significance. Close to 80 years ago Boulder Basin was similar to the Grand Canyon, with farmlands, small towns, and ancient Anasazi petroglyphs on walls that extended over 500ft up from the base of the Colorado River. The construction of the Hoover dam changed everything, and everything they used and did to build the dam are now historical dive sites and artifacts. For instance, the **Clarified Water Station**, misnamed the **Batch Plant**, is a 100ft circular 8-10t ft high bowl for clarifying water used to wash rocks and make cement at the real batch plant back in Black Canyon. Water heavy in particles and debris were washed away down the adjacent sluice. Cleared water was also held in a huge cement box while waiting for trucks to return and refill. These structures are still down intact and home to rare freshwater sponges. A diver from Scuba Views Dive Shop can be seen hovering in this site in a video on Youtube. Other known sites of historical importance include the **Train Hopper** at 95ft at 1097elev.with 8x10ft tunnels with 4x4ft vertical roof top openings. You can find bore holes, cables, and rock fragments near certain walls, but keep in mind that during the construction of the dam these sites were hundreds of feet off the ground where high scale men drilled in to the rock cliffs, and set charges. Meanwhile, men with jackhammers crack the blasted rocks into more manageable sizes.

I asked Bill Duckro of *Scuba Views*, which is also the only dive shop to currently operate a dive charter boat, what were his favorite dive sites in the lake and he just laughed and said there were just too many to name. He showed me a picture he had taken the previous weekend of two big bass battling for a piece of rocky reef. The fish out there are awesome too, he said. You can find parental male blue gill as big as a dinner plate. If you approach them too close, they will swim away, but if you let them approach you, then you slowly back away, then they will swim right up to your face mask to greet and say hello to their reflection.

Besides the fish and dam construction sites, there are lots of boat sunk in the lake as well as one deep **PBY Catalina**, and a **B-29** super fortress. These two planes are beyond the reach of recreational divers and currently no one has a permit to take even tech divers out to the B 29. Some of the coves also go down to 120+ft before coming to a short shelve, then dipping down some 500ft deep. Other sites like **Kraken Cove** are only 50ft deep at 1097 elev. There are also some pinnacles, roads that follow down towards the entrance of the cofferdams, and the ruins of three towns; the biggest of which was St. Thomas that submerged back in 1938.

One other thing about the lake, and that is the weather. While winds are low in Las Vegas, winds can be sweeping up big waves on the lake. So even if you plan a dive on the lake, you are literally at the mercy of the winds as to whether you will actually get to go out or not. This makes it very hard to run a charter operation on the lake at certain times of the year, but even more difficult for those boaters that are inexperienced with Lake Mead.

Lastly, get an early start if you are meeting up with a dive charter service at *Las Vegas Boat Harbor*. As you come down the hill on US route 93 in *Boulder City*, allow time to stop at *Hemenway Park* off Ville Drive and take pictures of seventy or so big horn sheep that may walk right by you as you sit on a park bench. On the way back from diving, leave time to shop and dine in the small eclectic antique filled downtown area of Boulder City. It's also home to *Scubafy*, the closest dive shop near the lake, and the *Boulder Dam Brewery*, where there is nothing quite as refreshing as a Dam beer after some Great Dives!

147

Lake Tahoe
Altitude Diving; The Clear Choice

If you're like me, you may driven by Lake Tahoe countless times and noticed that the water visibility was extremely clear, but never thought a putting a toe in the water. Keith Chestnut from *Sierra Diving Center* in Reno, who has been diving since 1968, when asked what it is like to dive Lake Tahoe likes to joke and say, " Well, what you can't see, you can see forever." But it's easy to see if you know what you are looking at. Lake Tahoe is filled with countless fish, crawdads/crayfish, and underwater artifacts left by modern man and ancient Native Americans.

The Lake Tahoe Basin first uplifted 2million years ago like a pair of hands held vertically together and rising up with water slowly accumulating in the narrow deep gap between them. The current altitude of the lake is 6,228ft. The water surface covers 193sqr miles with 70sqr miles of water being in Nevada and the rest of the lake in California. The only outlet is the Truckee River and it's 18ft tall dam. It takes about 650 retention years for a drop of water to make the journey out of the lake. Tahoe never freezes over and the surface temp may reach more than 68° in the summer, but it is always 39° below 600ft deep. At 1645ft deep, it's the second deepest lake in the U.S.A., and the visibility ranges from 45 to 75ft. Most dive sites have a small park fee from $5-$8. The lake is currently home to brown, brook, volcano creek, Lahontan cutthroat, and rainbow trout. Kokanee salmon, and Mackinaw over 26lbs are also caught here. Washoe American Natives have lived in this area for at least the last 6000years.

As for diving, Keith tells me that the number one request is the PADI Altitude Diver Specialty. From 8am to 2-230pm, divers get to do two dives with a local instructor and get an Altitude Diver certification when all is wet, said, and done. Because of global warming or just warmer weather,

Keith has seen an increase of skiers taking a day off from one of the 12 surrounding ski resorts such as *Heavenly*, and instead adding a day of diving to their ski trips and Reno vacations.

Keith's favorite place to dive is the wall at **Rubicon Point**. The vertical granite wall drops down to 800ft. Access to this dive site is closed in winter until the snow melts around Memorial Day weekend. To visit this site, enter D.L. Bliss State Park; pay a small fee, then turn to your right towards Calawee Cove Beach. It's easier to go here by boat if you don't like long stairs, hiking with dive gear, or waiting for the snow to melt in spring. The wall is due south from Calawee Cove after a 150yrd surface swim.

I asked Chuck Webber, who has been diving since 1988 and is the owner of *Tahoe Dive Center* in Carson City which is also a PADI 5 Star training facility and the closest dive shop near Lake Tahoe, about Lake Tahoe dive sites and he mentioned the Rubicon Point wall too. Chuck's also uses **Sand Harbor** state park, which is a mere 24miles from his shop, for open water training, and **Hurricane Bay** for advanced training. June to September, for local boat diving, Chuck plans to team up with Chris Bartish of *River City Diving Co.* and the 26ft 6pack boat named "*Scuba Mood*." You can be part of some of his dive adventures by visiting *The Tahoe Dive Center* face book page.

On a side note, I asked him about the potholes found all over the lake at different depths. Chuck told me that long ago, the water level was lower by about 80ft. The Washoe Native Americans would burn small fires on top of the granite to soften the rock. They would then grind acorns and Pinon nuts on the flat granite surface using a handheld stone like using a mortar and pestle. Eventually the granite mortar foundation would take the shape of one of the numerous submerged 6" to 12" wide bowl holes that you find today.

Now before I mention the other dive sites, I just wanted to mention: On the Nevada side, "**Do not dive without a dive flag**." Fish and Game Officials will give you a hefty fine and they make lots of money this way, but they make even more money off the boaters and jet skiers who ignore the boating rules and come too close to floating dive flags. The law has made diving safe on both sides of the lakes.

As far the dive sites go, clockwise on the Nevada side we have: **Sand Harbor**. You'll see lots of grinding holes/mortars underwater here. Depth is 30ft until it slopes. 100ft from shore on a heading of 275° there is an old barge. **Cave Rock** has a depth of 30-35ft out to red markers. This former volcano opening and sacred Tribe Shrine is a good place to see trout and crawdads/crayfish. Lastly, **Zephyr Cove** has a sandy bottom with depths between 20-25ft. Old bottles have been found here. By the way, invasive crawdads first established themselves in Tahoe around 1936. There are currently 220 to 360 million crawdads in the lake. Crawfish Etouffee anyone?

Starting on the top of the lake and turning counterclockwise, we have **Speed Boat Beach.** Next is **Bucks Beach,** is small hidden beach and a popular night dive site. Shallow until you go 500ft out; max depth is 20ft with plenty of grinding holes. **Carnelian Bay** has a max depth of 25ft and is home to a sunken barge, motorboat, logs, and the giant 20ft long black-eyed carp is 900yrds from shore at 30-40ft. After a 40ft surface swim at **Sunnyside,** at Kent State Park, the bottom drops off at 60ft at a 45° angle. **Hurricane Bay** is home to a 40ft long sailboat at 50-60ft. Depth is 40-100ft and has large trees, silt, and sand on the bottom. **Blackwood Beach** has a huge drop off. Remember, at this altitude, 96ft=125ft at sea level. **Meeks Bay** has a sandy bottom with dead trees and a rock ledge at 60ft, then angles down to the abyss. Minnows to Mackinaw hang out here. **Ribicon Point** is next going south on Hwy89. **Baldwin Beach** is 1.5miles in length, vis is down to 30ft near Tallac Creek. Some of the submerged trees here are 6,400 years old. Emerald Bay has two sunken barges near 35ft and old china plates from the 1928 34-room tour site, *Vikingsholm.* The ruins of the associated Teahouse are still visible on **Fannette Island**. Lastly, **Stateline Wall** is the 2nd best wall dive on the lake. There are boulders down at 35ft before it drops off.

So there you go. Plenty of sites to try out once you've been trained as an altitude diver, and plenty of reasons to take a day off from skiing and instead go diving. Lake Tahoe has millions of years of history for you to explore and excellent visibility to see it all. That's why Lake Tahoe is the clear choice every time. Great dives.

Las Vegas, Nevada
Get Tanked On Desert Diving

If New York City is the city that never sleeps, then Las Vegas is the city that never sleeps...on steroids. In Vegas, things always seem to be bigger, more is more, and where eye opening surprises, fantastic floor shows, and once in a lifetime adventures are booked on a daily basis: 24-7, 365. One thing people from out of town are always asking me is what's a marine biologist doing living in Vegas? Perhaps the following will help answer that question.

First of all thanks to people like the folks from ATM, *Acrylic Tank Manufacturing*, who are based in Vegas and the stars of the TV show "Tanked", there are more aquariums in this town than just about anywhere else in North America. They make small 200gal tanks or 200,000gal tanks. They make tanks 24inches tall to over 24ft tall. You can get a tank 48inches long or one 48ft long. You can get a tank made in the shape of a bubble gum machine like the one that was at *serendipity 3* at Caesars Palace, in the shape of a nail polish bottle, or incorporated as part of half a car or working bus. The point is, that aquariums are everywhere in Vegas, and so are salt water creatures, and since all aquariums are not created equal, here are a few tanks that you must see, could get a thrill swimming in, or may like to plunge inside right now.

Starting out at the **Silverton** Hotel & Casino south of the strip there is a 110,000gal tank filled with a simulated coral reef and thousands of tropical fish from butterfly fish to stingrays. It's a cool looking tanks, but what makes it even cooler is that the resident marine biology staff at set times answer questions from tourists and talk about the creatures they care for. Also, at set times, women dressed as mermaids swim around the tank, interact with tourists and especially with kids, as they occasionally take breaths of air off of inconspicuous hookah set ups. The costumes are so well made that it's hard not to remember that the mermaids are not real; or is that just my own personal problem? Anyway, besides this huge tank the

Bass Pro Outlet, 30ft away, has a waterfall system and a very
large sturgeon and channel catfish can be seen gliding beneath
the surface. Inside the Bass Pro there are other tanks with trout
and other assorted fresh water species of fish, and hanging
from the ceilings above the fishing section, you can see
casts/models of thresher sharks and great whites chasing after
schools of tuna while marlins and sailfish dart after other prey.

Our next stop or stay would be at The **Golden Nugget**
Hotel and Casino in old downtown off Fremont Street. Here,
guests get to swim in a pool shaped like a giant donut and in
the middle is 200,000gal tank with five species of sharks and
many schools of large fish including one humongous grouper.
Guests can swim right up to the transparent walls and look
right in at the fish, or swim along with a 9ft long sandbar shark
as it makes its way around the inside of the tank. This in itself
is a cool experience, but because this is Vegas, they have
stepped it up a notch. Slanting down through the middle of the
tank is a long see through tube. Guests walk up three flights of
stairs for the pleasure of sliding down through the tube and
being expelled into the main swimming pool far below at the
other end. You go through the water tube fast, and as you do,
you see glimpses of sharks swimming right beside the tube. To
outside observers you look like a fast paced bullet zipping by
the sharks. Caution, do not take a seven year old on this ride, or
like me, you could be climbing the stairs up to the top of the
tube at least a dozen times. Oh, and on the backside of the pool,
the silhouettes of the sharks are fantastic, and if you look up at
the see through ceiling, you may see stingrays swimming above
you. You can also watch the sharks from the Jacuzzi, near the
open outdoor fires, or from the H2O bar. Unfortunately, from
the 15 private cabanas and the *Hide Out* lounge and bar area,
you can't really see the sharks: just trim lined bathing suits. Oh
well.

Moving on to something bigger, we have the 54ft long
200,000gal tropical aquarium behind the front desk of the
Mirage Hotel. The 1,000 total fish that include at least 60
different species are impressive, but a hotel on the strip that has
a nightly erupting volcano trumps this fantastic fish exhibit by
having a family of 10 dolphins living in 2.3million gallons of

salt-water as part of *Siegfrieds & Roys Secret Garden and Dolphin Habitat*. Yes, you can say it, "Lions, white tigers, and dolphins oh my!" Two of the dolphins are over 30yrs old, and the youngest one was born here just last summer. Not only can you view these dolphins, but also for $550 and if you are over 13yrs of age, guests can sign up to become "Trainer For A Day." This is a special interactive experience where you really will feel like you have become acquainted with these remarkable intelligent creatures on a whole new level.

Next, it just wouldn't be a complete trip to Vegas if you didn't spend a little time at the *Shark Reef* aquarium at the **Mandalay Bay Resort & Casino**. Here you will find fish from Brazil, Africa, piranhas, an albino crocodile, a tropical reef fish exhibit, rays in a touch tank exhibit, a lionfish exhibit, octopus exhibit, jellyfish tank, plus seven species of sharks, and two sea turtles. I've only been here about fifty times, so that's all I can remember off the top of my head. Perhaps with a $40 annual pass I can do better next time. So Shark Reef sounds impressive, but for $650 or $1000 for two, guests can sign up in advance to go scuba diving in the 1.3million gal Shipwreck tank with the sharks. All you need is a swimming suit, your own mask if you prefer, and they supply everything else including chain mail garments that guarantees the sharks stay on a "fish only" diet. They even video the event for you, so all you have to do as a certified diver is just gaze in total amazement at your new 6 to 14ft long dive buddies. Oh, and the sea turtles are cute too. Total preparation and dive time 3-4hrs, but the experience will remain with you forever; take that Shark Week!

Finally, the Las Vegas **Natural History Museum** has some small live sharks, tropical eels, a frogfish, Maine lobster, and a few other sea creatures on display. Tourists and especially divers, have lots of options and opportunities when they come to Sin City, but from a marine biology perspective it's only a sin in this city if you come to Las Vegas and don't get tanked. Great Dives.

New Hampshire
The Heart of New England Diving

New Hampshire is the sixth smallest state in the union and has barely 19miles of coastline, but you would be surprised how many dive sites are packed inside such a tight space. To get an idea of the variety of diving New Hampshire offers, I talked with Jay Gingrich owner of *Portsmouth Scuba*, who also runs boats out to some of the more popular spots. Jay said some of his favorite diving spots are out at the **Isle of Shoals**. To be honest, some of the islands out here are on the other side of the border and fall inside the boundaries of Maine, but if you come out here to dive one of the nine islands, you better come out and dive them all, as each island has at least one or more unique dive sites. Jay likes diving with the playful seals at *Duck Island* and diving the 300yrd long ledges & caves at 105ft deep around *Star Island*. He says that there are still many places still unexplored out here. During Scallop season the shoals and other offshore areas are like a giant Easter egg hunt for adults.

Some of the dive sites around the Islands include: **Jimmies Ledge** at 45ft at *Duck Island*. **Gosport Harbor** on the NW side of *Star Island* where the bottom may be mud, but it's the spot where you can find artifacts such as bottles and clay pipes. Now before I go on, Jay said that some of the items they find on their dives vary from 400year old European to 10,000-year-old Native American artifacts, and his collection is large. Back to the islands, out at *Appledore Island* there are ledges at 75ft in **Broad Cove**, 90ft at **Babbs Rock**, **Devils Gorge** at 35ft, and **Pyramids Valley** at 60ft at the mouth of the cove and 25ft deep inside. **Cedar Island** has sand at 60ft, and ledges, boulders, and granite slabs going down to 140ft.

For another fun dive and also a wild ride, Jay said you have to do a drift dive down the Piscataqua River, which has 10ft tide exchanges and really moves you along.

Judy Leclerc of *Divers Den Dive Shop* in Manchester likes to do shore dives, and she said they like to dive in front of the **Coast Guard Station** in Portsmouth where you can find assorted debris in the harbor. She likes **Great Island Commons**, aka "**Newcastle Commons**," around the jetty. The vis can range from 5-8ft, but that's good enough to find a lobster in eel grass. She also likes **Sunken Forest** which is a cove just south of Odiorne Point State Park, but this cove may only get 10ft-18ft deep on high tide, but 60ft deep if you follow the telegraph cable that use to connect to Europe.

Moving South along the coastline is **Pulpit Rock** that has a rocky to sandy bottom with plenty of sea life and a max depth of 30ft. **Seal Rock** is just south of here with a sandy bottom and also 30ft max. North of Ragged Neck State Park at **Foss beach** is another 20ft deep dive site. **Fox Hill Point** north of New Hampton and **Plaice Cove** are shallow dives with lots of life around the rocks. **Sea Brook Beach** south of the Hampton Bridge gets 40ft deep and a good spot to find lobster. As with all New Hampshire shore dives, foot placement is crucial when navigating your way out from the beach to where the water gets deep enough to put on fins, and tides and currents are crucial once in the water. Ask a local dive shop about the latest dive conditions, so you know before you go.

Occasionally, members of Divers Den go up north to Maine and **Nobulet Light House** where there is easy entry, a max of 60ft in depth and great night diving as well. They aren't the only ones that go out to this site though, shops like *Aquatic Escapes Dive Center* in Londonderry routinely go out of state dive sites, such as Nobulet Light House as well as traveling south to Old Garden Beach in Massachusetts where there is and easy pebble beach entry, the vis is good, and the depth around 30ft.

Now apart from salt-water dive sites, New Hampshire has plenty of fresh water dive sites too. At **Lake Winnipesaukee** with up to 45ft of vis. Some of the local dive sites include **Clark Point** at Mckiney Park with a max depth of 50ft. Weirs Beach has a steam barge at **Doe Point** at 45ft. One mile north of Weirs Beach is the **Train Wreck**: an engine and a few cars. The 135ft long **Lady of the Lake** wreck at

Glendale Cove rests at 60ft and is used all year round, even for ice diving. Diving around Diamond Island you'll find the **Empty Pockets** wreck at 60ft. You can find all sorts of strange stuff in Lake Winnepasaukee courtesy of the U.S. Navy underwater laser testing team.

Some other lakes you might like to dive include: **Nubanusit Lake** with a max depth of 60ft and lots of bass. **Lake Sunapee** is 30ft deep and divers go in the water at *Blodgetts Landing.* **Dublin Lake** is 2 hrs from Boston so many out of state divers like to come here. This 240acre lake is spring fed and 110ft deep and has several entry points. Lake Dublin is said to contain some underwater caverns where unknown monsters prowl. Big Foot has also been seen splashing along the shoreline. Apparently, a diver went missing here and was found naked four days later, so my advice is don't set your clothes on tree limbs before you go diving, but secure them in a vehicle, and rinse your gear well after the dive, as there is nothing worse than Big Foot hair clogging up a second stage. The substrate is glacial boulders, with silt at depth. At 30ft deep it can be 68°. **Lake Winnisquam** on the other hand, has a video on Youtube that clearly details the rock bottom and shows that this site is a great place to feed bass with no threat of monsters, or the weird strange and unexplainable eerie camera crews that monsters tend to attract.

To sum it all up, New Hampshire has lots of dive sites to explore. You can do beach dives, dive around islands and play with seals. You can hunt for scallops, lobster, and fish, or dive and collect ancient fossils and artifacts from Native Americans Indians forward. There are several freshwater lakes with wrecks of various sizes and they double as great ice diving locations too, and if all this isn't enough, New Hampshire is surrounded by nearby dive sites just north or south across the conveniently located state borders. Great Dives.

New Jersey Ship Wrecks
Over 4000, But Who's Counting?

There are some 4,000 to 7,000 wrecks for divers off New Jersey to choose from and that doesn't include natural or artificial reefs, so to limit the scope of this article I narrowed down the list to some of the favorite places charter boat captains like to dive and here is what I found:

Capt. Jim Wilson of the 50ft boat, *Gypsie Blood*, likes the *R.P. Resor*, the *Great Isaac*, and the *Stolt*. The 445ft long oil tanker **R.P. Resor** sank in 125ft of water after being torpedoed by U-578 Feb 27, 1942. It rests 30miles off shore and is lightly defended by lobster and a 6inch gun mounted on the stern foyer. The **Great Isaac**, once part of the Normandy Invasion, sank in 1947 to 90ft and rests on its port side. Occasionally coast guard china is found on the wreck. The 582ft long tanker **Stolt Dagali** sank Nov 26, 1964 after a collision with the Israeli liner *Shalom* and now rests 18 miles out at 130ft of depth. Jim says that on artificial wrecks, everything of value has been removed to pay for the sinking, while on natural wrecks you may find a lighter personally marked that formerly belonged to someone from the past. The divers out here find artifacts and catch fresh seafood and enjoy the atmosphere aboard the boat; it's a small price to pay for by having to wear drysuits and using wreck reels.

Capt. Dave Walker of the 31ft 6 pack *Finders Keepers* likes to dive the *Mohawk*, the *Brunette*, and the *Delaware*. The 387ft long **SS Mohawk** sank to 80ft on Jan 25th, 1935 after a collision with the Norwegian freighter *Talisman*. The **Brunette** (Door Knob Wreck) sank to 70ft in 1870. She contained doorknobs and locks with keys wrapped in wax paper, among other things. The 250ft long **Delaware** sank 75ft July 9th, 1898.Capt Dave found the leather of a woman's size 7 shoe with the stitching disintegrated. After preserving the leather, he re-stitched it to see what the fashion was at the time. He also found a pewter spoon and cup on this wreck. He says that wreck diving never gets boring, and that fewer miles out is better, as bottom time is everything; when you are searching, sifting, and looking for artifacts.

Captain Brian Larsen of *Atlantic Charters* likes the *Almirante*, the *San Jose*, and the *Varenger*. The **Almirante** (Flour wreck) sank to 65ft on Sept 6, 1918 after a collision. She was carrying china, tiles, and kerosene lanterns. Her load of flour washed up on the beaches. She left a big debris field and is a good place to find brass objects, fish, and lobster. The 330ft long **San Jose** sank to 110ft Jan 17, 1942 in a collision. She was dynamited in the 1950's. Brian and his brother spent 8 dives removing one porthole from a hull plate. They had to saw the bolts off a little at a time because of the short bottom time at depth. Brian likes the 470ft long **Varenger** that sunk to 140ft June 25, 1942 after being torpedoed by U-130. His grandfather was one of the fishermen from Sea Island Inlet that rescued the Varenger's crew.

Captain Roger Hoden of the 42ft *DinaDeeII*, likes the *Great Isaac* for fish, mussels, and artifacts. He likes the Spanish steamer **Viscaya** for lobster and fish. This was a rich Cuban ship that sunk to the low 80's Oct 30, 1890 after a collision. The ship quickly went down with sixty fatalities, silver bowls, platters, coins, and personal jewelry.

Capt Paul Hepler with the 46ft *Venture III* likes the *Mohawk*, *Stolt Dagali*, and the *Pinta*. The 194ft **Pinta** was a freighter from the Netherlands that sunk May 8th, 1963. The bow was salvaged, so the wreck is 142ft long and rests between 65 to 130ft deep on its port side. Paul has found lots of old stuff digging around wrecks including a brass capstan with a brass base 3ft in diameter and 3 1/2ft tall and 18 pairs of cowboy spurs from around 1854. Capt. Al Pyatak of the 36ft *Sea Lion* and *Atlantic Wreck Diving, Inc*. Has brought up many artifacts over the years. He has plotted over 2000 potential wreck sites called piles,with 500 solid sites. He said he couldn't tell me his newest secret site, but he did say that, "New Jersey has the best wreck diving in the world by far".

Capt. Tony Donetz of the 35ft *Blue Fathoms*, likes the 280ft **Tolten** at 95ft for fish, the 430ft long **Gulf Trade** at 60-

90ft for fish and scallops, and the inshore 200ft long **RR Barge** at 55-70ft for mussels, lobster and other fresh seafood.

Capt. Ben Barina of *the Independence II* and *Deep Expeditions* loves tech diving on the 252ft long **U-869** submarine at 240ft, the *RP Resor* for scallops and lobster, and the380ft long **SS Carolina** at 240ft. Divers study the wrecks during the winter months and know them intimately before descending where time at depth is everything.

Capt Howard of the *Lady GoDiver* likes the **San Saba,** which sunk 75ft October 4th, 1918 from a mine from U-117. He also likes the *Great Isaac* too; it recently opened up in areas that were previously blocked off and divers are now finding artifacts in these formerly unavailable locations.

Capt. Rich Benevento of the *John Jack* and *Sea Going Adventures*, likes the *Resor* for lobster, the Delaware and *Mohawk* for air dredging for artifacts, and the *Stolt* for photography. Late in the season Sept-Oct, vis can reach 80-100ft. After storms, the vis may be 1ft, but that's when artifacts are freshly exposed. Professional Captains know the weather inside out and use their years of experience to understand the weather such as wind direction and the size of the waves in correlation to the height and speed; a 6ft wave at 12sec intervals, is only a low swell.

Capt. Gene Petersen of the *Miss Lindsey* and *Atlantic Divers* likes the **SS Miraflores** and it might be because the team at *Atlantic Divers* discovered this 1942 wreck some 15years ago. It was officially identified in 2008. Gene has recovered many items from many wrecks including china from the famous *Andrea Doria*. Gene also has one of the best websites on local shipwreck information.

New Jersey has over 126miles of coastline making it easy to shore dive from flat sandy beaches, off jetties, and along rock walls. Even though spearfishing is good near shore for stripers and tautogs, you may never ever hear a local diver mention shore diving and that's because wreck diving and all its associated underwater activities is king in the garden state. Many of these Captains have donated artifacts to museums. Some like Capt. Dan Berg have written several books on diving off New Jersey. Going with a charter boat operation instead of a private boat means much more than a securely anchored boat to the site, it means a higher level of safety is in place during all phases of a dive, and that just makes the local wreck diving even better. Great dives.

New Mexico
Close Encounters & Diving

When I first mention diving and New Mexico in the same sentence people usually give me a glossy eyed look like I wasn't from this planet. Sure, people are more than willing to believe that extraterrestrials crash-landed near Roswell, but they are skeptical about the actual affirmable local dive sites. Perhaps it's because most of the dive sites are from 3,000 to 7,200 feet above sea level. Perhaps it's because most of New Mexico's dive sites are in reservoirs/lakes or water filled in sinkholes. Perhaps its just the fact that the local destinations are so filled with historical passages and questionable irreconcilable mysteries that diving here has had a hard time making a splash in the national headlines.

To start off, the most well-known dive site in the state has to be **Blue Hole** in Santa Rosa. Blue Hole is oval shaped on the surface: 80ft by 60ft. It widens with depth like a bell or Erlenmeyer flask to about 130ft in diameter down at 100ft of depth where a steel grate keeps divers from descending into the cave system that feeds 3,000 gallons of fresh water per minute literally to the hole area. This flow rate exchanges the water in Blue Hole approximately every six hours and gives divers over 80ft of visibility. One thing to note is that the water temperature is a constant 61-64degrees year round, so if you get cold easily, a 3ml wet suit with hood should be considered bare plus minimum to keep you from turning blue when you dive Blue Hole too.

The first non-local visitors to Blue Hole were the conquistadors who came with Francisco de Coronado in 1541. They must have looked like aliens from another planet to the local natives: as some tourists still do to this day. It is said that Billy the Kid stopped by here and possibly the great Apache Chief Geronimo too. Fortunately, you don't have to be a famous outlaw or memorable chief to stop by here, you can drop by just about anytime or century, but diving here at Blue Hole is only open on the weekends, and you need a permit that you can purchase for a reasonable price at city hall, or at the Santa Rosa Dive Center. Diving here without the necessary $8 weekly minimum permit can lead to a hefty fine that was last heard over $300 dollars, which is steep even by cattle rustler standards.

      You can either take the stairs down to the water level, of take a 12ft leap of faith into the water, either way, you may find yourself approached by invasive species of almost menacing gold fish. Meanwhile, crawdads, or crayfish, lurk on the substrate. You have to plan your dive here as a high altitude dive and keep in mind that the roads are not flat from Albuquerque, so a quick trip from there and back isn't going to happen. After a dive here you need to off gas before you cross the 7,000ft pass. A trip to the Billy the Kid Museum, the Fort Sumner National Monument, and/or a stay at the Quality Inn near the airport, can help pass time and gas . . . uh, nitrogen that is.

      If you want to get a little more dive time in around Santa Rosa, the city of natural lakes, then visit **Perch Lake**, another $8 permit location. Here you can dive a twin-engine plane down at 50plus feet. The plane was last used above water for sky diving classes. That's right, above water when it was in perfect condition, people couldn't wait to dive out of it. Now that it's below water, people can't wait to dive inside it. I can't blame them though, how often do you get to board a plane without being searched by TSA officials? Here, you won't hear, "Remove your dive knives and fins please…"

      Lastly, there are two other lakes divers are sometimes, by permission only, able to dive near Santa Rosa. Both **Swan Lake** and **Rock Lake** are on private land, the Butler Quarter Ranch to be exact. Debbie Ladyhawk is the owner. Swan Lake is 60ft deep with lots of usual suspect fish. Rock Lake is the real reasons divers flock here. The Lake is 285ft deep and technical divers from Albuquerque to Denver schedule trips here long before and well in advance. My local friends tell me that Debbie is hard to get a hold of, so they dive on her property by joining up with in state and out of state dive shop training teams who already have permission and scheduled dives at Rock Lake. Fortunately, this is a deep dive site, but you only have to go to 30ft to see freshwater sponges, fish, and turtles.

Northeast of Santa Rosa is **Conchas Lake State Park** its 4,200ft in elevation and maxs out around 158ft deep. Petroglyphs mark the canyon walls, sand and rocks fill the substrate, and you'll find some good spear fishing spots near the Conchas Dam on the Canadian River.

12 miles east of Roswell is **Bottomless Lakes State Park**. There are 8 lakes here, but Lea Lake is the only diveable lake. For a small park entrance fee you can dive down 80 to 90ft and have 50 to 75ft of visibility. You might see a canoe or boards from boats, but the main attraction here are soft shell turtles, or rare species such as the Pecos Puff fish, Rainwater Killifish, and Mexican tetras besides others not so endangered, but still on the unusual side. In the summer it's 84 on the surface and 61degrees on the bottom.

South of Albuquerque is **Elephant Butte State Park.** This is a 40,000 surface acre lake filled with bass, catfish and walleye, among others. The lake dips down to 165ft of depth. The remnants of the old volcano make up an island in the lake. During dry spells the island gets bigger and the water level goes down as local water consumption goes up. Use a dive flag, as boating and fishing are big sports here. The geothermal activity still goes on around here, so try out the hot springs in the town called *Truth or Consequences*.

On the north end of the state we find **Heron Lake**. At 7,200ft high, it's a 5,900 acre "no wake lake", 4miles long and 3miles wide. Here you can dive with salmon and trout, but keep an eye out for sailboats. The marina has showers and camping facilities.

Lastly, we have the **Navajo Reservoir** and **Navajo State Park**, or at least 2/3rds of it. Colorado shares the other 1/3rd the lake. At 6,100ft high, and 35miles long with 150miles of public shoreline, there is an entry point for just about everyone not already leaving from the Navajo Lake marina. Kokanee salmon, northern pike, and brown & rainbow trout are the usual suspects here.

To find more about New Mexico, check with the local dive shops. After all, if the government can cover up the alien landings at Roswell from outer space, there's no telling what they're keeping from those of us exploring inner space. Great Dives.

New York
Big State, Big Wrecks, Great Dives

If you take the New England states of New Hampshire, Vermont, Connecticut, Rhode Island, and Massachusetts, and combine them into one big state, then this new state would be roughly the size of New York State. Only Maine is larger in size, but unlike Maine, New York is the only state to have shorelines that extend across two great lakes (**Lake Eerie & Lake Ontario**), the **St. Lawrence River**, the **Long Island Sound**, and the **Atlantic Ocean**. When it comes to (not so great) lakes, New York shares **Lake Champlain** with Vermont and has an exclusive hold on the **Finger Lakes** just southwest of Syracuse or southeast of Rochester. I've written an article on the Finger Lakes for Dive News Network and the Northeast Dive News edition, but even small lakes like **Lake George** have books written about them because of so many historical wrecks and military exploits took place near or on these smaller lakes. Just in Lake George alone, there is the **Sunken Fleet** of 1758 at 40ft of depth. The 52ft long **Land Tortoise**, scuttled by the British in 1758 is the oldest intact sunken warship in North America and rests at 105ft. For something a little more recent, the **Forward** tour boat built in 1906 and sunk in 1930's rests at 40ft. For more background on the military history of Lake George, I recommend *Lake George Shipwrecks And Sunken History* by *Joseph W Zaryinski and Bob Benway*.

As for Lake Champlain, I mention a great deal about this lake in an article I wrote on Vermont. As for the great lakes, I mention Lake Eerie in articles on Pennsylvania and Ohio. Lake Ontario I wrote about in my Ontario, Canada article. Long Island sound I mention in my Connecticut article, but for one of the best sources of shore diving here, I recommend *The Long Island Shore Diver* by *Daniel Berg*. If you want to find jetty dives, dives in front of nuclear power plants, or dives right down the street on Long Island, then this is your source book.

Now I've written about some of the many thousands of wrecks off the Atlantic coast, but compared to *Gary Gentile* and his series of wreck dive books' I'm a real slacker. With 58 books covering the Great Lakes, New York wrecks, Technical Dive Instruction, the Andria Doria which sank in 1956, and the USS Monitor, Gary by pen as well as dive light, has covered the east coast wrecks like no other writer or diver. The cruise ship Andrea Doria is called the Everest of wreck diving, and most wreck divers dream of diving just once in their life on this magnificent almost 700ft long wreck. Some divers just want to touch the wreck, while other divers have "china fever" and will dive 240-260ft down in hopes of finding a flower designed cup or a blue lined plate. Gary has done more than 200 decompression dives on this wreck. Another excellent book that just came out in 2012 that describes the life of divers, the crew of the *Wahoo* Dive boat, and the personal history side of passengers on the final voyage of the Andria Doria is *Setting The Hook*, by *Peter Hunt*. Take about a small world, Peter worked for the same airline I did, and he took his IANTD technical training from Ron Akeson at *Adventures Down Under* in Bellingham, Washington. My IANTD Advanced Nitrox Instructor, Don Kinney, also took lessons from Ron. Later I also worked for Ron as a recreational PADI Master Instructor. Peter and I never connected all the dots until we had a chance to chat at the 2012 DEMA Show (Dive Equipment & Marketing Association) in Las Vegas. You might say that in our small diving world, you are only connected three people away from every other diver in most of North America.

Before I forget, the *Wahoo* built in 1982 is now called the *R/V Garloo*. Hank Garvin who was originally a deckhand, worked his way up and is now the owner and Captain. Under his accumulated experience, the Garloo still goes out to the Andria Doria as well as several other sites that I will mention in a minute. I should add that I met Capt. Garvin at the Northwest Dive and Travel Expo last year in Tacoma, Washington. He brought some Italian china pieces such as a teacup and saucer that had been covered in silt for at least 25 years, and now shined under the lights at the convention center. As a marine biologist, I'm usually more concerned about the creatures on the wrecks, but for a brief moment, as I looked at the print design and the words "Andrea Doria", I could see how easy it was to become enraptured by the overwhelming historical mystique of china fever.

Back to Peter's book and Gary's books too for that matter, the most notable wrecks off New York's coast besides the 100 mile out Andria Doria include such wrecks as the 503ft long armored cruiser **USS San Diego** built in 1904 and sank in 1918 after hitting a mine most likely planted by U-156 and coming to rest in 70-115 ft of depth. The 518ft long **Oregon** built in 1883 was sold to the Canard Line in 1884, and sank two years later in 1886 after being hit by the schooner *Charles R. Moss*, which was never seen again. The Oregon sank 8hours after being struck giving everyone time to safely depart the stricken vessel. She now rests in 85-130ft of depth. There is also the 290ft **Grecian** freighter that was rammed in fog by the *City of Chatanoga* in 1932. The White Star liner **Republic** was rammed in fog by the *Florida* in 1909. The crew of the Wahoo in 260ft of depth discovered the resting site of the Republic. Many vessels sank in collisions in these waters, but the Andrea Doria is one of the very few vessels to join this select group while being outfitted with radar to prevent just such disasters. The combined speed in a heavy fog bank between the *Stockkhom* and the *Andria Doria* proved to be too much for the primitive radar system or perhaps the radar system was so state of the art for its time that the crew relied too heavily on it.

The Garloo also makes routine visits the site of the U-853, which I wrote about in another article. After reading Peter Hunt's book, "Setting The Hook, "Down the hatch," will have a complete new meaning for you.

As you can see, there are tons of books and stories on diving in New York State, and tons of wrecks in both fresh and saltwater locations. There is also lots of room for more articles and books on the local rivers, lakes, and the Atlantic Ocean. I don't know about you, but I plan on thumbing through a few books and taking advantage of some of these local dive sites. The fact that the waters can really warm up when the summer tropical currents push northward, makes diving here even more irresistible. Great Dives

Finger Lakes
New York State

You can't quite put a finger on the best lake diving in New York State. You need six fingers to do this task justice. The six bodies of water that comprise the Finger Lakes were long ago formed and carved out to various degrees by past saltwater seas, glacial scouring, and glacial deposits. Four Nation tribes such as the Iroquois lived near the lakes for thousands of years, but they had the misfortune of aligning sides with British loyalists "Tories" in the Revolutionary war, and some forty of their campsites were destroyed during the Sullivan campaign in 1779. Major General Sullivan's force of 3500-armed troops broke the will of 1000 loyalists and the Iroquois nation. There are still rumors of artifacts and gold lost on the east end of Seneca Lake dating back to this period. As a reward for expelling the loyalists, military participants and settlers were granted parcels of the newly vacated Indian lands around the lakes. Early Homesteads sprouted everywhere, but they have given way to wineries over the past thirty years. Today you can still find beautiful forests, historical farms, and European looking vineyards tucked in, around, over looking, and encompassing the lakes. So what are the names of these lakes and what can you expect to find while diving here? Let me just start in no particular geographical order.

Seneca Lake. At 618ft deep, 38miles long, and at an elevation of 440ft, Seneca is the largest and deepest of the six lakes. Because it's so deep, the water temp is a steady 39°F at depth, but the 10-15ft near the surface can reach up to 70-80° in the summer. The deep waters make it easy for channel catfish and lake sturgeon to thrive here. FLUPA, the Finger Lake Underwater Preserve Association, has a buoy by one sunken 1800"s canal barge here. Offshore from Watkins Glen there are several mapped locations of barges and small boats to dive on and explore.

Cayuga Lake. 435ft deep. It's just over 38miles long making it the longest of the lakes. It has an elevation of 382ft.

Channel catfish and sturgeon are found her too, along with several species of trout including: lake, brown, and rainbow.

Skaneateles Lake. Pronounced "Skinny atlas", is 315ft deep max, 16miles long, with a surface elevation of 863ft; making it the highest in elevation of the six lakes. Skaneateles Lake has a shale and rock substrate with natural springs flowing up giving this lake the purest water of any of the nearby lakes. While diving you can find remnants of horn corals 300-400years old. Invasive Zebra mussels encrust old barges and other sunken objects. Members of FLUPA have been busy weeding out Eurasian milfoil from this and the other local lakes. While diving, FLUPA members pull out the milfoil one handful at a time, bring it all back to shore where they let it dry, and then use it for mulch.

Canandaiga Lake. 276 max depth, 15 1/2 miles long, and at 688ft elevation. This lake typifies the glacial sediment with separate delineated clay beds, sandy beds, weed beds, and rock beds. Besides several species of trout, this lake is known for muskee, walleye, and mudpuppies. Mud puppies "necturus moculosus" are nocturnal salamanders that grow over 18 inches long and have fringing external dark red gills sticking out behind their neck region. In the daytime you can usually find them only under rocks, but at night you can find them out, swimming about, searching for crayfish and small fish. The island on the north end is called Squaw Island named after the four nations women and children who fled here during Sullivan's expedition. The island has eroded and is considerably smaller than it was 200years ago.

Keuka Lake. 186ft max depth, 20miles long, and at an elevation of 700ft. The lake is Y shaped and flows into Seneca Lake. Besides being home to lake trout, brown trout, rainbow trout, small mouth bass, large mouth bass, and yellow perch, this lake is also home to land locked salmon. The old paddleboat has disintegrated and sunk beneath the silt, but you can still find barges between 60-70ft deep. Finger Lakes Scuba of Auburn has a satellite store located on the north shore of Keuka Lake at Penn Yan where you can get last minute air and dive supplies. Mike Morehouse runs the satellite operation. He starts off his technical dive classes right in the lake, but for his student's final dives before certification, he prefers to move them over to the St. Lawrence River. You could say it's all part of a well-rounded and adventurous aquatic education.

Owasco Lake. 177ft deep max, 11miles long, and at an elevation of 712ft. Because it is the most shallow of the lakes, it warms up the most in the summer and you may need only a 3ml shorty to dive here. The only caveat being that when the water gets warmer, the visibility gets lower. On the other hand, the colder the water, the better the visibility. So if you want to see past 20ft under water, then winter could become your preferred season to dive.

Another thing to keep in mind about the Finger Lakes is the old adage that one person's garbage is another person's treasure. That means that old broken arrow heads several thousand years old are valuable, 200year old bottles are worth collecting, bottles from boot leg days are coveted, and water logged 16lb bowling balls are nearly priceless. Perhaps the order is subjective, but you get the drift that I'm not just kicking up silt. The Finger Lakes are a treasure trove of past human endeavors spanning close to ten thousand years.

Local dive shops, dive clubs, FLUPA members, and boat charter operations dive this area routinely, so ask ahead if they have a dive coming up in one of these lakes. Many of the shoreline areas are privately owned, so a boat comes in handy when wanting to dive certain areas. Some of these lakes are big, long, wide, and deep.

Videos on U tube can give you an idea what the visibility is like around some of the sunken relics. The videos also show you what a mail boat with walls of zebra mussels looks like, and what a barge cleared of zebra mussels looks like too. There are several videos of different divers trying to ride a sunken motorcycle. Needless to say, they don't get far; probably due to a flooded engine.

On the serious topside, a trip out to the Finger Lakes should take you longer than expected. The land is filled with college towns, wineries, vineyards, resorts, state parks, and other recreational areas. The scenery is the perfect setting for some great dives and great places to relax after the dives. The

Finger Lakes are just another prime example of why diving with air is so addictive and habit forming. Great dives.

North Carolina
On the Fringe of the Caribbean

No matter what you read, they always portray North Carolina as the *Graveyard of the Atlantic*. It is true that there may be well over 5000 shipwrecks off the coastline, but North Carolina waters should not be compared to Atlantic waters. The waters here can range in temperature between 76-80 degrees. The lobsters are spiny, not heavy clawed. The fish are tropical. The ledges are coral gardens, and the diving is generally more typical of the Cayman Islands than it is comparable to Maine, New York, or Newfoundland.

I've never tried to personally count all the wrecks off North Carolina, but I do know someone that probably has or is in the never-ending process of charting them all. Dale Hansen of Discovery Diving in Beaufort has mentioned some of these wrecks to me over the years that I've known him. He and a dedicated group of divers have been collecting data on the existing wrecks as well as finding new wrecks. I believe the team is currently in the process of getting ready to announce a newly discovered wreck just as soon as they make sure that all parties concerned get due credit for the discovery. Dale is passionate about wrecks and as it turns out, he couldn't have picked a better location for his passion. It turns out that storms, high waves, and mechanical failures have helped sink more ships here than we could ever do alone due to human errors and making artificial reefs. From the sixteenth to Eighteenth centuries ships routinely sank in heavy seas without any trace or record. One of the most famous wrecks from this early time is **Queen Anne's Revenge** Captained by the pirate Blackbeard (Edward Teach) that ran aground by Top Sail Inlet. With a bell marked 1709 and 21 cannons strewn on the substrate, there is little chance that it could be any other ship that stranded on a sand bar and went down around that time. Oh, don't bother looking; the pirates took all but a few specks of gold with them.

During the Civil War the most famous ship to go down off the coast was the **USS Monitor**. With only twin 11inch guns based on a turret, the Monitor faced off and stale matted in battle against the 10 fixed guns of the ironclad **CSS Virginia** "the remodeled **USS Merrimac**". This battle ended the days of the tall sailing ships. My brother, a war historian, points out that more importantly it was the end of fixed gun emplacements. The industrial North replaced the Monitor with three new ironclads within six months. The Agricultural based South on the other hand destroyed the only iron clad they had so it wouldn't fall into Northern hands. You can see that it could take a book just to do justice to all the wrecks of North Carolina, lct alone just these two mentioned wrecks or even the 184 historical wrecks located near Cape Look Out. Rod Farb is the author of *The Guide to Shipwreck Diving: North Carolina.*

One of the most famous wrecks to dive here has to be the German submarine **U-352**. The VII-C Class is 218ft long and rests at a max depth of 110ft. The outer hull is still in good shape. Besides the sub, schools of fish live here and make a great backdrop for photo images. The U-352 was one of a dozen ships and submarines sunk off the coast during the war years. The **U-124** sunk several tankers over 400ft long. The **U-588** torpedoed a 162ft long British armed trawler. The U-352 sunk the **Atlas** Oil tanker. The **U- 158** sunk the **Caribe Sea** freighter. The **U-552** sunk 5 vessels by itself. Other U-boats created other disasters almost to the point where any vessel sailing these waters during the war years was an artificial reef waiting for a place to happen. This added to North Carolina's notoriety as the graveyard of the Atlantic, but on these dives expect to see wrecks dotted with groupers, sea turtles, barracuda, lionfish, and sometimes cool looking sand tiger sharks. The **U-85** near Nags Head has lots of attractive coral growth on it and you can still see where the **USS Roper's** depth charges buckled the hull.

After the war, the carnage and sinking continued with such notables as the 298ft long **USS Tarpon**, a shark class submarine, that sank in 1957 at 140ft of depth and the 406ft long passenger freighter **Proteus** with 46 state rooms that sunk in 1958 at 120ft of depth. Suffice to say, that you could spend several years diving the waters of North Carolina before you even saw half of all the known wrecks. Ships continue to sink here in bad weather and I should mention that more accurate assessments have deduced that the shipwreck called the **Hutton** is actually the oil tanker **Ario**. The tanker **Papoose** is actually the tanker Hutton, and the Papoose is deep off the Oregon Inlet. Also, like any good menu there are lists of wrecks to choose from so you can choose between freighters, fishing trawlers, tankers, coast guard cutters, cable ships, submarines, or armed trawlers.

But don't order yet! If all this wasn't enough, North Carolina artificial reef projects include the 441ft long **Liberty Ship Theodore Parker** in 30-60ft of water, and a 328ft long landing craft repair ship called the **USS Indra** in 35-70ft of water.

So you are not a fan of wreck diving? No problem. North Carolina has miles and miles of 5 to 20ft tall underwater ledges full of coral and fossil artifacts. While **6-mile Ledge** and **8-mile Ledge** hint at how long they are, **Lobster Ledge** hints at what you might find here. **Fossil Ledge** is famous for divers finding 6.5inch teeth from prehistoric 60ft long sharks that used to patrol these waters. Fortunately it's safe to go back in the water now and with a little luck you may find a fossilized tooth that doesn't quite fit in the palm of your hand. Dive trips to fossil sites vary greatly and you have to shop around to get the best price. Also, they don't guarantee that you will come back with a large prehistoric tooth, you just have to keep your eyes open and hope for some exposed serrated artifact to be pointing out of the sandy substrate, but even if you come back toothless, it still could be good experience as well as another fun dive to log.

As far as shore dives go, the most famous beach dive is **Radio Island** near Beaufort. It's a jetty dive with up to 43ft of depth. You might see dolphins playing on the surface and stingrays just beneath.

As you can see, its no wonder why they call this area the graveyard of the Atlantic, but it baffles me where the

Atlantic part enters into the picture. Tropical pirates, tropical reefs, tropical fish, and tropical storms all suggest to me that the best kept secret in North Carolina is that you are diving in the Caribbean without having to take an over water flight to get there. Great Dives.

U-Boats of North Carolina
Predator & Prey Dive Sites

During WWII German U-boats infiltrated the waters off the coast of North Carolina on many long-range missions. Most were sent to seek out and destroy ships and interrupt the supply line to Europe, while others were sent over for more clandestine operations. Out of the nine U-boats mentioned in this article, three remain diveable off the coastline. One was lost off the coast of North Caroline and presumed to be in deep waters or buried under sand. Three U-boats inflicted casualties along the coastline, but were then sunk elsewhere, and at least two survived the onslaught of the war, but were scuttled elsewhere rather than surrender the military vessels to the Allies after the death of Hitler and defeat of Germany. Here is a brief list of U-boats starting with the ones you can actually descend beneath the waves and explore. The other U-boats left carnage in local waters and the sunken vessels have in their own right become popular N.C. wreck dive sites. With seventy years of underwater activity, some of these sites have become popular not only as submerged vessels, but as thriving isolated sea gardens filled with tons of fish and invertebrate life.

U-352 is probably the most well known submarine sunk off the coast. The hull is in relatively good shape and the plethora of sea life makes a great backdrop for underwater photos. It rests at 90-110ft in waters that range from 75 to 80° in the summertime. Commander KL Rathke fired 4 torpedoes at one ship that never hit or detonated. A few days later he fired two more torpedoes with the same effect on what turned out to be the Coast Guard Cutter *Icarus*. After five depth charges, the U-352 surfaced to abandon ship and Rathke gave orders to scuttle the already damaged vessel on 5/9/1942. *Dale A Hansen*, a diver from Discovery Diving in Beaufort has made a CD with pictures of the U-352, the prisoners taken, video clips of the wreck, and photos and names of many tropical species of fish that inhabit the wreck. He also has a book at the dive shop on some of the major wrecks in the area including what they looked like, and what the wrecks look like now from a diver's perspective. Several charter operations frequently run dedicated trips to this site.

U-85 near Nags Head and the Bodie Island Light house can have warm water at the surface but is can cool down to the 50's at the 100-110ft depth of the wreck. This submarine has more items removed from it than the U-352. A hatch from the U-85 is displayed at the Cape Hatteras Lighthouse museum in Buxton. Two oak boxes with enigma code machine parts were recovered from inside the wreck in 1997. It's the only VIIB class sub in American waters. It sunk 3 ships before the *USS Roper* depth charged and destroyed it on 4/14/1942. The *R/V Go Between* makes two runs a week out here when weather is favorable.

U-701 sank 9 ships before a Lockheed Hudson A-29 drooped 3 depth charges and sank the u-boat on 7/7/1942. Commander KL Degen sank the small-armed trawler YP-389 with his 88mm deck gun on 6/19/1941. The trawler rests in 300ft of water off North Carolina Degen also sank the tanker SS William Rockefeller. The U-701 remained hidden under shifting sands north of Diamond Shoals until discovered in 1989 by Uwe Lovas. His crew kept the site a secret for 15years. By 2004 the site coordinates became public and looters soon took a heavy toll on the structure and resting spot of many crewmen; 17 crewmembers escaped the abandoned vessel, but the coast guard picked up only 7, including Degen. The conning tower, the stern, and deck gun have been exposed above the sand for quite some time. The vessel lists on its side by 45 degrees. Amber Jacks and sand tiger sharks frequent the wreck. Strong currents may make this site undiveable at certain times.

U- 576 fired four torpedoes sinking the motor merchant *Bluefields* in deep water and damaging two other vessels off the N.C. coastline, but was then depth charged by a US Kingfisher aircraft and lost near Cape Hatteras on July 15, 1942. The U-576 has never been publicly seen or heard of again.

U-158 sunk a total of 17 ships before being sunk near Bermuda by a PBM Mariner on June 30th, 1942. Off N.C. the *Caribe Sea* was sunk on March 11th, 1942. The tanker *John D.*

Gill was sunk 25miles off of Cape Fear on 3/13/1942. The *Ario* was sunk near Cape Lookout on 3/15/1942. Many other vessels were badly damaged by the U-158.

U-124 had an impressive record with 11 patrols and 46 ships sunk. Off the N.C. coastline U-124 was responsible for sinking the *W.E. Hutton* on 3/18/1942, *Casandra Louloudis* on 3/18,1942, tanker *E.M. Clark* on 3/18/1942, the *SS Papoose* on 3/19, 1942, *SS Naeco* on 3/23/1942, as well as damaging other ships such as the *Acme*.

U-402 sunk in the middle of the Atlantic 10/13/1943. Off N.C. U-402 sank the 412ft long Russian tanker *Ashkhabad* on 4/29/1942 off Cape Lookout. The ship came to rest in 55ft of water, but had to be blown apart as it was a navigational hazard. Boilers and parts of the bow section remain for divers to explore.

U-552 was scuttled May 2nd, 1945. Off N.C. U-552 sank the 435ft long American steamer *Tamaulipas* on 4/2/1942, the *Bryon D. Benson* on 4/5/1942, the motor tanker *British Splendor* on 4/7/1942, and the 446ft long *Atlas* on 4/9/1942.

U-71 was scuttled May 2nd, 1945. In N.C. U-71 sank the 485ft long *Dixie Arrow* near the outer banks on 3/26/1942

As you can surmise, 1942 was a deadly year for Allie ships near North Carolina. By the end of 1942, Axis u-boats were more likely to be destroyed by planes than by ships, and because of this fact, u-boat deck guns were no longer installed on newer models. From now on the primary defense of u-boats was to dive and hide. Also, torpedoes were just as likely to miss or run wild, as they were to detonate as planned. Minefields laid off the N.C coast by u-boats were almost as deadly as the torpedoes themselves. Many ships went down off the coast during the war years, and many lives on both sides were lost. The vessel remnants are both diveable wrecks as well as the final resting place for many a crew. The prey ships and predator u-boats have currently become reefs for millions of fish and invertebrates, knowing the background behind these dive sites makes the diving here even more interesting, more thought provoking, and above all, a more personal underwater adventure and discovery experience. Great Dives.

North Dakota
Fish, Fossils, & Freshwater Diving

Your summer diving schedule might not have included any where outside of the Caribbean, but you might have to change your plans to include North Dakota if you are into spear fishing. You see, blocking off the Missouri River with the Garrison Dam and building the Garrison Dam National Fish Hatchery has created the 178mile long 6 mile wide Lake Sakakawea filled with fish. The Garrison Dam is the fifth largest earthen dam in the world and generates up to 583 megawatts of electrical power and controls annual flood levels. Meanwhile, the National fish hatchery raises some 10million native fish annually. Native species include: Northern Pike, Pallid Sturgeon, Shovelnose Sturgeon, and Walleye. Non-native species produced here include: Chinook salmon, brown trout, cutthroat trout, bass, paddlefish, sauger, small mouth bass, and yellow perch. Many of the cool water fish species here are also later supplied to other states. Divers who want to spearfish can hunt both Pike and Walleye, and when last checked, the limit on walleye was 5 a day, but check with local fish and wildlife regulations and restrictions before you enter the water. For the other species, you can fish from a boat. The Pallid Sturgeon averages 30-60 inches long and weigh 85lbs, and are the third largest fish in North America. Going by the name of Pacific, Oregon, or White Sturgeon, the Pallid's bigger northwest cousin can get up to 20ft in length and weigh over 1700lbs, but average size is slightly less. While the cartilaginous sturgeon group is 175million years old, the Pallid Sturgeon off shoot group is a mere 70millions years old, which puts them in the rivers during the Cretaceous time when Tyrannosaurus Rex ruled the surrounding lands.

Lake Sakakawea at an elevation of 1,817ft is less than 200ft deep and because of past droughts is more like 150ft deep, but closer to 28ft deep is all you need to go to fish for walleye. They tend to stay farther away from divers than other species of fish, but with vis from 10-15ft, they are easy to spearfish. The hard part is actually keeping the bass out of your face and obstructing your real target. Keep in mind, that even though walleye may be easy to hunt underwater, most people aren't trained as scuba divers and have some $2000 tied up in gear to spear a fish. It's just easier for most people to buy a boat, on a hook add bait, then sit and wait. The point is, that spearfishing divers take a relatively minute percentage of the annual total fish population harvested.

Lake Sakakawea State Park marina is the best place to launch a boat. The lake gets its name from the Hidatsa spelling of Lewis and Clark's Native American female Guide. The name means, "Bird woman." The Northwest pronunciation uses the Shoshone word *Sacagawea* that means, "boat launcher. Most likely, she sang like a bird while translating languages, therefore . . . Sakakawea wins the local pronunciation debate. The Marina has a snack bar, store, and restrooms and is next to a 300-site campground. Motels are close by in Pick City.

I talked to Randy Kraft owner and operator of *Scuba One* about 75miles away from the Dam in Bismarck. Not only does Randy have the closest dive shop, but also currently it is the only dive shop in all of North Dakota. You see business has comeback to North Dakota with such a boom that at least one other dive store has closed down because the lucrative construction business was just too irresistible. Randy on the other hand also owns and operates an international travel agency. Occasionally he works for the government as a consultant on underwater pipelines and inspecting former bridge sites. If not busy enough, he has also spent the last twenty years as a travel and dive operations consultant for dozens of Caribbean Dive Resorts. Check out the Scuba One web page if you are looking for a warm water destination.

Now as for Lake Sakakawea, Randy told me that besides spear fishing, he likes to keep an eye out for Buffalo bones and skulls; he collects only fishing tackle and things gone overboard from boats. If you are looking for something even bigger to search for, there is a **F-106 Delta Dart** that crashed in the ice and came to land on the river's dark substrate surrounded by 30ft tall submerged trees still standing in place from when the dam first filled in 1954.

Just below the Garrison Dam is the 17ft deep **Tailrace** of the Missouri River that becomes the 231mile long Lake Oahe and continues to flow out of North Dakota and half way down through South Dakota. The Tailrace waters are from the cold deeps of Lake Sakakawea and the vis can reach 30ft. The water rushes out at 1.5 to 4knots, making it a fast fun 15-25minute-drift dive with a live boat pick up; Randy uses a 27ft Carolina skiff. Not only will you see plenty of fish including big paddlefish on this dive, but you will also see remnants of cable and aggregate material when they were building the dam. About a mile down stream around the sunken tree stumps is a good place to hunt walleye.

Devils Lake in Ramsey/Benson Counties is another good place to dive. It is the largest natural body of water in the state and sits at an elevation level of 1,454ft. This lake is an endorheic or closed off lake and last drained into the Sheyenne River about a thousand years ago. Because of this lack of runoff, the lake has accumulated minerals, nutrients, organisms, and is saline similar to the Great Salt Lake in Utah. Because you can't drink the water, the Lakota name was Bad Spirit Lake, but the settlers didn't figure out the bad to drink connotation, so it became Devils Lake. The lake constantly changes shape as water runoff accumulates then evaporates. From 1993 to 1999 the Lake doubled in size and flooded 300 homes. In 1984 the shape of the lake looked like a leafy sea dragon. In 2009 the outline of the lake looked more like a thick-clawed lobster. As for fish, the lake holds walleye, Northern pike, and white bass, and is one of the top 5 lakes in the U.S. for perch weighing more than 2lbs. The max depth is about 60ft. Devils Lake is a good site for ice diving, but has low vis in the summer due to algae blooms.

At the beginning of summer Randy says they start diving over at **Spiritwood Lake** in Stutson County where there is easy access and the fresh water is really clear. The lake elevation is 1,450ft and the max depth around 50ft.

183

So there you go, there are tons of dive sites in just four mentioned lakes. Two of the lakes on the Missouri River give you hundreds of miles of shoreline to check out. There are tons of fish to spear or catch, fossils to view, and Scuba One is the only dive shop in the entire state that you can easily find online or currently reach by phone. The water temp can range from freezing up to 60degrees, but for diving anything warmer, you can make all your worldwide reservations at Scuba One. Great Dives

Ohio Rocks

Diving in Ohio rocks. Not the kind of rock as suggested by the music emanating from the American Music Hall of Fame in Cleveland, but from the water filled remnants of rock quarries whose contents were used to pave the Ohio roadways making it easy to go from one dive site to another. Scuba diving is big in Ohio. I don't really know if it's because there are so many local places to dive that local divers are more inclined to stay active, or if it's because so many local divers are active that they discover, create, and proliferate so many local places to dive. Either way, you have a wide assortment of dive sites to choose from both lakes, quarries, and in one case, even salt water. Starting from north to south here are a few:

Nelson Ledges Quarry Park is near Garretsville. Here we have bass, blue gill, fresh water jellyfish (too small to sting), crappie, and catfish. There is a cabin cruiser to dive. Local clubs have Halloween and treasure dives at this site.

White Star Park in Gibsonburg. This 800-acre park has a 15-acre lake that has a 40ft depth going down to 50ft in the center. With one hole at 60ft and another at 80ft. Besides a sunken cabin cruiser, there is a Frito Lay truck, a phone booth, sail boat small boats, and a car that needs some repair plus a good wash and wax.

Portage Quarry Recreation Club Inc, in Bowling Green. This is the home of the Portage Quarry Air Force consisting of one Hamburger Flug Zengbau Gmbh. This corporate 8-12 passenger jet currently has reduced seating fees for scuba divers. Other frequent flyers include large and small mouth bass, northern pike, blue gill, walleye, turtles and crayfish. If you would rather drive underwater, hop in the Ford bronco or on the motorcycle. A silo goes up 55ft under the water's surface. Max depth is around 70ft Three sides of this quarry have a carved stone ledges. Zebra mussels have cleared up the water and dive club members from Milan Michigan have put together an underwater navigation course. D.A.N. has an annual barbeque here in July.

Gilboa Quarry in Ottawa. This 14acre limestone substrate has a shallow side 5 to 65ft deep. The non-shallow side dips down to 130ft. A Grumman plane, and a Sikorsky helicopter are home to paddle fish, koi, trout, and turtles. D.U.I. has an annual D.O.G. rally at this site.

Natural Springs, formerly known as France Lake, is near the southern Ohio city of Paris. Here you may encounter bass, catfish, blue gill, grass carp, and freshwater jellyfish.

Circleville Twin Quarries, brought to you by Todd's Scuba, encompasses 10 acres of water. It has a school buss and a Cessna 421B. Call ahead if you want to dive here to make sure that the gate will be unlocked.

Many of these parks have small fees and waivers to sign. Some have camping, cottage, RV, or other overnight facilities. Including dive service centers, and gift shops. Some have semi enclosed gearing up areas while others have heated changing rooms including access to hot showers. Many state parks also have potential dive sites.

Now if all this isn't enough for you, then head back up to Cleveland or along the Ohio shoreline of Lake Erie. The lake averages only 62ft deep, but has hundreds of historical shipwreck sites as well as some nice islands. For divers, the underwater preserve around Kelly's Island is the resting place of three vessels. The steam ship *Adventure* rests in 5-15ft of water in North Bay. It was a schooner from 1875 until 1897 then it was converted to a steam barge in 1897 and sank in 1903. It rests 200ft off shore. The *Hanna* a scow schooner sank in 1886 in 3-8ft of water, and the *F.H. Prince*, a propeller steamer sank in 5-18ft in 1911. Built in 1890, she was converted into a sand dredge vessel in 1910 and sunk a year later. It seems that ships converted for other duties did not last long after the conversion process in these waters.

Other popular ships to dive along the coast include the *Mecosta*, which was a 281ft long wood propeller steamer that was scuttled about 9 miles from Cleveland after she was stripped of anything of value at the time in 1885. The ship, that was named after where her wood building material was harvested in Mecosta, Michigan, came to rest in 48ft of depth.

Near Port Clinton rests the 135ft long prison ship *Success* in 16-20ft of water. This teak wood Barquetine burned and sank in 1946, but the ribs and keel are still visible. There is also the 60ft long ship the *Detroiter* that sank in 20ft of water in the 1980's.

Just a few years ago using side sonar, divers located the *Anthony Wayne* near Vermillion, Ohio. The 155ft long side-wheel steamer sank in 1893 while carrying passengers, wine, and livestock. She was reported to have gold in her ship's safe and in the captain's safe as well. She currently rests in 50ft of water.

Now for an interesting adventure in salt water, locals help out at the **Cincinnati Zoo**: in the salt-water manatee exhibit to be more specific. What could be more rewarding than helping out with an 8 to 15ft long sea cow that can weigh up to 3,500lbs?

For more aquatic adventures locals can cross the state line and visit the **Newport Aquarium** in Kentucky and be part of the D.I.V.E Program. The real name is Dive Interactive Volunteer Educational Program. You can help out by preparing meals, cleaning habitats, working with fish, and working with visiting tourists almost all simultaneously. Other out of state dive sites include: **Summerville Lake** in Indiana which can drop down to 300ft near the base of the dam, but averages around 20-50ft, **Dream Lake** at Hidden Paradise Campground which boasts 4-5ft long paddlefish, **Phillips Quarry** near Muncie which drops down to 55ft with lots of fish and algae covered objects, and **France Park** in Logansport, Indiana where you can find a 1940's school bus, a pickup truck and other assorted objects people have donated over the years.

So you probably can tell that by the great number of local places to dive, the only excuse not to dive is in the winter when the snow is too deep or you are not quite yet a dry suit diver, but the water clarity may be over 70ft of visibility in the winter, so even then, divers in Ohio can be found in the local quarries and lakes. When the mild weather returns, the boat dive charter operations are once again busy on lake Eerie and the annual cycle continues, and perhaps this helps explain why the local divers dive so much and why diving in Ohio rocks. Great Dives.

Oklahoma
The Homeland Of Hearty Lake Divers

Oklahoma has over 200 artificial lakes, giving one the impression that it has more dam dive sites than just about any other state in the union. Unfortunately, the visibility in many of these lakes can be quite low as one local diver solemnly explained to me. He said that 6ft to 8ft of visibility is considered good, and anything above 15ft was down right spectacular, but I think you may find sites where the vis is even better. So if you're ready to get your dive gear wet, then here is a list of some of the better-known dive spots in the great lake state of Oklahoma:

Lake TenKiller near Gore heads the list because this lake also has a designated scuba park. The lake covers 1,650 acres, has 130miles of shoreline, and rests at the foothills of the Ozark Mountains and was formed in 1953 by the construction of the Tenkiller Ferry Dam. The maximum depth is 165ft. The vis can get up to 20ft at certain depths and sites. Some of the best dive spots are reached by boat.

On the east side of **Skunk Island** there are ledges that drop down in 12-15ft increments down to 120ft. This is a great spot for spear fishing. The lake is filled with black bass, white bass, stripped bass, sunfish, crappie, catfish, and walleye. Keep in mind that spearfishing is only for non-game fish, and even with catfish, the season for flathead catfish is shorter than channel catfish, so be sure and check the current regulations before you go diving. To date, the biggest catfish caught in the lake weighed 65lbs.

On the west side of Skunk Island underwater you will find slabs of cement where once houses stood before the old town of *Cookson* was flooded to fill the dam. Around the slabs expect to see old bottles and horseshoes. Farther down the slopes expect to find remnants of horse carriages, and many structures still standing; nothing can be removed as per state law.

Goat island is easy to spot; look for goats. Underwater, walls are on the south side, and slopes, ledges, and trees are on the north side. Max depth is 150ft. The **Old DX Landing** and **Crappi Point** are two other local diving sites.

Now in the Pine Cove Recreational Area at Fisherman's Point is the **Tenkiller Scuba Park**. Here you can swim by an old ski boat, fishing boats, a school bus, and a big coast guard helicopter fuselage. Max depth is 91-100ft.

Overall, with 24 boat ramps, 10 marinas, 14 parks, cabins, cottages, tons of primitive campsites, and the Pine Cove Marina and Clearwater Café, Lake Tenkiller has something to offer everyone.

Lake Elmer Thomas Recreation Area (LETRA) is a no wake lake west of Medicine Park. The lake is actually inside Fort Sill military base, so when you want to enter the park, you may have to pass through a military gate and say, "I'm going to LETRA." It's that easy. You can go camping, fishing, play at the family water park area, golf, or go canoeing. There are buffalo and deer in the nearby Wichita Mountains or visit the US Army Field Artillery Museum. Underwater, the max depth is 95ft and you'll see wide mouth bass, crappie, and catfish. The best diving is on the north side of the dam. Many dive classes train here, and the vis here the last few years has been better than just about anywhere else in the state.

One thing to remember here, is to wear at least a 5ml suit or warmer. In the winter the water temp can be 46° at the surface with no thermo cline, but in the summer the air temp can reach 95° while the surface is 78°. At 35ft of depth it is 69°, at 55ft it is 60°, and at 78ft it is 53°. Another thing to keep in mind is to carry a flashlight and backup light for any dive below 45ft where it gets dark and rocky.

Lake Murray, south of the Arbuckle Mountains and Ardmore, opened in 1938. The lake has 67miles of shoreline and covers 5,700 acres. The substrate consists of silt and clay. 300 million years ago, this area was a vast sea. Lake Murray is known for its small mouth bass. The most notable dive site is on the southeast end at Marietta Cove Landing. There are a couple of boats and a car between 15-25ft of depth. If you swim way out along the channel, the depth gradually goes down to 45ft. Over at the old pump tower you can climb down to a dive site where there is a platform down between 60-70ft. While the surface maybe 72° at 70ft the spring fed water temp dips down only to 62°. Besides diving, you can camp, golf, or go horseback riding. The Tucker Tower Nature Center is home to fossils including the skeleton of a Mammoth found at the Washita River 35 miles away and is also home to the fifth largest meteorite in the world; which is cut in half. The 77ft tall Turner Falls in the Chicasaw National Recreational Area is near by, as well as the Arbuckle Wilderness Exotic Animal Theme Park.

Lake Broken Bow is in Southeast Oklahoma. The water temp gets down to 40° at 100ft. There are cliff walls, and isolated coves to dive with rock, pebble, sand beaches, especially northwest of Beavers Bend Marina on Stevens Gap Road where trails make it easier to get down to the water's edge. Max depth is 140ft by the dam spill walls. Some divers also dive in Mountain Creek River just below the dam to see water dogs (salamanders), and catch crawdads (crawfish). On the lake you can rent houseboats, and jet skis, which reminds me that you need a big dive flag when diving in Oklahoma. Not the normal garden variety, but one that is 20"x24" and has a 4" diagonal white stripe. It may seem too big, but the fine for not having a flag this size is even bigger. Another thing you will need is a knife to cut away any stray fishing lines.

Lake of the Arbuckles, 6 miles southwest of Sulphur, has 36 miles of shore land and 2,350 surface acres. Spotted bass, catfish, crappie, and sunfish are the local residents. In addition to diving, you can swim, play on the beach, use the biking trails, go bicycling, or go jet skiing here.

Besides these lakes, if you ask nicely, you may be able to enter one of the many privately owned flooded quarries around the state.

So there you go, a short list from over 200 lakes, but still lots of lakes, rivers, and quarries to dive. Bring a larger than life dive flag and you're set to go. In Oklahoma, enjoy seeing a wide variety of fish underwater, and seeing plenty to do on the surface too. You'll quickly see that in Oklahoma, for a great time diving, all you need are just a few friends, the right gear, and extra ice for the day's catch. Great Dives!

Oregon
Pacific& Non-pacific Diving

Oregon has one of the most beautiful stretches of coastline in the world. I'm not just saying this because I'm a fifth generation Oregonian, just ask any one of the millions of tourists that have stood at the edge of a rocky overlook or traversed the sandy beaches and witnessed the awe inspiring power of the Pacific Ocean, but besides the natural scenic beauty, there are the seals, puffins, seagulls, invertebrates, fish of all sorts and sizes, and washed up Japanese glass fishing floats to keep one spell bound for days on end. Now although I recommend everyone visit Oregon and the northwest at least once, I only recommend diving off the coast of Oregon to those divers that are physically fit and already have acquired and refined good diving skills. Those magnificent waves may have sections connected to powerful undertows, and currents can run very strong, plus there can be unexpected sneaker waves too. You may also have to carry your equipment a mile down to the beach, or swim way out from shore before you begin your dive. Some day, visibility can drop to almost nothing and leave one with only a compass as a guide. In response to all this, Oregon divers have become extremely physically fit, and typically dive from shore only at high slack. They also dive closer to piers, jetty walls, around the mouths of rivers, and bays, where direct contact with the Pacific's powerful waves are greatly reduced: especially when not diving from a boat.

Now that I've warned you, I will say that while there is only one dive site on the Washington coast that I can think of where scuba divers routinely go, but I can name at least three-dozen shore dive sites off or near the Oregon coastline. So starting at the northern most end of Oregon, I have made the following list of cities where dive sites are close by:

Manzanita is just south of Cannon beach and home to *Oswald State Park* and **Short Sands Beach** or (Shortys). It's a long walk down the path for less than 8 ft of vis, but Floyd Holcom of *Astoria Scuba*, the closest dive shop within 100 miles, says there is a nice reef on the left side and rocks on the north side, but watch for currents.

Garibaldi is part of the **Tillamook Bay** and you can see *Three Graces,* as you are just about to enter into town. Some divers cross right across the railroad tracks and down to the water's edge, while others like to start from the small park at Pirates Cove. The Graces go down about 40ft and vis is between 10-30ft. It's a good site to view a wide assortment of underwater creatures including wolf eels, octopus, and other favorites. *Pirates Cove* and the *Lumber Dock* are two sites for catching crabs and clams. If you have access to a boat, a third site is directly across from Pirates Cove at *Crab Harbor* and around T*he Old Lighthouse*, many man made souvenirs and artifacts have been found. Charter boats go out of Tillamook Bay to *Cape Lookout*, and down to Pacific City to *Haystack Rock* at Cape Kawanda, which is 100ft taller than the Haystack Rock at Canon Beach. Two interesting phenomena have been reported in Tillamook Bay: First, harbor seals watch for crabbers, and they have learned to dive around flat circular crab nets and eat the salmon bait and do not even bother swimming near box traps. The second phenomena is that particular divers that dive extremely close to crab buoys tend to bob their heads around when they surface, similar to harbor seals that have just raided a flat crab pot. The fact that these divers have full crab bags when they surface does nothing to ease the local fishermen's suspicions; just another reason to be careful where you dive.

Newport is home of the Yaquina Bay and on the south side of the Newport Bridge at the **South Beach Park** is the *Fingers*, a set of what look like miniature rock jetties to explore for sea creatures; max depth 34ft. Close by is the *Crab Dock* a the **Newport Marina** that has been there since 1910. The *Wacoma Dock* is another near by site, but may be busy with NOAA stuff. By charter boat you can dive *North Pinnacle* that starts at 40ft underwater and goes down to 100ft. Bring a flashlight to see all the colors and tons of critters including rock scallops. *Johnson Rock* is the 2nd largest pinnacle and has ridges, gullies, deep holes, and crevices where animal life thrives. The 1983 Korean oil tanker "*Magpie*" wreck is right next to the north jetty, but is very hazardous due to strong currents, sharp broken objects, dangling debris, and tangling kelp. *Seal Rock* at **Seal Rock Park** 10 miles south of Newport is great spot for viewing aquatic mammals of some sort.

Waldport at *Yaquina John Point* is max 45ft deep and a good spot to find crab in the sand, but watch out for the boats.

Florence at the *North Jetty* there are crabs, and gaper clams at 35ft max or at Crab Hole at 65ft. The *Siuslaw River* is 40ft max. *South Jetty* has clams around a sunken jetty.

Winchester Bay, south of Reedsport, has the *Crab Dock*. Look for the **Windy Cove Park** sign and dive between the parallel running dock and the jetty.

Coos Bay is great for Dungeness crabs anywhere except the main boat channels. Vis may be only 10 ft and depth 60ft max. Remember to dive at slack or don't come back! By boat you can go out to *Simpson Reef* or *Baltimore Reef*. Charter boats go out of **Bandon** to these reefs too.

Port Orford has **Nellies Cove**: small bays with beaches and rocks, a jetty, and shower facilities. If you have a boat, then you also have 2 square miles of rocks, and sea lion colony playground to explore including: *Large and Small Browns Rocks, Fox Rock, Island Rock, Orford Rocks, Tichenor Rock*.

Brookings has *Whales Head* Beach 7 miles north of town it looks beautifully untouched, and with a long hike and 100yrd swim out to the rocks, it's not for the feint of heart. *Twin Rocks* or *Lone Ranch*, is 4 miles north of Brookings. *Mill Beach* is a small sandy beach behind the A&W root beer restaurant with a 35ft deep cove and vis around 5ft.
Did I mention all the places to dive? No, I didn't really have room or time. I didn't even get to mention fresh water lakes like the volcanic ash formed *Clear Lake* near **Mill City** or 7,000 high *Crater Lake*, which has a sunken helicopter down at 1,500ft deep. *Woahink* is a state designated dive park at **Honeymoon State Park**. Parts of the *Smith River* and *Illinois River* are diveable sites. Actually, many Oregon lakes are great dive sites, but don't dive the high cascade lakes like I tried

30yrs ago: the water temperature decreases by twenty degrees with every half-inch of depth. I know, live and learn, and in the mean time, have some Great Dives.

Astoria Scuba & Kayak

It seems every year around the 4th of July I find myself surrounded by friends and family and the beauty of the Oregon Coastline. During my last visit I stopped in at Astoria Scuba & Kayak to say hello to Floyd Holcom. Floyd and his family own and operate Pier 39 in Astoria. This wooden pier has a narrow two-lane road that extends out from 39th street into an 84,000sqft structure that for 135years was the home of the Hanthorn Cannery and the Bumble Bee cold storage facility. Currently, Pier 39 is home to the Fishermen's suites, Office suites, Art loft rentals, the Rogue Ale Public House, Coffee Girl, live crab holding tanks, boat storage, a coin operated Laundromat, Astoria Scuba and Kayak, plus the Bumble Bee museum and displayed fishing boats of a by gone era. It's a lot to take in on just one visit. Fortunately, the Rogue Ale Public House has plenty of seating with food and beverages to reenergize any weary diver or tourist. At Coffee Girl from quiche to cake all they seem to do is bake. In fact, I believe their motto is "Let them eat cake!" Their coffees are topped with handcrafted artwork, and the back patio Columbia River scenery is hard to leave even after the sun finally sets.

Now as far as the dive shop goes, Floyd has been filling air tanks and working with NOAA, military units, and the local Sheriff's department since 2004. His son, Nate Holcom, is the current president of the dive shop. If you go on Youtube, I have a video of Nate under mike hughes scuba where he explains the Heed 3 spare air system specially made for helicopter divers. The day I was at the shop Nate's sister, Victoria, was working behind the dive shop's counter. Floyd deeply believes that if you are going to have a next generation of divers, then you have to get them involved with diving while still in their teens. Together, they have not only made diving a family way of life, but they are also one of the very few NAUI Pro Platinum Facilities in the United States: a very prestigious award in its own right. The shop itself carries many name brand items in one section and there is a state of the art service and air fill section right next door. The air here is cleaned an extra step to military specifications. They also have a hydrostatic test facility. Whether you have a small boat or a Naval Ship, there is plenty space to dock and visit Astoria Scuba & Kayak

As far as the kayaks go, this is a popular activity around the Oregon and Washington coastlines and allows divers to venture into coastal areas that would otherwise be off limits due to currents or to distances. Even while I was there trying to take pictures, a family was busily deciding which kayaks would suit them best.

I should also mention that right in the dive shop is a hardhat diver suit and helmet similar to the ones used by some of the first west coast divers who cleared underwater snags along the Columbia River. In addition, at the Columbia River Maritime Museum just about a mile away is a complete Snag diver in helmet exhibit, as well as charts and maps showing the locations of hundred of wrecks near the mouth of the Columbia River. The museum is home of the Light Ship Columbia, as well as miniature replicas of ships that plied the local rivers and Pacific Ocean. One of the wrecks on Floyd's to do list is the wreck of the Isabella. The *Isabella* was a Hudson Bay Company supply ship built in 1825 and sank in 1830 in 40ft of water off Cape Disappointment.

One wreck is known as the *Beeswax*, and no one knows exactly where it rests, but every so often after a storm, blocks of bees wax appear on shore. The pollen in the blocks comes from flowers in Central Luzon in the Philippines, and 1670AD is the radiocarbon date of the wax.

To sum it up, Floyd and his family have created a Pier 39 for Astoria reminiscent to Pier 39 in San Francisco, but with flavors, flare, and plenty to offer locals as well as tourists. Now, sometimes the family steps out of the dive shop to run other errands around the pier so just give a call if you arrive at one of these "back in a moment" instances, or call ahead if you prefer, as the next dive shop available is likely to be more than 100miles away, and it's down right impossible to get a pizza, pastry, air fill combo, at any other Pier along the Oregon Coast. Great Dives

Pennsylvania
Rich In History; Great Dive Diversity.

Sure, Pennsylvania is rich in history with such sites as the Liberty Bell bearing an ever-widening crack and resting on display right near Independence Hall in Philadelphia. There is also the national military park and battlefield of Gettysburg where Robert E. Lee tried a northern advance. 51,000 casualties were the result of the endeavor. The death, destruction, and divisive nature of the civil war led and inspired then President Abraham Lincoln to write and orate one of the most famous speeches to ever be recited in American history. There is also the Fort Necessity National Battlefield, and the Valley Forge National Military Park. On a lighter note, Pottsville is the hometown of the oldest brewery in the country; a German immigrant started The Yuengling Brewery in 1829. But for scuba divers alike, the real history revolves around the 1700 ships, freighters, schooners, and other vessels that have come to rest at the bottom of Lake Erie. You can dive some of these wrecks straight from shore, but to see the rest you have to go out on the charter vessels that usually operate between the months of May and October.

The biggest airport on the west side of Pennsylvania is Pittsburgh. Inside the airport before you even get to baggage claim you have to pass between a statue of a Pittsburgh Steeler and George Washington. Going down the escalator you are met with a full replica statue of a Tyrannosaurus Rex. The city itself has green hills of trees separated by rivers and reminds me a lot of my native hometown of Portland, Oregon way out west. Philadelphia on the other hand has an older airplane terminal where businessmen roam the high ceiling sparse halls. Lots of high buildings and the humid Atlantic coast driven air in downtown Philadelphia remind me of New York City in the summertime. It's the distinctive aroma and taste of Philadelphia cheese steaks being cooked on corner grill stands, though that makes the tropical humidity worth bearing. And just like there are two different types of Pennsylvania airports, major cities, and climates, there are even more types of variations in local scuba diving activities, locations, and dive sites. Many dive sites are former quarries that have been filled in with water. Some of them have been seeded with wide selections of fish. Then to make the sites more attractive, other manmade attractions have been added to make the bottom topography more interesting. Other dives are in natural lakes, rivers, and streams.

One of the biggest dive locations has to be **Dutch Springs** in Lehigh Valley. This 50acre lake has an Aqua park and a Sky Challenge course in addition to a picnic area, and other facilities. Underwater there is a Sikorsky H-37 helicopter: 88ft long 27ft wide, 22ft high, and suspended in the water. There is also a school bus, a 1946 trolley, fire truck, a Cessna airplane, and many more boats and artifacts; max depth 100ft.

Willow Springs quarry boasts a sunken 72ft trawler, SS Minnow, a steam shovel crane, a fire truck, a caboose, a school bus, and may more objects that strategically found their way to the bottom of the lake; max depth 55ft.

Bainbridge Sportsmanship Scuba Club is a former quarry turned lake that offers a bus, truck, airplane, building structures, diving platforms, and a depth down to 130ft.

Guppy Gulch in Delta, Pa near the Maryland state line is a former quarry with a depth of 80ft, which boasts 5 platforms to train on. Speaking of trains, they have those too, as well as trucks and other items sunk in the lake. They even treat the water for better visibility.
Many of these lakes require a day use fee for scuba diving. Private lakes and quarries such as **Blue Hole** require permission to cross private lands. Some parks and lakes you will have to contact ahead of time to find out all the requirements and parking areas.

Other notable dive sites include the Old Williamsport Dam, the Jay Street Bridge area on the Susquahanna River near Lock Haven, and many public, as well as private beaches along various creeks. The local dive shops can give you numerous tips on places to go near and far.

Far for a few Pa divers however is a relative term. Some divers like to go to West Virginia to Mount Storm to do a high altitude dive at 3,380ft above sea level. Besides following the altitude dive tables, you have to stay away from the power plant water intake pipes down at 120ft of depth.

Some Pa divers just like to dive the local quarries while others travel around the entire state. I asked Instructor Dennis Zahradnik from Dive World where he likes to dive and he said, Strawberry Quarry, Lake Erie, and the St. Lawrence River. The Strawberry Quarry has three main dive sites and is the spot where a few years ago the boy scouts built a suspended artificial reef made from wooden pallets as an Eagle project to help protect smaller fish find safe havens in different thermo cline layers. Now lake Erie as his second choice, sounded reasonable. Once you know the history of past storms and shipwrecks. When Dennis said "The St Lawrence River", I had to ask him why? He said, "Because it was "Refreshing"". I wasn't sure what he meant by that until I looked it up online and read about all the different types of diving you could do up north. I found that the list included wall dives, deep dives, wreck dives, and drift dives. So now I have another place I have to investigate.

It's not all about going up north either; many Pa divers hit the shores and charter operations off the coast of New Jersey. Driving from the Philadelphia it's a short hop over to what William Penn and the early settlers called the Western Ocean, but then again, in those days Philadelphia was called Philada, and Pensylvania only had one "n" in the name.

So the landscape of the land where George Washington first resided in his presidential residence may have undergone many changes including quarries and dams, but the diving has just gained more places of access, better onshore facilities, and tons of underwater structures and attractions. And while not all underwater structures have been sunk on purpose, they have all added to the growing popularity of Pennsylvania diving. For warmer weather and perhaps a greater concentration of dive quarries, turned resorts, you have the Philadelphia area dive sites. For green forests, cooler weather, and a chance to discover sunken wrecks hundreds of years old you have the dive sites surrounding Pittsburgh and up on Lake Erie. Either way, there is plenty of public dive sites and private dive clubs to keep any diver historically busy.

Rhode Island
Wreck Divers Gone Wild!

Rhode Island is a state smaller than the Clark County School District in Nevada, but even though it is small, the Ocean State contains over 400 hundred miles of coast line, and that makes for tons of potential dive sites. A thousand times you may have heard the phrase "Rhode Island is Wreck Divers Paradise", but one of the employees at *Andersons Ski and Dive* in East Grenwich summed it up best by stating that there's an artifact in every square foot of the bay. I asked him what his top three dive sites are and he jokingly said, "*Those I only keep to myself*", but he did fill me in on some of the regular sites as you peruse in the article.

Charlie Walpole of *Narragansett Pier Dive Shop* said that the top dive in all of New England has to be the **U 853**. This German 252ft long WWII submarine is fascinating to divers on so many levels. It sits relatively in tack with the stainless steel periscope still shinning in 130ft of water 7 miles east of Block Island. The mystery surrounding the U 853 is why did Capt Helmut Fromsdorf, a 24yr old *Knights Cross* recipient come so close to shore that he only had 30ft of water under the sub and fire one of his six torpedoes at the **SS. Black Point** one day after acting Furer Donitz ordered all submarines to cease fire as Hitler had a day earlier committed suicide and continued aggression was pointless? Even stranger is the fact that Capt Helmut waited in the area for 90minutes afterwards until US warships arrived. He kept submerged so he couldn't fire his deck guns, didn't fire any more torpedoes, and didn't try to abandon ship until finally all 55 men aboard were killed by depth charges; a sort of "*death by navy*". As for the SS Black point, the 369ft coal ship that you could hear before you saw it, was armed with one 5inch gun, was broken in two by the torpedo explosion and now rests at 105ft. 12men and a chimpanzee went down with the coal supply ship and 34men survived. Each wreck of Rhode Island has an interesting history behind it, and even on these two wrecks, I barely skimmed the, no pun intended, sub surface.

Another dive spot Charlie mentioned was the **Pinnacle** off Block Island. Smooth cylindrical granite rocks at the forefront of a glacial advance over 10,000years ago formed this rock wall that juts up 35 to 75ft from the bottom. This is a haven for photographers with up to 40-60ft of vis.

Warren Eddi from *Giant Stride Dive Shop* in Warwick likes the 120ft tug wreck the **Idene**. It was scuttled in 1991 and sits upright in 90ft of water like a Hollywood Wreck set. He also likes the 80ft tugboat **PT. Teti** at 100ft that sunk while in tow. Divers have recovered portholes and other objects from this wreck. Red Godin, from *Giant Stride*, likes the **Arches** off Gooseberry Island. Also formed by glacial deposits off the tip of the island. You will see lots of different fish here including flounder and blue fish; it's the Caribbean of Rhode Island in the summer as Gulf Stream currents raise the water temp to 70°. Red also likes **Kettle Bottom Rock** near Mackerel Cove on the south end of Jamestown. It's a haven for fish, kelp, and anemones. **Horsehead Cove** has a nice wall dive depending on tides; both of these sites are considered boat dives.

Hymie Beaufort of *Newport Diving Center* likes the **Dumplings**. This should also be considered a boat dive due to currents, and boats traffic around the marinas. He likes the structure of the almost cave like setting near the house on the rocks. The area is covered with rocks, sand and eel grass. You'll see lots of lobster, anemones, and tautog. Tautog is a blunt nose white chinned fish that is found almost exclusively in New England waters. Average fish are 2-4lbs and 6-10years old, but males get up to almost 23lbs and max out around 35yrs old. At night they are inactive and you can catch them using your hand. Hymie also likes diving off **Ledge Road** to find Stripper and Black fish, and **Ft. Adams** for the fish, lobster, and weird and strange stuff like railroad carts.

One of the representatives from *Kalypso Dive Shop* in Smithfield said that one of her favorite dive sites was **Bull Point**. There's a nice wall that extends down to 100ft and basically contains all the regular Rhode Island suspects, critters, and fish. Like most others she also mentioned **Kings Beach,** as it is the easiest entry beach and a great spot for novice divers. With a depth between 25-35ft, and lobsters, eels, skates, flounder, and tautogs, there is plenty to see in the eastern cove and not so much in the eelgrass of the western cove. **Ft. Wetherill** in southern Jamestown offers easy entry diving via a small boat ramp in the right cove, and on the far left side of the left cove there is an anemone-covered wall that drops down to 70ft. **Beaver Tail Park** is large and exposed at the southern tip, and the exits can be tricky so look on both the western and eastern side for calm waters before hiking down, and if the waters are too rough for advanced divers, drive over to Ft. Wetherill instead.

For something a little on the adventurous side try a shark cage dive with *Snappa* Charters. It's a 46ft long boat run by captain Charlie Donilon. He usually takes groups and individuals for a total of 10 divers out between mid-June to October. It's about a 10-hour trip round trip from shore and along the way don't be surprised to see turtles and dolphins. Out at the appointed site the main sharks you will see while safely in the submerged cage and/or the surface cage are oceanic blue and mako sharks. Its a cool blue water experience to get close to these apex predators and don't forget to take photos to show the folks back home.

Other wrecks to visit include: The 341ft long **USS. Bass** submarine at 155ft, the 165ft long **L-8 submarine** at 105ft, the 200ft **Metis** at 130ft, the 70ft **Mary Arnold** tug at 55ft, the 252ft **Larchmont** paddle steamer at 135ft, the 275ft **Onandaga** steamship at 50ft, the 110ft **Heroine** trawler at 80ft, the 340ft **Rhode Island** side wheeler, the **USS Revenge** sunk in 1811 commanded by Oliver Hazard Perry. Plus the tanker **Lightburne**, steamer **Essex**, schooners **Montana** and **Two Brothers**, the **Black Diamond**, the freighter **Grecian**, and more.

As you can see, there are tons of wrecks to explore, but don't remove anything over 10 years old as it is against Rhode Island law. The problem with the current system is that no one wants to show off what they've found or preserve the artifacts publicly, and the historical significance of the artifacts may be lost forever, but for now, leave bubbles and take lots of pictures, as Rhode Island is truly the land of countless wrecks. Great Dives.

South Carolina
Revolutionary Diving Experiences and more!

South Carolina may not have the 100ft visibility waters known to Florida, and sometimes the river visibility may be best measured in inches, but what South Carolina lacks in visibility, the waters make up for in view. I'm talking about the chance to see and dive around Civil War wrecks, Revolutionary War relics, ancient American Indian artifacts, and prehistoric preserves. Sounds intriguing? But what if I told you that the South Carolina Institute of Archeology and Anthropology also allows you to obtain a *Hobby Diver* license so you can collect said artifacts? Now, throw in lots of wrecks, tons of fish, breath taking Blue Ridge Mountain views, historical war sites, a few aquariums, and barbecued pork with a sauce custom made locally with mustered instead of ketchup, and you have one great recipe for a true dive adventure.

For those unfamiliar with diving in South Carolina I've divided the Palmetto tree state into three distinct regions. Starting at the northern end on the Atlantic side we have Myrtle Beach, which has cornered the market on most of the state's sunken ships. Some dive sites list the top 20 wrecks in the area, while other web sites list over 60 wrecks in the area. Carey Alford, of *Nu Hurizons Dive & Travel,* says that his favorite dive site in the area is the **Bill Perry Reef System**. There are quite a number of things to dive here. The Bill Perry is a tugboat sunk 21 miles off shore at around 65ft of depth, but near by it rests 44 New York subway train/cars, a navy landing craft, and a shrimp boat. This collectively makes this reef system a must dive destination. Small fish like to embark and disembark the subway trains in finicky fashion, groupers seem to conduct the movements of schools of fish in harmonious headings, and between soft corals, agile algae, and the occasional policing the area by small bands of barracuda, typical subway graffiti has never been an issue. Now if you want something larger to dive, the **BP 25** is in the same area. This 160ft long British Petroleum oil tanker is down at 90ft and is home to tons of sea life.

For even larger wrecks you'll have to visit other sites such as the 470ft long **USS Vermillion** rests between 90-140ft of depth. She was built as a liberty ship, used as a troop transport, and her last designation was an attack cargo ship. The 290ft long **City of Houston**, a passenger/freighter sunk while carrying Christmas goods in 90ft of water, but she is 55miles offshore, so diving her is and all day excursion.

As for older vessels, several rank in the 1800's including the 200ft long **Sherman** which was a blockade runner during the Civil War, but sank during a storm in 1874 in 52ft of depth 6 miles from Little River Inlet. **The Pipe Wreck** is a paddle wheeler sunk in 80ft with side-wheel shafts and a boiler exposed. **The Governor** was another paddle wheeler that sunk in 80ft, 22miles off the coast. The 200ft long Governor may have hosted Southern gentry and Southern soldiers, but currently is booked to the gills with Southern stingrays.

If all this isn't enough to wet your appetite, then you'll have to have to visit some small reefs loaded with landing craft, military armored personnel carriers, and barges, such as the artificial reef **Barracuda Alley,** or other reefs such as **Greenville Reef, Georgetown Reef, Will Goldfinch Reef**, and **Wayne Upchurch Reef**. Oh, and don't forget the reef them selves such as **Table Top** 17miles offshore with 4ft ledges. So did I hit all the dive sites up near Myrtle Beach? No, but the ones that I did mention should keep you satiated long enough.

Down by Charleston is where the diving diverges. I asked one anonymous employee from Charleston Scuba what his favorite dive site was and he said, "The Ledges." He liked the natural reefs over the wrecks as natural reefs have a natural abundance of colorful fish life such as **Indigo Ledge**, but he was quick to point out that others in the dive shop preferred wrecks like the **Y-73**. The Y-73 was a 180ft oil tanker that went down in 100ft of depth. There is also the great lake icebreaker, **Comanche**. Down at 100ft. One wreck, the **Frederick W. Day** is the ultimate model for artificial reefs.

This 200ft cargo ship went down in 1914. At the time it sank, it was filled with cement. All around the world, cement artificial reefs are being sunk, only here, the ship went down too.

So Charleston has wrecks and ledges as well, but what sets this area apart is the river diving. If you don't mind mere inches of visibility, temperatures down to 40degrees in the winter and 90degrees in the summer, and sightings of alligators and snakes in the warmer months, some of the best black water diving is found in South Carolina. What you will get for you efforts are finding prehistoric Megalodon shark teeth, mammoth and giant sloth bones, Native American Indian pottery chards, bottles, Civil War and Revolutionary War buttons, buckles, and bullets. Case in point, the **Cooper River Underwater Heritage Trail** has 2 miles of underwater sites from the old 1781 British military **Strawberry** shipwreck to remnants of the **Mepkin** plantation dock pilings. Other rivers have also given up artifacts to hobby artifact divers, it's not surprising when you remember that hundreds of skirmishes between British & Loyalist troops and later when General Sherman marched the Union army from Georgia through South Carolina and up to North Carolina in what is referred by many as 66 days of hell.

Now for a real fresh water look at diving you need to visit the western side of the state. Lake Jocassee is a 7,500acre reservoir with vis from 15-50ft, and temperatures from 45-78degrees depending on the time of year. Dive sites here include **Big Wall**, **South Wall**, and **Jenny's Drift**. Mike Atkins, from *The Scuba Shop* in Spartan, recommends diving **The Junk**, a Chinese junk sunk at 40ft. He also recommends making a weekend out of the diving experience here. *Devils Fork State Park* is adjacent to the lake and with six waterfalls, remnants of the quarry, and a view of Tennessee and the Blue Ridge Mountains; Lake Jocassee sights are breath taking above and below the water line.

Lastly, visit the **South Carolina Aquarium** in Charleston, which holds 385,000 gallons of saltwater in its two story tall *Great Ocean* tank. The **Ripley's Aquarium** in Myrtle Beach has a 340ft long moving walkway to aid in your exploration of *Dangerous Reef*. Plus those interested can see what it takes to swim or dive with stingrays without having to book a flight to Grand Cayman first.

As you can see, South Carolina has something for every diver. So add a little history to your dive logs and share your next dive experiences with the flavor of southern hospitality and great South Carolina dive sites.

South Dakota
Great Prairies, Great Dives

South Dakota is known for many things including Mount Rushmore, Badlands National Park, Crazy Horse Memorial, and the motorbike capital of Sturgis, but more important to divers, South Dakota is one of only six states that allow spear fishing of game fish except for paddlefish and sturgeon, and if there is one thing that South Dakota has, it is plenty of fish. You see the Missouri River runs down right through the middle of the state and is separated into three large lakes (Oahe, Sharpe, & Francis Case) inside the state, and Lewis and Clark Lake sharing the SE border with Nebraska. And while as a Scoutmaster I had to pick up my canoe and walk it over to deeper water on the Missouri river some 50miles east of Fort Benton Montana, here on **Lake Oahe**, the river can get as deep as 205ft. Two popular entrance sites include Spring Creek Marina, and Okobojo point State Recreation Area 17 miles north of Pierre.

Now you won't have to go that deep to spear fish according to Colonel Echols of *Land Shark Scuba and Snorkel* in Sioux Falls. Most spear fishing takes place within 4 to 28ft of water. Colonel says the trying to spear fish here on scuba is like bow hunting with a 9 piece marching band, but if you don't look directly at the fish, and keep the camera flash to a minimum, then you can get close enough for a good shot. Sometimes when the vis is low the walleye look like a shadow with white fins making them easier than other fish to spot. Besides walleye, the lakes are filled with large mouth bass, buffalo carp that can get up to 50lbs, northern pike, white bass, white crappie, yellow perch, channel catfish, and babot. The Babot is the only freshwater member in the cod family. They can get just over 25lbs in weight and they look like a slippery lingcod. They can open their mouth and almost swallow a trout or salmon as big as themselves and because of this reason most

211

states want you to catch & cook, but don't release them. Fortunately, babot taste almost as good as their saltwater cod cousins. In Finland, babot fish roe is sold as caviar.

Before I forget, Lake Oahe is the 4th largest reservoir in the nation. The dam opened in 1962 and provides electrical power for several surrounding states. The lake elevation is 1,596ft, 231miles long, has 2,250miles of shore land, and the Oahe Dam is 245ft tall.

Near Billy Goat Jump and the spillway, is the **Scuba Dive Park**, which according to Caleb Gilkerson, of *Steam Boat Skin and Scuba* in Pierre, consists of 5 boats sunk in various positions. Steam Boat is also known for its charters to **Tailrace** in the Tailrace Recreational Area. The max depth here is 26 to 30ft. This a drift dive site immediately south of the Oahe Dam where divers do a drift dive as the dam is pumping out water. The vis is 16-20ft and the water races at 3-6miles per hour. The Trailrace dive lasts about 45minutes before you are retrieved by a live boat pick up. During the day you can race with the trout and you may see a 6-7ft shadow of a paddlefish swim by as they are not afraid of divers. On night dives you might see the babot actively feeding on smaller fish, plus, the flashlights really light up the walleye. Steamboat has charter boats that will accommodate up to 50 passengers or down to 12.

Tailrace turns into **Lake Sharpe**, which is almost 80 miles long, covers 200miles of shoreline, has an elevation of 1,444ft, and is 78ft deep max. Lake Sharpe halts at Big Ben Dam. Below Big Ben we find **Lake Francis Case**, which flows 107miles down to Ft Randall Dam. Lake Francis Case has 540miles of shoreline, an elevation of 1,368ft, and a max depth of 140ft. The folks from *Donovan's Hobby and Scuba Center* plan weekend boat diving trips to Pickstown just north of Fort Randal Dam where there are rock and shale outcrops and more rock beds than mud on the lake's substrate. They use a 24ft custom dive boat called the "Scubaspearit" that carries up to six divers. Last year they made some 35 trips what they like to call "Safari" trips and in the summer, they went on Safari every weekend. Donovan's not only dives lake Francis, but also they go up to Lake Oahe, and frequently over to Okoboji in Iowa as it is only some 90miles away.

Below Fort Randall Dam the water flowing out returns to the name of the Missouri River, somewhere before Santee the waterway turns into Lewis and Clark Lake until it pushes against Gavin Point Dam. Lake Lewis and Clark is 16miles long and 45ft deep, but has very low vis.

On the west side of South Dakota is Pactola Lake, which is the largest lake in the Black Hills and has an elevation of 4,580ft. In 1875 the town of Pactola stood here, where now rests the reservoir. Scott Willams of *Black Hills Scuba* in Rapid City told me that people come from all over to dive the Pactola ruins as described online, but the truth is that all the town buildings are gone, and about 8 years ago silt covered up any remaining evidence of foundation indentations. There are some remains of a dynamite shack at 20ft, but that's about it. Vis is always good here, usually between 10-40ft. The water temp is between hard (frozen) to 74°. The lake is 158ft deep when at full water capacity. The spear fishing is good here, so bring a boat and try and catch a large fish like the 14oz state record trout caught here in July of 2003.

Scott also recommends, for something out of the ordinary, diving at **Cox Lake**. This lake is little more than a sink hole that has bubbling rocks down at 60ft, but you are diving in the middle of a prairie and who knows what might be grazing nearby by the time you surface. Scott also said to watch below the dams for signs of fresh banks caving off and exposing, fossils, buffalo skulls, and other interesting recognizable artifacts.

Some other diveable sights include **Granite Springs** in Alexandria that is 50ft deep, and has a fish hatchery and 20-30ft of vis. **Hunter Quarry** in Milbank has a max depth of 120ft and vis of 16-20ft to view suckers and trout. There are many private quarries too.

In summary, thanks to Thomas Jefferson buying this land in 1803 from Napoleon for a whopping $15 million dollars, and Lewis and Clark exploring said purchase on their way to the west coast, hundreds of millions of dollars worth of electricity is generated each year in South Dakota. This stretch of the Missouri River system has become one of the best areas in the nation for spear fishing, and to top it all off, South Dakota has several other unique Black Hill, Prairie lakes, and manmade quarries to explore. Great Dives.

Tennessee
Reasons To Dive All Seasons

Tennessee is home to several lakes and water filled quarries. Some of these dive destinations are open year round and some are open seasonally or by request only. Some of these sites are filled with huge numbers of various species of fish and others sites are filled with man made artifacts. Anyway you look at it, the local dive sites are so interesting that divers from other nearby states make annual pilgrimages to explore Tennessee's waters. After perusing this short list of diveable sites, you might want to too.

Martha's Quarry east of Nashville has something you don't find too often underwater so let's start here. It's open Saturday and Sunday, April thru September or by appointment. It's home to a four-story tall rock crusher whose roof is a mere 8ft under the surface. You can dive down 50ft to the substrate. Max depth in the quarry is 60ft with the viz average between 16 to 20ft and sometimes up to 30 to 40ft. Next to the rock crusher is a three-story shaker whose roof is at 16ft under water. There are also two pump houses, a greyhound bus that you can swim through, and a truck. The truck moves around a lot as it is the favorite object to use for search and rescue classes. There is an u/w kitchen down at 45ft complete with a washer, dryer, and refrigerator, which seems ironic since there is no electricity at the quarry. Dress warmly as the water temp dips down to 50° at depth.

As far as animal life goes, you can see blue gills, sauger, spotted bass, and Catfish. Miss Kitty, at 65lbs, is the largest catfish in the quarry. Past the under water forest of trees and in the southwest corner, where most divers don't venture over to, you can find milling groups of fish and turtles. Sauger fish, by the way, are a cousin of walleye, their most discernable distinction from walleye are the spots on their dorsal fin.

Philadelphia Quarry is a 3acre spring fed dive site that has training platforms at 17,25, and 75ft. There is a buoyancy course and in October an u/w pumpkin carving contest is held here. The quarry is open year round for around $10 admission. Vis can be 25ft. Divers can enjoy bathrooms and changing rooms above water and see a boat, mailbox, wheel chair, and stacked turtle replicas at depth.

Loch Low-Minn Dive Resort is a 10acre lake surrounded by 60 acres of woods in McMinn County. Rich and Stacy Low run the resort. Some 20 dive shops and centers converge at this site; including dive groups from Kentucky, Georgia, North Carolina, and Alabama. There's a wooden dock that gives you a walk-in entry down to 45ft. There are two 10x20ft platforms down at 20ft, a 3x16ft culvert, a 100ft line for measuring kick cycles, small boats, a porcelain toilet, and figures of David, a deer, a donkey, a 5ft life like alligator, and most recently, a great white name "Sharkey". Now besides all the silly fun stuff, there are some cool prehistoric paddlefish that are around 5ft long and weigh up to 60lbs. The biggest paddlefish on record goes to a 198lb behemoth from Iowa. Paddlefish can live up to 50yrs and have been around 300 to 400 million years, which makes them older than most dinosaurs and career politicians. There are also catfish, blue gill, and bass in the quarry. The deepest point is Boulder Hole at 74ft of depth. While the surface may be 70 degrees, you may encounter a thermo cline at 35ft. Three different springs cool the water as well as keep the visibility up from 40 to 60ft in the winter.

On the surface side they have a bathhouse with changing rooms and hot showers, plus a rinse tank and toilets. There's a wooden deck with a pool and spa for non-divers. There are two cabins that hold 4 to 6 people each, and plenty of room for tents. They're open 9-6 May thru October and have a rental tanks and a limited save a dive gear as they don't want to compete with their friends at the dive shops. Park entrance fee is $15, $10 for non-divers, and under 12yrs of age are not admitted unless enrolled in a scuba dive training course.

Dale Hollow Lake covering 27,200 acres is interesting in the fact that the lake straddles the Kentucky border, so you can dive two states on the same outing; depending on where you decide to dive. Some of the more popular dive sites include the steep banks of Ashburn Creek, Pleasant Grove Cliffs, Diver's Rock near the outlet at Sulphur Creek, Spring House near Dale Hollow State Resort Park, and the u/w ruins of the Willow Grove School House which became submerged when they dammed the Obey River. Now one local diver told me, for shore diving, to dive the rock walls to avoid silting up the water. At Willow Grove Marina, you can rent a boat, pontoon boat, or houseboat, depending on if you are looking for speed or overnight accommodations. The max depth is 130ft. Vis is anywhere from 11-30ft in the fall. Local inhabitants include small mouth bass, large mouth bass, Kentucky bass, gar, trout, crappie, muskie, and catfish.

Some other local dive sites that you might like to visit include: **Jeff's Quarry** which has cars, a boat, a platform, city bus, tires, and a van, max depth is around 40ft. **S. Holston Lake** has a max depth of 150ft and shore diving off of S. Holston Dam Rd. **Pickwick Lake** is 90ft deep max. **Parksville Lake** has cars, house chimneys, and a boat; max depth is 96ft and temp 38degrees. **Cherokee Lake** has a cabin cruiser; max depth is 45ft. **Normandy and Fontana Lakes** are notable dive sites, but i'm still looking for more dive intel on these lakes; so many places to dive, so little free time. Finally, if you have never dove an u/w bridge, go to **Chilhowee Lake** and under 15ft of water parallel to the 129 bridge lies the fairly intact remnants of the old Abraham bridge. You may notice that some cars have an uncanny way of accidentally rolling into lakes; max depth 45ft.

Besides all the lakes and Quarries, try a river dive near Townsend in the Smokey Mountains National Park. The vis may be only 10ft, but that's all you need to find a 2ft long Hellbender Salamander. These wrinkled looking creatures have been around for approximately 65million years, and as far as I'm concerned, anything that out survived T Rex and his claw toed raptor buddies deserves our utmost admiration and respect.

217

So there you go, lakes, quarries, rivers and such. Tennessee is a magnet for divers from several surrounding states. Bring a dive flag, and a knife or line cutter and dive a bridge, a rock crusher, or play with the fish, what ever you choose, the diving will keep you entertained during the day, but save a night or two for places like Nashville or Memphis, as it seems that music in Tennessee is a big hit too. Great dives!

Tropical Diving Texas Style

You might think that I have had one too many salt-rimed adult beverages when I begin talking about Texas and tropical diving in the same sentence, but you would be wrong. Texas has had tropical coral reefs next to its shores for thousands of years. Today there are a total of 36 banks (or reefs). These areas are currently home to parrot fish, sea turtles, nurse sharks, and whale sharks.

Thousands of years ago the sea level was hundreds of feet lower than it is today. Salt pooled, then dried as the oceans receded. Eventually minute fossils and debris hardened in different layers over different spans of time into clay stone, sand stone, siltstone, and limestone covered this layer of salt. Reefs formed on these substrates and in some locations the trapped layers of salt bulged, forming reef mounds. Closer to shore, depressed areas became fresh water drinking holes for mastodons and other prehistoric creatures.

Today, the gulf's saltwater level has risen and the inland waterways, marshlands, and mudflats are the home and migratory rest areas for countless species of bird as well as crucial nursery grounds for many species of fish and invertebrates.

Close to the Texas mainland shore, Padre Island is the longest sand beach in the USA. Here you'll find birds such as pelicans, herons, and cormorants. Depending on the time of year, you'll also find bottlenose dolphins and loggerhead turtles swimming in the water, and endangered Kemp's Ridley turtles nesting on the beach.

The Flower Garden Bank National Marine Sanctuary has to be one of the most notable dive destinations off the coast of Texas. Most dives here require one or two nights away from shore aboard a charter boat. The Flower Gardens are home to huge coral heads in various stages of growth and erosion. Here you may encounter manta rays, grouper, several species of turtles, and on very rare occasions see a silky shark, sand shark, or a hammerhead shark. Of course you will also find small angle fish, gobies, and blue-headed wrasse. Scientists are still discovering new species of fish; some found only on the banks, such as the bright purple, yellow, and green colored terminal male phase *Mardi Gras* wrasse.

Boat diving is a real bargain out here because you are diving with Caribbean fish, yet you don't have to fly to get there if you are already from Texas, and the live aboard costs are less than typical hotel and restaurant expenses you may expect to find even south of the border. Keep in mind that some of the charter operations may only allow bookings through local dive shops and some trips out to the banks fill up quickly.

Stetson bank is the second most notable bank for encountering sea life. Some banks are less than 100ft deep while others descend past the 300ft mark. At around 240ft in some locations you can see rivers of dense layers of briny salt water slowly pouring onto brine lakes and ponds of concentrated salt water. They have been doing this for thousands of years and the pressure at depth assures the process will continue on for quite some time to come.

At least one bank has been drilled and excavated by salvage operators in search of buried Spanish treasure. A few other bank locations are barren or ooze with volcanic mud and little else to enthrall a diver. To make up for some of these lack luster and to enhance the over all Texas dive experience, Twelve artificial reefs have been created using 400ft plus long liberty ships built during WWII. They are located at five different sites. The Freeport reef has 2 liberty ships, 3 ships are located at the Mustang liberty ship reef, and 3 sunken liberty vessels comprise the Matagordaa Island Liberty ship reef. The Port Mansfield Liberty ship reef has 3 ships, the MV Worthington rests by its self, 1.5nauticle miles off Aransas, and the George Vancouver sits alone in 40-60ft 9nmiles from Freeport.

The Freeport area also is where the 523ft oil tanker, the VA Fogg, split in two and sank after an accidental explosion occurred while cleaning Benzene residue in 1972.

The latest ship to reef inductee is the 473ft long USTS Texas Clipper, 17nm off of South Padre Island. She sits on her side 66ft below the surface. Her greatest historical point of usefulness occurred when she was transporting combat troops to Iwo Jima and turning with wounded soldiers back during WWII.

Besides the ships, Texas is known for its rigs to reef program: oil and gas rigs that are turned into coral reefs. Discarded rigs are home to countless big fish including grouper and sharks. Several thousand metal structures span a distance of some 500 plus miles from Texas to Mexico, and over to Louisiana. While some are quite deep, many are less than 120ft deep making them I deal dive sites. The iron reefs, as they are called, are the safest dive spots around because divers can control their depth by gauging their position next to the rig structure. Any slight movement up or down will easily catch your eye. Rigs standing erect allow you to dive three different zones with three distinct critter habitats. Down at the substrate, 120 to 80ft of depth, you'll find ivory coral, poisonous red cone shells, shrimp, octopus, oysters, flounder, stingrays, and just a wide assortment of bottom crawlers and bottom feeders sifting for food in the mucky waters. Midlevel, 80ft to 30ft, expect to find game fish such as amberjacks, spadefish, grouper, barracuda, queen angelfish, dolphins, silky sharks, and whale sharks. Attached to the rig there are colonies of barnacles, sponges, and tons of other invertebrates. The surf zone, 30ft to the surface where waves and currents drive the bigger fish away, expect to find wrasse, sergeant majors, damsels, file fish, stonefish, blue tang, soap fish, and more barnacles.

Texas A&M students use a former rig platform as a research station. The above surface accommodations are used for studying and sleeping. The actual sub surface part of the rig they do their research on, runs 863ft deep. The rig is called the "Snapper Platform". Tech divers also prefer such deeper rigs where they can test their gear and look for larger pelagic fish all at the same time.

Other artificial reef programs include welded pipe tubes, cement and ash blocks. National Geographic in their February 2001 issue in their article *Relics to Reefs* mentions Texas in particular. See the fold out on pages 100-101 of the gas platform and tell me if that doesn't look awesome. Texans are amazingly generous and big on artificial reef programs and when it comes to quantity and quality of local marine creatures, size really does matter. So the next time you are in the mood for Caribbean diving, but fix'n to stay close to home, Texan tropical reefs, as well as the local artificial reefs, are in a big class, as well as a deep league of their very own. Great Dives.

The Texas Caribbean Flower Garden Banks National Marine Sanctuary

Two reefs discovered by fisherman long ago in the middle of otherwise deep water became known as the West Flower Garden Banks Reef and the East Flower Garden Banks Reef. The Flower Garden Banks are actually sites where salt accumulated 170million years ago into bulging salt domes and 10-15thousand years ago, coral reefs comprised mostly of brain and stone corals formed on top of the domes; some 70ft below the surface. 30miles NW of Flower Gardens is Stetson Banks at 60plusft. Other Banks such as Geyer Bank rise to only 130ft beneath the surface and deeper than the recreational dive limits.

Now no one is intentionally trying to keep the Flower Garden Banks a secret, it's just that by being located 110miles offshore from Freeport Texas. You need a big well-equipped sea going vessel or you need to book with a dive shop that charters boats out of Galveston or the 100ft long *MV Fling* from Freeport, Texas to get there. On this trip, I chose the MV Fling out of Freeport. It takes only an hour to drive southwest from Houston to Freeport. The MV Fling typically runs two to three day charters. The three-day trip I went on boarded at 8pm on Friday night. After an initial onboard welcome/briefing, our Nitrox/C Cards checked, fresh homemade snacks eaten, and once our gear was set up, divers slept while the Fling made its way out to our first dive site. Saturday was our initial day one of diving, and after a light pre-breakfast of pastries and fruits, we were ready for dive one. I should say right off the bat, that if we weren't diving, we were eating, resting, or both. There was food before and after the dives, and sometimes even more food if the rest between dives was too long. The two cooks, Mathew and Wendy, did a great job of making everyone forget about dieting. Wendy was the junior member of the crew with

223

3 years on board. Captains Bland, Kurt, and Admiral Ken worked full time, but the rest of the crew were all volunteers. When not working as a cook, Wendy is a chemist. Tank filler Neal, is an electrical engineer. It seems everyone had degrees and/or tons of diving and boating experience, but most of all, they just plain loved being on the boat and being part of the crew. Wendy summed it up by saying that some divers take the trip, and never come back, while other divers never seem to leave. I have to say though, that on this trip many of the guest divers I met had been on the MV Fling several times before.

Our dive masters JT and John briefed us well before every dive. Our first two dives were at West Flower Garden Banks. There are 19 buoys total between Flower Gardens and Stetson Banks. The boats hook up to the buoys so there is no coral damage due to anchors. The currents on the surface were moving faster than a diver could swim, but currents were reduced at depth. This made the buoys extremely important as in some cases we had to pull our selves hand by hand along our guide rope over to the buoy then follow the buoy chain down some 50ft before the currents subsided. It wasn't hard to do, you just had to do a giant stride entry into the water then slowly work your way along the rope, and in the meantime, you were looking down with 70-100ft of visibility at the coral. I won't say that you have to be an experienced diver to do these dives, as a few divers were relatively new; you just have to be a comfortable diver: comfortable with your gear, the ocean, and your physical shape. Down below I saw some divers swimming all over the reef, while others remained close to the buoy taking pictures and filming quite contently. The first thing you'll notice diving out here is how amazingly healthy these reefs are. White splotches of bleached dead coral are minimal, and the abundance of fish and invertebrate life is maximal.

West Flower Banks is not big on the map, but with 23 species of coral blending in seemingly endless mixed patterns, it's easy to get turned around or find yourself near a side that ends by sloping down to 160ft. We never did go beyond 90ft, as there was so much life to see around the corals or in the small sandy valleys. Tube and barrel sponges were quite prevalent. Besides the traditional 300 species, and the quantity of each species of fish found locally, rare golden smooth trunk fish are known to hang out here, and even more important, the Flower Garden Banks is where scientists first discovered a new species of wrasse called the "Mardi Gras Wrasse", because of the bright purple, yellow, and green colors on the adult male.

After a cool dive with loggerhead turtles at an oilrig, we hit East Flower Garden Banks where the topography is slightly different with bigger valleys of sand where conch hung out between coral heads, and where there were deeper cracks and crevices for fish to hide in. On the night dive here our team got to see bioluminescent organisms, the night shift of fish, daytime parrotfish sleeping in cocoons, and a loggerhead turtle resting on the bottom in a trancelike state.

After late night ice cream sundaes and a good night's rest, we did one more dive here then headed over to Stetson Banks. Stetson Banks has few corals, as the water is seasonally a bit too cold for them to proliferate. What you do find though are layers of clay stone and sand stone jetting upward vertically as if someone punched their fist up through the sand and left the rocks on end. Fragments of the rock will mush between your fingers without very little force applied. As for the fish, this is where adults seem to come and mingle, where angelfish look like they took growth hormones, and spotted eels and moray eels like to hang out in the open. The sponges were mostly low-lying varieties and algae covered the flat substrate area. Big schools of fish randomly hung around us. In and around the algae we found several types of cone shells, hairy tritons, Atlantic thorny oysters, and a bright yellow Atlantic cowry. At night the group encountered bearded sea cucumbers, urchins, brittle stars, crabs, shrimps, and one rather large lobster.

These are just some of the creatures we saw, but if you wait till winter when hammerheads or mantas are migrating, or in the spring when the spotted eagle rays pass by, the view changes radically. Around the first full moon in August the MV Fling does a special 4-day cruise to enjoy the spawning of the corals. Basically, anytime you can book a trip to see these gems in the Texas Caribbean, is the best time to dive. I would so like to be one of those annual divers that the crew of the MV Fling just can't seem to get rid of. Great Dives.

Texas Liberty Ships
37 Years As Artificial Reefs

Twelve Liberty Ships were scuttled in the Texas Gulf between August 1975 and October 1976. The Plan was to make 4 artificial reef sites with 3 liberty ships at each site, but things don't always go as planned when your dealing with mother nature. The fact that these ships made it through World War II was a feat in itself. 2,581 Liberty Ships were completed before the end of the war. They were built on an assembly line system based similar to what Henry Ford did for cars. The ships were identically and simultaneously built at several shipyards around the country. Like giant Lego blocks, they were put together quickly in set stages, then welded together instead of the slower process of bolting the pieces together. At the top of the nationwide production they were producing 57 liberty ships a week. Some welds would later crack open especially in cold north Atlantic waters in hind sight, but the goal of producing cargo ships faster than the enemy could sink them was an overwhelming success.

Each of the Liberty Ships were 441ft and 6 inches long and 57ft wide. Typically they were armed with, two 3inch guns and eight 20mm antiaircraft guns, plus torpedo nets that could be lowered over the sides of the ship, this way potential incoming torpedoes could be detonated before they impacted against the sides of the ship. The theory didn't work so well for the SS Jose Navarro when it was hit by a torpedo just forward of the anti torpedo net by U-178 in the Indian Ocean.

Each liberty ship had two crews. One crew consisted of merchant marines that consisted of engineers, stewards who cooked, served, and purchased ship stores, and dock men. The other crew was navy service men, radio crewmen, gunmen and deck hands that were in charge of protecting the ship. The two groups of crewmen didn't always see things eye to eye and some times the Captain would have the final decision over whether to pay the merchant marines overtime to set up the torpedo nets, or side with the navy and keep up the readiness state at all cost. There were some ships where both crews managed to run extremely well together, and that had to have helped both sides of the combined crew with surviving the war.

Each Liberty Ship had five giant cargo compartments, and when they were full, the ship sailed smoothly, but when the holds were empty and ballast was light, Liberty Ships were known to bob in the water like a cork in a whirlpool. Eventually extreme buoyancy would cause injuries among the crew and increased the likely hood that metal hull plates might crack. The rides could sometimes get very rough, but it was all about getting massive amounts of military supplies from point A to point B. Admiral Chester W. Nimitz summed it up as: which ever side supplied the most oil, bullets, and beans, would win the war.

To supply the troops, the Liberty Ships went through a gauntlet of enemy assaults. From the sea submarine torpedoes attacked them and mine fields lay in wait. From the air fighter planes and bombers that carried machineguns, bombs, and torpedoes attacked them. At Port they could encounter canon fire, V1 buzz bomb, and V2 rocket attacks. V1 buzz bombs they could shoot at, and canon shells made noise as they spiraled downward, giving the men at least time to duck their heads, but V2 ballistic missiles were so silent and swift that one second the ship tied to the dock in front was having its cargo off loaded, and the next second the ship was destroyed and the cargo crew considered lucky if they were only wounded. Even smoking onboard the ship was dangerous, as it could cause an exhausted seaman to carelessly catch a bunk bed on fire, and when a fire breaks out is not a good time to try and remember if your cargo that day was High test aviation fuel, 500lbs bombs, or garden variety troop ammunition, grenades, and cans of kerosene. Sometimes the men got lucky and the ship's cargo was something less destructive such as lumber, sugar, or civilians. But no matter the cargo, just docking at ports such as in Tewfik, Egypt could expose the men to Bubonic Plague; so setting foot onshore at some destinations was forbidden. Fortunately, within a few years after implementing the liberty ship project, the war ended. Most of the ships that survived the war were sent home or used to re-supply the peacekeeping forces remaining around the world; especially in Germany and Japan. Later, these ships were put into reserve or brought out again to use during the Korean War.

When the Texas Department of Parks And Wildlife got on board the artificial reef program, there were many things that had to occur. The ships were cleaned and stripped down to a mere 27ft in height and large holes were cut in the sides of the ships to help them sink upright. In addition, the ships were to be sunk at a depth of just over 100ft to keep 50ft of depth cleared for passing ships, which put the artificial reefs far from shore: especially from Galveston. The *George Vancouver* was the last ship to be sunk, but it sank on its own during a storm and those in power let the ship remain sunk at 60ft at a reef of its own name. At the Freeport Liberty Ships Reef the 553ft long T-2 tanker V.A.Fogg, and remnants from several oilrigs joined the *William F. Allen* and the *B.F. Shaw*. At the Matagorda Island Liberty Ship Reef rests the *Dwight L. Moody*, the *Jim Bridger*, and the *George Dewey*. At Mustang Island Liberty Ship Reef rests the *Conrad Weiser*, the Rachel Jackson, and the Charles A. Dana. All the way down at the Port Mansfield Liberty Ship Reef rests the *George L. Farley*, the *Edward W. Scripps*, and the *Joshua Thomas*, plus other rigs to reef artifacts.

Because these ships do not have their superstructures in tact, other ships like the 473ft long *USTS Texas Clipper*, the 447ft long tanker *SS John Worthington* or the thousands of working oil rigs in general, are the preferred sites that divers like to visit. But just like studies proved with fishermen, the Liberty Ship artificial reefs are great places to go for fish. These reefs have given fishermen places to fish when other sites have been exhausted or when fish have migrated. These sites have also proven to extend the overall fishing season. So whether you visit these artificial reefs because you want to do a little spear fishing, check out the over all coral growth, take some pictures of the local creatures, or for some reason just can't make it to your primary dive site, it's just good to know a little about the Texas Liberty Ship Artificial Reef Program, and a little bit about the historical background that led to where these ships currently rest today. Great Dives.

Padre Island, Texas
The Great "American" Barrier Reef

Padre Island is the second longest island in the United States. The north island is home to the Padre Island National Seashore with close to 70 miles of hiking trails and beachfront where 380 species of birds migrate yearly and where sea turtle science and recovery has led to the re-introduction of kemp's ridley, leatherbacks, loggerheads, green, and hawksbill sea turtles. The north island is also home of the Malaquite Visitor Center where you can find out more about these local inhabitants and so much more.

As for recreational activities and the best diving sites in general, the south island is the ultimate destination for annual diver migrations. I asked a representative of *American Diving* what the top three spots off South Padre Island, (SPI), were and he said that the number one site had to the **Texas Clipper**. This 473ft long ship was sunk as an artificial reef on November 17th, 2007. It currently rests on its port side in 60 to 130ft of water. There has been a lot of growth on the wreck in the last five years, and besides all the big ling and snapper, the latest family to move in and take up residence on the ship is a family of stingrays. The ship is so big that you can't see it all on even a couple of dives. Not only that, but while you are looking at tropical fish on one end of the ship, divers in the middle may be watching dolphins catching bait fish right above them, and at the other end of the ship divers are busy photographing invertebrates and oblivious to the silhouette of a passing whale shark; so no two divers or groups of divers, ever experience a dive on the Texas Clipper quite the same way. This is why diving here has become the number one attraction in town.

Now before four million was spent on clean up and removal of 700tons of metal and debris from the ship to ensure it would be creature and diver friendly, the Texas Clipper served as the USTS Queens as an attack transport to carry troops to Iwo Jima and wounded away from the island during WWII. It was also part of the occupation force in Sasebo,

Japan. From 1948-58 the ship was converted to a cruise liner as the USS Excambien with the American Export Lines, and carried passengers and cargo to the Mediterranean. In 1965 it was loaned to the Texas Maritime Academy at Texas A&M University in Galveston where it was used for 30years as a merchant marine training vessel. This explains the big A&M lettering on the sunken ship.

Besides the Texas Clipper, sometimes charters will do a second or third "tons of steel dive" at one of two iron reefs such as the gas rig **Little Sara** at 105ft deep max or **Seana's Rig** at 126ft deep max. Both of these rigs have tons of life on the horizontal beams at 35ft-65ft of depth, so whether you want to find damsels, sergeant majors, or octopus, just look around the horizontal beams. Pelagics are known to swim around the rigs on a routine basis: up to and including whale sharks. **Los Torres** is another well-known oilrig, but at 240ft max, this is a tech dive. Expect to see pelagics such as amberjacks, hammerheads, silky, and white tip sharks here.

Some other (SPI) wrecks you may wish to see include the shimper boats **Deep Six**, **Pat's wreck**, and the **Dona Nelly**. Deep Six is an 82ft long boat at 60ft 11miles from shore where rays, red snapper, and turtles are usually spotted. Pat's Wreck is an 80ft shrimper 22miles offshore in 138ft. Dona Nelly has a deck at 85ft and descends to135ft. The **Albatross** wasn't a shrimper, but this boat went down 80-105ft with machinery cargo and 10,000lbs of shrimp.

For other wrecks that are really big, but might take a two day dive trip to explore, you have the (Mustang Island) three 441.6ft long liberty ships 18nm from Port Aransas up north which include the **Conrad Weiser**, the **Rachel Jackson**, and the **Charles A. Dana**, or you can visit the three Port Mansfield liberty ships 23nm from SPI or 15nm from Port Mansfield which include the **Edward W. Scripps**, the **Joshua Thomas**, and the **George L. Farely** at 96-100ft, in addition to 9 rigs to reef structures down at 50-60ft. Tarpon, tigers, black tips, grouper, and cobia are found at these sites.

Last but not least, we have the **Texas Underwater Park,** which has tugboats, 2 oilrigs, a US navy work barge, and 32 reef balls 65-73ft underwater.

As for natural reefs, the **Sponge Gardens** is a seamount at 150ft deep so out of reach for most divers, but **7 Fathom Reef** is made up from a series of four distinct rises and between 24-45ft deep. This sandstone area 2miles offshore was an ice age coastal fresh water lake when local waters were 350ft lower than they are today. Mammoth, mastodon, and fresh water snails can be found imbedded in the stone substrate. Invertebrates such as tubeworms, sponges, bryozoans, mollusks, and crustaceans now call this place home.

As for shore dives, they say you can find sand dollars in **Dolphin Cove**, and numerous critters around any of the jetties, but the truth is that the vis can get really low next to shore unless blue waters have moved in next to the coast line. Hence, the visibility is usually better the farther out from shore you go and that's why dive boats, charter boats, and private boats are so popular here.

Another thing to keep in mind with diving South Padre Island is that you may want to set aside at least a day off from diving, as there are so many other local activities to do. Families love the *Schlitterbahn Beach Water Park*. It's a tropical theme park with a variety of splash rides, a lazy river, and white sand beaches. You may also want to take a dolphin tour or visit the *Dolphin Research and Sea Life Nature Center*. *Sea Turtle Inc* Rescues, recovers, and rejuvenates unfortunate sea turtles. You can see the turtles close up and personal, or help with their hatch and release program. South Padre Island has a *Birding and Nature Center* as well as an *Island Equestrian Center;* horse riding on the beach anyone? You can even walk on the 1,500ft long *Laguna Madre Nature Trail* boardwalk and name the migratory birds, but don't try to count them.

As you can see from the list, you could spend a week on the boat and not see all the dive sites, you could spend a week on shore and not see all the land sites, and maybe that's why, besides the birds and turtles, so many people return here on an annual basis.

You can drive here from Houston like many dive clubs and dive shops do, or you can fly into Brownsville at the BRO International Airport and drive across the Isabella causeway to

South Padre Island. Either way, have a great time and great dives.

Utah's Hot Sites
Dive Year Around

Like most people, you hear the word Utah and visions of skiing and past winter Olympics come to mind, but not too many people would think of scuba diving; especially while it's snowing, but if you go to Utah and just ski, you'll be missing out on two extremely unique hot scuba dive sites as well as many others in the summer time.

First on the list is **Bonneville Seabase**. This warm springs site was a former bath site, then a dumpsite for early western settlers. In 1988 George Sanders and Linda Nelson purchased the site and after a lot hard work fixing, cleaning, digging, building, plumbing, cementing and just about anything else that ends in "ing", they were able to have a warm water site that they could use year around for their dive students at Neptune Divers in Salt Lake. At Bonneville, the warm water naturally combines with salt crystals on its way to the surface, so by the time it reaches the three main pools; the water's salinity is almost exactly identical to what you would find in the ocean. A mile away, Great Salt Lake is almost four times as salty. What happened next at Bonneville was the introduction of some tropical fish that grew too big for private aquariums such as the two male nurse sharks that were donated at 18inches, and now are 9ft long. Fortunately, they will stop growing when they reach 15ft. Crevalle Jack and Pompano that were mere inches and weighed next to nothing when they went into the water, now look over 3ft long and some probably weigh 50lbs. There is a large grouper though, that could eventually overtake all the other fish in sheer weight. In all, there are 70 different species of tropical fish in the water. If you get to Bonneville Seabase before feeding time in the morning, you can watch Lynn Findlay feeding the nurse sharks, one at a time, what appeared to be nice slices of salmon? This it the best way to see that one nurse shark is really pinker and one is slightly bluer than the other. Meanwhile, Ron Simmons tosses freshly cut pieces of tuna to the jacks and other big fish. My daughter had a chance to feed the minnows. During the rest of the day, divers are encouraged to bring along romaine lettuce with them to feed angel fish, damselfish, or whatever other fish one encounters.

Before you can dive in, all first time guests are required to see a short film about Seabase. The film lays down the basic rules like "don't puff up the puffer fish", and gives a good description about what to expect in the three main pools. The Abyss pool is the smallest of the three pools, but goes down to 62ft. The 14ft deep White Rock Bay is enclosed overhead making it the warmest area and also where fish congregate and divers gear up during the wintertime. The largest setting, Habitat Bay at 24ft deep, has an air filled habitat underwater at 15ft exclusively for divers. The *Sheer Joy* wreck is in Habitat Bay, and this is where the stingray was hanging out the day we were there. The water temp dips to 68° on the surface in the winter, to 85° in the summer, and up to 90° at the inflow vents. Bonneville Seabase has an enourmous rental selection. Make reservations in advance, and check online for hours and fees. The vis is typically 7-10 ft. Wear a 7ml or drysuit in the wintertime: 5ml or less in the summer time. Use a red covered lens light on night dives. Altitude 4293ft.

Homestead Crater in Midway, Utah at 90-95° temp is an even hotter spot to dive. The crater is a 55ft tall calcite mountain with a wide opening at the top to peer down at the half filled naturally carved out hourglass interior. In 1995 Dr Jerry Simons blasted a tunnel in the side of the domed calcite structure so that people could easily gain entrance inside to the warm springs pool formerly physically off limits to so many. The 60ft wide bathing pool is 65ft deep with a 10,000year old layer of silt 8-14ft deep at the bottom. There are three diving platforms from 20-35ft. From the surface you can see two of the platforms. Whether you swim or dive here, it's cool to watch the clouds move above and over the opening in the ceiling. On one side of the floating T dock, there is a half

submerged benched and floored area for training new divers
and on the other side, a small sitting area for soaking up and
relaxing in the warm water. In the past, thousands of coins and
a few guns have been found in the silt far below. Divers are
reminded to stay off the bottom so that the visibility remains
clear. Because of the fresh water's mineral content, there are no
fish or mermaids to contend with. You can rent dive gear here.
Jerry's son Craig Simons is the manager and has worked on
site since the crater's dive and swim theme first inception. I
recommend bringing a suit, a towel, and a waterproof camera:
relax, float and shoot. The Homestead Resort and Golf course
is right next door. Reservations recommended and check online
for hours and fees. Altitude 5714ft.

Belmont Hot Springs has a 2acre area for divers in the
winter that's 30ft deep and 90°. In the summer it heats up to
115° and so is closed to divers. Dive buddies include fingerling
trout. Check for open times. There is a clubhouse and changing
room. Altitude 4,319ft.

Cold water diving sites include: **Flaming Gorge** at
6023ft on the NE border with Wyoming. The vis can be 20-40ft
and the water 68° in the summer. There are walls and
pinnacles, Osprey and Gilligans Island, plus 208miles of
shoreline. Near the Cedar Spring boat ramp there is a 1949
truck at 100ft. On the southwest end near Nevada and Arizona
is **Sand Hollow** at 300ft altitude. Vis is 14-20ft. There is a
Cessna 310 at 40ft and an old VW bus at 30ft. Park fees apply
to swim with bass and bluegill. **Fish Lake** at 9,000ft is the
largest natural lake. Stay north of the marina and enjoy 35ft vis
and find fishing gear. The trout will thank you. **Bear Lake** at
5,924ft, **Deer Creek Reservoir** at 5417ft, **Tony Grove Lake** at
8,500ft, and **Big Sand Wash Reservoir** at 5,585ft are also
notable local dive sites**.**
Diving the Homestead Crater and Bonneville Seabase can both
be done in a single day as they are only 70miles apart, but as I
found out, spending more time at each location, as well as
visiting the other dive sites of Utah will be an on going
personal quest. In Utah, the surrounding mountain scenery is
breathtaking anytime of the year. On an 80° day, you can take

images of spring flowers with nearby snow-capped mountain ranges in the background. I also strongly recommend viewing the local fossil museums during all surface intervals; the dinosaurs liked this area too. Great Dives.

Vermont
Many Ponds, One Big Lake Champlain.

Lake Champlain is such a big lake with so much history that I've kept it separate in its own article. Besides Lake Champlain, Vermont divers have many ponds and smaller lakes to dive and enjoy. **True Blue Quarry,** a marble quarry, in West Rutland has a car at 40ft another car at 80ft, plus cave diver tunnels to explore that go more than 130ft deep. **Sunset Lake** near Benson and *Green Mountain Scuba* is known for clear waters, rainbow trout, perch, northern pike and pumpkinseed fish. **Mirror Lake**, or **#10 Pond** near North Calais, is around 50ft deep and has good visibility in early spring before the algae blooms: do not touch the civil war canon balls, as some are still live. Two miles up the road from Mirror Pond is **Nelson Pond**. Large boulders, ledges, and walls are home to bass, trout, and pumpkinseed fish. This is also a good spot for scavenger hunts. **East Long Pond** is a dive off a private dock into 10ft water that quickly goes down past 25ft. Large boulders and a wall are found out here. **Dog River Pools** near Northfield Falls are 18ft deep and home to some very large trout. You'll need permission to dive the last three mentioned sites. Ask the Vermont Scuba Diving Club coordinator to set any of them up. Basically, anywhere there is a potential swimming hole, there is a dive site, and Vermont lists some 86 swimming holes in all. For another 100 potential dive sites, read my article on Lake Champlain. Great Dive

Lake Champlain.
A Historical Treasure-trove

So what's so fantastic about a small 12mile long lake on the boarder between Vermont and New York? It's only 95ft above sea level and 405ft deep. The visibility can go up to 40ft, but more often than not is 10 to 15ft and you will see land locked salmon, northern pike, sturgeon, and walleye, but none of these items seem unusual for any other eastern lake. What does set this lake apart from the rest, and I mean by hundreds of millions of years is the sheer history of an ancient sea that turned to freshwater then became home to some 300 ship wrecks from dull boats carrying stones and coal, to Benedict Arnold's fleet that sunk, but delayed the British long enough for the Americans to regroup and win the war in 1776. Benedict was actually a great patriot until the Continental Congress decided not to pay him for services rendered. As history shows, getting even didn't work too well for him either.

Back to ancient history, up at Isla la Motte, one of the 70 islands on this lake, we have the fossilized remains of the Paleozoic Chazy reef. At 480 million years old this is one of the oldest coral reefs known on the planet. It is part of the Iapetus Ocean that once flourished with squid like creatures housed in shells: as if you took a nautilus shell and rolled it out to a pointed cone. Now the Goodsell Fossil Preserve is flourishing with these specimens to view first hand.

About twenty thousand years ago the salt seas vanished and freshwater filled the basin between the newly raised Appalachian mountain range. Local farmers however still find bones of beluga whales and seals in their pastures.

To see the current fresh water life of Lake Champlain I recommend a visit to ECHO Lake Aquarium and Science Center in Burlington right next to the water's edge. I've been there a couple of times and It's a great place to see the elusive 5 to 6ft long adult sturgeon, muskellunge, channel catfish, and many local species of amphibians, and reptiles. They also have a good display on what the invasive specie of zebra mussels has done in a devastatingly short period of time.

One last spot to visit before you actually dive the lake is the Lake Champlain Maritime Museum. Here you can see artifacts from Benedict Arnold's exploits plus relics of some of the 300 known other wrecks in the lake. You can even see a replica of the schooner *Louis McClure* complete with main sail, fore sail, and jib. Once you've been here you will now have a keen eye for wreck debris, know the history behind the seafaring tragedies, and a better understanding of where you are while diving on some of the more popular wrecks.

One particular interesting wreck according to Stephanie Farrell of **The Waterfront Diving Center** is the Schooner *O.J. Walker* that was built in 1862 in Burlington and sunk in 1895. The Walker is 86ft long and 14ft wide and at a depth of 65ft. There is still a mast on her, a wheelbarrow, a stool, and the load of bricks the doomed Schooner was carrying when she went down. Her even less fortunate cousin the 88ft long, 14ft wide schooner rigged *General Butler* built in 1862 in Essex, NY, rests near the southern end of Burlington breakwaters. She went down in a storm Dec 9, 1876. Since she doesn't even lay two thermo clines beneath the surface at 40ft, she is in a warm water zone and covered with zebra mussels.

According to one diver from **Victory Sports** the schooner *Water Witch* is the most intact wooden ship in the lake. It was 83ft long, 18ft wide, and was a steamboat converted to sail. It was built in 1832 and sank in 1866 with a load of iron ore. It's still intact possibly because of the depth of 90ft, currents, and because removal of artifacts here is illegal.

The diver I spoke with also recommends the *Burlington Horse Ferry*, because there is not another one like it in the world. Horses walked around a large turntable to power two paddle wheels whose remnants are still there. The ferry was 63ft long, 23ft wide, and in 50ft of depth. This type of ferry peaked around the 1840's on short routes across the lake.

Speaking of steamboats, the *Phoenix*'s charred remains rest at 60ft on the bow and 110ft on the stern. She was 146ft long, 27ft wide, and burned from a suspicious fire supposedly starting in the Galley. No one has ever proven whether she succumbed to the indirect flames of careless candles or to the direct flames of careful competitors.

If you are into barges then you might consider diving the *Diamond Island Stone Barge*. 93ft long, 14ft wide, up to 25ft deep, and carrying possibly too many stones for said nautical conditions. The *A.R.Noyes Coal Barge* is 90ft long, 14ft wide and descending from 60 to 80ft of depth. I think you've already figured out the contents when she went down.

Pat Jones from **Jones' Aqua Sports** in Willsboro, NY, on the other side of the shoreline, thinks that the *Pinnacle at Ferris Rock* at Schuyler Island is an interesting dive because it descends from 30ft to 150ft and contains fish, fossils, and shipwreck fragments. She also likes the *Swim Thru at Garden Island Shoal* because here, from shallow to deep, are the rock remains of saltwater seas and how many divers have you ever heard of that can say with pride that they have dove on a 480 million year old Ordovician reef?

There are some shore dives you can make in the lake. Right off of **Tompson's Point** the water descends to one of the deepest parts of the lake, which coincidentally makes this site the deepest wall dive in the lake. The problem with some of the shore dive sites is getting past the zebra mussel beds. You have to wear gloves to prevent cuts, as these mussels are sharp. It's also a good idea to carry a knife and scissors to cut lines. A dive permit may be in order to dive certain wrecks and no penetration of historical wrecks, as they are more fragile than my hairline. A yellow buoy typically marks the location of an underwater preserve. Going out with a charter operation or booking through a local dive shop is a good way to go dive the lake sites and make sure you are within all the local rule compliances, and not accidentally setting an ordinary anchor on a one of a kind national treasure.

As you can see from this article, Lake Champlain is not just your typical northern lake. It is packed with more history than it is with water. Ancient saltwater seas have left divers something quite unique to explore. The lake's position next to Canada and past British battle sites made the lake a national security hot spot, and it's weather, wind, and waves, have left hundreds of wrecks sunk at various depths; some relatively still intact. What more could any diver ask for? Great dives.

Virginia Is For Lo. . .
Divers!

Virginia is home to the CIA and quite possibly the MIB, "Men In Black", if you were to believe the local rumors, but this isn't surprising considering all the legally registered aliens and foreign diplomats that commute daily from here to Washington, DC. What may surprise you though is that Virginia has over 132miles of shoreline and 7,200sq miles of tidal bays, giving local scuba divers plenty of space for close encounters in salt as well as fresh water environments. I asked some locals where there favorite spots to dive were, and the following is a list I put together from some of the responses I got.

Kathy Clancey of *Kathy's Scuba* in the Shenandoah Valley just got back from playing with dolphins in Rangiroa, Tahiti, and shooting through passages from the outer reef into the inner lagoon with untold visibility when I asked her about her favorite dive site in Virginia. I know . . .timing is everything. Anyway, she told me that locally she likes 20 acre **Lake Rawlings**. The water temp can rise to 85° in the summer, and fall to 40° in the winter. The visibility on the other hand is lower in the summer time, 30-65ft, and up to 100ft or more in the wintertime. The depth is 65ft Max. The lake was a former granite quarry, so the visibility here is typically better than other quarries mined for limestone. Beside the typical bus, sculptures, cars, cabin cruisers, and the boat from the movie " The Replacements", Lake Rawlings has a blackhawk helicopter airframe. The lake has several introduced species of fish including bass, bream, and bluegill. Since this is a no fishing lake, the fish are abnormally large compared to other similar sized lakes. There are also crayfish, plus two species of clams that have become endangered due to divers using knives to feed the clams to the fish. Dive knives are no longer allowed in the lake and there is a $300 fine if you accidentally forget this restriction. Besides diving, this lake has great camping sites, from tents, RV's, to cabins; plus coin operated hot showers and other host facilities. Diving fees are currently $25 per person. Like most parks, camping is optional and requires modest additional fees. For more information see www.lakerawlings.com

A spokesperson from *Virginia Scuba* in Manassas told me that besides diving of off the coast of North Carolina, she likes to dive **Lake Millbrook**, which is also known as Millbrook Quarry. The vis in this 12 acre limestone quarry is generally 10 to 20ft, but it's a great place to train as it goes down to 93ft. There are cars, a bus, various sized boats and platforms at various depths. At 70ft there is a single engine plane with the propeller still attached and a Winnebago at 80ft. The lake was inundated with zebra mussels at one time, but the state used a solution of Potassium Chloride to wipe out the invasive species. I know, save the locals, but wipe out the aliens. It's the plot of every science fiction movie I've ever seen, but apparently this procedure didn't bother the local perch. Lake Milbrook is owned/leased by *"The" Dive Shop* in Fairfax, which is about 30min away from the lake. The lake is open to divers on the weekends and closed during certain times of the year except when they host the winter "Chilly Willy" dives. As of this writing, the dive fee is $30 at the main gate, or $19 if purchased at *The Dive Shop*. Over night camping is occasionally permissible. Check *The Dive Shop* schedule online for specific park rules, regulations, and hours of availability. *The Dive Shop* also arranges exotic trips as well.

As for salt water, Matt Hannum, a staff instructor at *Dive Quarters* in Virginia Beach has three favorite dive sites. He likes the 423ft long Liberty ship **John Morgan**, which sank to 100ft June 1st in 1943 after colliding with the SS Montana. The motorcycles are cool to look at, but Matt especially likes the tanks that are upside down, right side up, and with barrels bent. There are also Willy Jeeps, tractors, a ford truck, machine guns, P-39 airplanes, and ammunition littered everywhere.

Matt likes the 448ft freighter **Lillian Lucanbach,** which sank in 1943 after colliding with the SS Cape Henlopen. The Lucanbach rests on her port side at 105ft of depth. She was carrying war goods such as tires, and airplane parts with 50calliber machine guns still attached to P-40 wings.

As for finding collectibles, Matt prefers the 351ft long **Eureka,** which sank to 115ft 50miles out from shore after colliding with the SS Benison in May 1888. This four schooner-rigged mast wooden ship was carrying a wide assortment of merchandise, from silk, laces and linen, to porcelain doll heads, brass keys, and doorknobs. Sifting through the sand is all it takes to find something you may treasure the rest of your life.

Besides being great wrecks, Matt also wanted me to point out that these are also good sites for spearfishing. Virginia has many other wrecks just off the coastline as well as German U-boats just south off the coast of North Carolina. Some of the other wrecks include: The 250ft long **Trepca** at 15ft and known for lobsters, the 253ft long **York (Norvana)** at 110ft torpedoed by U-66 in 1942, the 110ft tug **Esteridge** sunk in 1962, the 60ft **Margaret Hanks** clam dredger, the **Gulf Hustler** fishing vessel, the **Kurn** on Tower Reef, the 605ft long **Marine Electric**, and at least a dozen more known wrecks and several found, but still unnamed wrecks. Added to all these are three liberty ships as artificial reefs: the **James E Haviland** at 100ft, the **Garrison** at 110ft, and the **Webster** at 120ft. Added to this artificial reef list is 115ft long Coast Guard Cutter **Cuyohoga** which was struck by the MV Santa Cruz in 1978, sank, lifted up, stripped, then sunk again as an artificial reef. Lastly there is the **Chesapeake Light Tower** with 40ft of depth around its legs.

Keep in mind that with any of these salt-water sites, you have cold water Atlantic fish touring during the 7ml or drysuit season, and transient tropical fish populations arriving in the spring until the end of summer during the warmer 5ml wetsuit season.

For more information on Virginia dive sites, I recommend the book *Shipwrecks of Virginia* by Gary Gentiles. Now I've been in Virginia when the rains come down, and not only do they temporarily ruin the water vis, but the heavy rains and lightening can shut down entire airports. This seasonal change in weather conditions maybe why so many local dive shops offer so many exotic and distant travel packages. Once the rain clouds move on though, Virginia has diveable sites for both fresh and salt-water lovers. Perhaps that's where the original state slogan derived from so many years ago: "Virginia Is For Lovers," but now it's for Divers too. Great Dives.

Washington State

There are so many great places to dive in Washington State that it took a book to cover most of the dive sites. My book *The Northwest Dive Guide* by Harbour Publishing goes into great detail about some of these sites, but I also have added a couple of recent articles that I did for *Northwest Dive News* Magazine and *Dive News Network.org* under this Washington heading that cover many of the popular Washington State dive sites. So please read the following articles and enjoy, and if you want more info, please get your hands on a copy of my book; available in selected dive shops, or on line.

Everett

Everett is a small town about 25 miles north of Seattle and is homeport to a flotilla of naval vessels that comprise a strike force, which could easily make Everett the envy of many a foreign navy and/or country. The largest vessel is a nuclear powered aircraft carrier named the USS Abraham Lincoln. To see the vessels first hand, I believe you either have to be a 12year old boy scout on a special assignment, or part of the navy family.

Naval Station Everett which they first started building in WWII isn't the only large facility in Everett, in the 1960's Boeing built a covered area for making planes such as the 747, 767, 777, and the 787. The structure next to Paine Field Airport is the largest building by volume in the world. But these aren't the only big things in the city; Everett also boasts the largest boat marina on the west coast with over 2000 slips. I guess you could say it's just a typical small town were they just happen to do things big. I should also add that from this marina many good dive sites are not far away.

Everett is flanked on the east side by the Snohomish River and on the west side by Possession Sound. Marysville and the Tulalip Indian Reservation are on the north end, and Mukilteo and Lynnwood border the south end. In Forest Park, the oldest Everett park, there is a swimming center where I spent many a day as a Dive Master then as a Scuba Dive Instructor preparing students with the skills that they would need to safely and comfortably enjoy the nearby local waters.

What I like most about Everett is the wide variety of restaurants they have Cajun and Creole food at the Alligator Soul, Italian cuisine at Lombardi's Cocina, and fresh seafood at Anthony's Homeport. The only negative thing about the Everett is trying to find a parking space during the holiday season when the Yacht Club and local restaurants are filled with private office parties, festive families, and cozy couples out for the evening.

As far as the local diving goes, Everett is the gateway to several boat dive destinations. If you have your own boat or sign up with a charter operation you can go over to **Gedney (Hat) island** where you can either boat dive the artificial reef on the south end of the island, where concrete slabs and rocks have formed a home for many varieties of sea life, or you can dive right in front of the **Hat Island Marina** and descend down to an upside down barge or a smaller barge down at 150ft of depth. Dive charters also may lead across the possession sound to dive off the southern end of Whidbey Island such as **Possession Point Fingers**. It's a wall dive with lots of cracks, crevices, and cavernous areas where a wide range of creatures call home. Be sure and bring a flashlight on this dive and watch your depth, because it's easy to pass a 100ft of depth or more when you're focused on finding giant octopus. You might also like to dive the wreck of the **Possession Point Ferry**. The Kehloken was a 240ft long passenger ferry and was sunk as an artificial reef in 1983. Take a two hundred plus foot ferry boat and burn it down to the water line then sink it at 80ft of depth, shake and stir with currents and salt water, and you have one fantastic artificial reef quickly filled with tons of fish and plumose anemones.

As for shore dives, with the Navy taking up part of the waterfront and the railroad taking up the rest of the shoreline, the nearest dive sites are down the hill in Mukilteo or north towards Marysville at Kayak Point County Park. Mukilteo actually has three dive sites to choose from.

The **Mukilteo T dock** is the most popular of the three sites. There is a sea wall on the right side of the Silver Cloud Inn and adjacent to the government instillation/ Marine Biological Research Facility. Sand has recently filled in the remodeled stairway so it's an easy walk down to the beach. Stepping in the water you have plenty of room to gear up before descending down a gravel slope that gives way to a steep sloping sand embankment. At 20ft you may come across a guide rope running parallel to shore. This is where a lot of dive classes complete their skills before touring the local area. Past this rope line you'll find tons of juvenile crabs with only their antennas sticking out of the sand. Down at 130ft the steep slope smoothes out and 2ft wide sandy ripples lead a long air consuming path down past 175ft and beyond. You can go deep here for training purposes or better yet, stay around 35ft and check out some underwater pilings, a geo-dome, and other manmade artifacts located near the T dock. If you go to your right past the T dock you'll find two consecutive shallow bowls of desolated sand. However, around the perimeter of these areas you'll encounter kelp greenling, lingcod, cabezon, stubby squid, sole, and flounder.

After swimming what seems like ½ mile or so you'll arrive at the **Oil Dock**. Around the Oil dock in less than 35ft of water you'll find a plethora of oversized crabs, perhaps even thousands. You have to stay a few feet off the substrate because the fine silt whips up here easily, but you can max out on your crab limit very quickly.

At the **Mukilteo State Park** Also known as **Lighthouse Park**, located to the left of the ferry terminal and adjacent to the picturesque postage stamp sized lighthouse, you'll come across a variety of diversified dive sites. A short walk from the beachfront restrooms into the water is a clay embankment at 30ft of depth and a second embankment at 70ft. Empty holes bored in the clay by former long necked clam residents give refuge to myriads of small invertebrates. This area is a good spot to see lingcods and octopus too.

Near the public boat ramp it's a steep sandy drop off past 150ft with nothing to see except artifacts discarded or lost overboard from passing boats, but it makes a great location to do decompression stops for technical divers.

At the park especially, you have to plan your dives according to slack tides to avoid strong currents. During salmon season sea lions patrol all these dive site areas in search of a never-ending supply of migrating fat and protein. Certain times of the year you can see gray whales close by and nuclear powered fleets off in the distance.

Kayak Point County Park north of Everett is a nice easy dive good for looking for crabs, or discarded crab nets over by the fishing pier. I once found a wedding ring here, but that was a planned recovery dive.

For more information on this and other northwest dive sites please see my book: ***The Northwest Dive Guide*** by Harbour Publishing. Great Dives!

Neah Bay To Port Angeles
Where The Wild Things Dive

     Heading out to Neah Bay requires you to pass by the unassuming town of Port Angeles. The drive along Hwy101 passes by grassy fields, elk crossings, and culminates in a town filled with shops, fast food restaurants, and the car ferry terminal where you can board the *COHO* to take you across to the city of Victoria, Canada during the summer season. Down on the waterfront next to the Marine Life Center is a small sandy beach where on any given weekend you'll see groups of divers heading in or out of the water. The depth in this part of the harbor rounds out to 50ft with sunken logs giving crevices for fish and shrimp to call home. It's a nice half moon bay beach adjacent to the *Red Lion Hotel*, a short walk up the sand to the Marine Life Center, and it is located about two walking blocks from *Sound Kayak and Bikes* where inside the building in the far right hand corner is the headquarters of Scuba Supplies owned and operated by Mike Kesl.

     Past the main town, turn off on Hwy 112 then go on to Camp Hayden Road, a total of 11 miles, you will arrive at one of the best and most beautiful dive sites in all the State of Washington; Salt Water County Park. During WWI & WWII this area was known as Fort Hayden. Near the top of the highest hill two 16" canons were mounted where now sits an empty heavily constructed lookout site and vehicle turn around area for tourists.

     There are three main trails leading down to the basalt shoreline. The trail by the visitor info board has the best gravel beach access. At the other end of the beachfront across from campsite 5 is another info board, but the trail here is steep. The middle stairway leads down to some small tide pools. A fourth stairway located by campsite 60 leads to a breathtaking view of *The Tongue Point Marine Life Sanctuary*, the main tide pools, *Crescent Bay*, and the small uninhabited island in the bay. On an average day you can look down right through the water at the passing sea creatures.

You'll need to be more than just advanced diver qualified to dive here during verified slack tides. This area is for the diver who is in top physical shape, and is ready for a possible strenuous swim. A diver here also has to have excellent navigation skills to locate entrance and exit points away from breaking waves. It also is advisable to set something large, colorful, and highly visible next to your entrance and exit points. In the water move carefully and have a few knives on hand in case currents make you play twister with the ubiquitous kelp.

500 yards off shore from Tongue Point lies the wreck of the **Diamond Knott**, a 360ft cargo vessel that sank in 1946. Strong currents make this Holy Grail of wrecks accessible by boat and only when currents permit. Very few charter boats go out here on a regular basis. You have to be in good physical shape for this dive as Mike has seen divers go through a tank of air while just descending down to the wreck. In recent years wave action has taken its toll on the hull and parts of the bridge, railing, and mid section have disintegrated. The shallow end of the wreck is a 100ft deep dive. The other end dips to 140ft.

Finally, up the road a bit, we arrive at Neah Bay. While diving here you'll feel like you are somewhere in the tropics with all the diversity of colors and abundance of animal life. If you set a finger down on the substrate, chances are you will touch a strawberry anemone, a white plumose anemone, or a lemon nudibranch.

Out here, **Duncan rock** is a popular destination for advanced divers. Situated in the middle of the Strait of Juan de Fuca and barely poised a few feet above the surface at high tide, this site contains a rich abundance of sea life. Below the surface this rock is cut into v-shapes slopes. On one side it goes down to30-50ft. The northwest side drops down to 120ft. Because of navigational and weather considerations this site gets fewer visitors than other sites, so don't be surprised if the marine life like the seals, are less timid and come out to check you out.

Not far from Duncan rock is **Tatoosh Island**. This is a wildlife sanctuary with interesting cutouts and rock formations. Stellar seals are known to join dive groups in this area. From Tatoosh Island you can look over to the water sculptured formation of **Mushroom Rock.**

You barely get to leave Neah Bay before you see **Whadda Island** forming the end of the jetty. There are three main areas to dive here, and **"the fingers"** section is one of the top rated dive sites in Neah Bay. You'll see tons of kelp and rockfish around the island, but at "the fingers" you'll also see large lingcod and kelp greenling perched on the sides of sloping ridges that extend from the surface near shore down to one hundred feet in depth. The ridges flow northward from shore and form wide canyons as they extend out and away from each other. The currents can quickly sweep you out into deeper water while exploring one canyon or bring you swiftly back towards shore while exploring another canyon. *Captain Bill Martin* of *Northwest Dive Charters* has been taking divers out here for the last seven years and fishing out here for the last 20years. Bill likes taking 4 divers at a time here. It's a nice relatively safe environment for advanced divers when tides are favorable, usually between May through August. Because Duncan rock can be a tricky dive, Bill doesn't like to take divers there unless the least experienced advanced diver on the boat is physically and mentally up for the task. He also likes all divers in this area to carry surface "sausage" markers and *Dive Alert* signal devices. A diver could drift away rapidly in these current and fog sensitive waters. Bill also recommends some boat dive sites near Sekiu in 30 to 70ft that are full of marine life, especially abalone.

As far as shore dives go, there's the **wreck of the Andalusia** in about fifty feet of water in front of Snow Creek Resort. **Sail and Seal rocks** are located in a partially protected bay. **1st, 2nd, and 3rd Beach** are a few notable shore dive sites.

There are several campgrounds and a few motels along the way to Neah Bay. Snow Creek Resort has camping areas. Curley's Resort & Dive Center, in Sekiu, is the closest place to get air fills and last minute dive related items.

The bottom line: From Neah Bay to Port Angeles the area is remote, the wildlife abundant, the scenery above poster quality, and this all makes for one of the best dive destinations in all the pacific northwest. Great dives.

Seattle
World Class Hometown Diving

If you ask a local from the state of Washington, they will tell you that Seattle has some of the best diving on the west coast. Divers in Seattle don't really dive the coastal shoreline as it's far away and consists of murky turbulent water. Divers in Seattle typically dive the calmer clearer waters of the Puget Sound. Captain George Vancouver in1792 first discovered the Puget Sound, which was a surprise to the previous Spanish explorers and to the local First Nations Indian tribes that had lived here for thousands of years. Anyway, the Puget Sound is an inland body of salt water where giant octopus, Orca whales, Gray whales, Harbor seals, Dungeness crabs, and various sized clams call home. The Puget Sound was one of Jacque Cousteau's top four dive destinations in the world, and Seattle sits smack dab in the middle of this prolific waterway.

Local divers don't really dive in Seattle. We tend to dive all around the Seattle area with the city of Seattle being the main reference point from where to start. For instance, 30minutes away on the other side of the water facing the Seattle Space Needle is West Seattle and the dive sites at **Alki**. **Cove One** is a shallow dive next to Salty's Seafood Restaurant where you can find plates and glasses tossed over board from weekend parties. **Cove Two** descends down past 110ft and it is down here that you may see a giant octopus or six gill shark. **Cove Three** dips down past 35ft and is a great training spot. It's also fun to look around for crabs and clams here.

Less than 30minutes north of Seattle is Edmonds. Downtown in the bowl north of the ferry terminal is **Bruce Higgins Underwater Trails**, the largest underwater park on the west coast. There are twenty-seven acres of marine preserve to explore here. Hundreds of tug boats, small boats, tires, cement structures, and rocks have been purposely sunk here to provide marine habitats where there was once nothing but sand. Miles of ropes crisscross this park giving divers a wide variety of trails to follow and explore. The largest lingcod in the state lives here. Squid come in the park at night; seals and salmon are also occasional guests.

My second favorite dive site in Edmonds was the "T" shaped oil dock, but the creosote soaked wooden pilings were ripped out of the site destroying the habitat for all the local sea creatures, and now all that remains is sand, a few loose rocks, and one out of hundreds of former poles for good measure that sticks out of the water. After the total destruction and removal of the pilings, no allowance was made for habitat, but a sign was posted on shore that reads "IT IS ILLEGAL TO REMOVE OR DESTROY MARINE HABITAT. ENFORCED BY THE CITY OF EDMONDS EMC 505.002." You can easily dive down to 135ft at this spot, but unfortunately that's now about it.

20 more minutes north and you can dive three different sites at **Mukilteo**. Sites include **Mukilteo Park** for deep dive, the **Oil Dock** for catching crabs, and **Silver Cloud Shoreline** right in front of the Silver Cloud Inn for training, deep, and multilevel dives.

Some 30 minutes south of SeaTac are a couple of dives sites in the Tacoma area. One of my favorites is around the pilings at **Titlow Beach**. There are lots of sea creatures around the pilings and in the crevices of the deeper clay banks. **Owens Beach** near the point defiance zoo is good spot for new divers that want an easy entrance location. A few miles up the road is **Les Davis Marine Park**, which has new artfully decorated steps leading down to the water's edge. Ceramic tiles display images of what you might see on your underwater journey.

Keep in mind that these drive times may vary by as much as an hour and a half due to traffic in Seattle. Think of the local traffic as similar to Los Angeles during rush hour, but moving much much slower. It's hard to build wide non-congested roads around so much beautiful waterways and scenic shorelines; it gets even more complicated when it rains.

Now if you are up for boat diving, then there are a plethora of local dive sites. Charter operators frequent the **Tacoma Narrows Bridge** area or they go south to **KVI Towers** where there are many octos residing at this man made cement pillar reef. The Southern bound charter boats also frequent **Zee's Reef** and **Sunrise Beach,** which are both marine preserves with lots of critters including wolf eels. One the northern route out of Mukilteo, Edmonds Marina, and even the Tacoma marinas, charters go over by Whidbey Island to dive the **Possession Point Fingers** that has walls, caves, and crevices to explore, or they may go over to the **Possession Point Ferry** wreck. **China Wall** at **Blakely Rock**s a short boat ride across the sound and just past the stellar sea lions on the buoy is also a good place to dive.

Now if all the mentioned dive sites don't quench your thirst for salt water and you don't mind driving two plus hours away from Seattle and/or taking a ferry, then there at least another half dozen spectacular dive sites to explore. From Mukilteo, take the ferry over to Whidbey Island and dive **Keystone Jetty**. The boulder-constructed jetty is home to wolf eels, giant octopus, and large lingcod. It's a cool night dive here because you don't have all the city backlight and the bioluminescence of the plankton really gets a chance to glow brightly. From Keystone you can take another ferry over to Port Townsend and go on an antique bottle dive or dive **Hudson Point** which use to be s submarine tending site and is now a top spot for underwater photographers.

An hour and a half or so drive North from Seattle on I-5 will even bring you to Anacortes, which is the gate way to charter boats heading for the San Juan Islands. There are hundreds of dive sites around these northern waters. **Sares Head** is a wall dive that is well known for life on the wall and in the crevices.

Right next to Seattle is **Lake Washington** and some boat charter operators take divers out in the fresh water to explore WWII airplane wrecks that still remain resting in the silted substrate. Here you can see crawfish, trout, salmon, and machine gun turrets pointed towards the surface.
Other dives sites definitely worth the drive time include those located in the Hood Canal such as **Sund Rock**, **Octopus Hole**, **Mike's Beach Resort**, and the boat dive to **Coleman's Pinnacle**. Dive sites to the Vancouver Bristish Columbia area are also reachable in less than a day, such as **Whytecliff Park**,

but I, like many others, prefer to spend more than just a day at a time up in Canada. So I'll mention some of my favorite sites up north in another article, or if you can't wait, you can read about many of them in my book, ***The Northwest Dive Guide***. Great Dives

Tacoma

Tacoma may have just nearly missed becoming the gateway to the gold rush in Alaska over a hundred year ago, but it is certainly the current gateway to scuba diving the southern Puget Sound. Out of four main marinas, and from docks along the Tacoma Narrows and Commencement Bay, dive charter boats head south under the Tacoma Narrows Bridge to KVI Towers, Z's Reef, and Sunrise Beach or all the way over to Budd Inlet to dive a sunken sail boat for that matter. Northward from the Tacoma marinas the possibilities are endless, but most often charter boats head out of here towards Blakely Rocks and beyond. It not just the dive sites that make diving in Tacoma so interesting, but what you see along the way as well. Under the Tacoma Bridge we have seen dolphins jumping out of the water and up north we have encountered enormous stellar sea lions lounging out on top of buoys as they soak up rays from the noonday sun. Sure, you'll also see Orcas whales, gray whales, harbor seals, and bald eagles, but for those of us from the northwest, these creatures are hard to spot, because we are used to seeing them all the time.

Southbound by boat I think my favorite dive is right in front of the **KVI Radio Tower** on Fox Island. You can dive shallow or past 100ft deep where a small boat rests. Large cement pillars extend down the bank like crisscrossing fingers and provide shelter for dozens of giant creatures. There are multiple octopus dens here. One only has to look for discarded clamshells and pieces of crab shells sequestered in front of cracks and crevices like welcome mats laid down in front of entrances to opulent octopus abodes. At this site, don't be surprised to find the octopus sitting out in the open. It's a good thing these 12-18ft long creatures are so docile. Large lingcod and plumose anemone also inhabit this artificial reef. There is no other dive site quite like it in the northwest. It is fun to go over and around the boulders and pilings just to see what creature lurks around the next corner or tucked away underneath the piled pillars and rock fissures. Best of all, you don't really have to swim that far before your camera is full of images.

Sunrise Beach is where I made my first boat dive out of Tacoma over a decade ago. This reef/wall dive is only about 40-60ft deep and runs from north to south (west is shore), so it is an easy dive for a wide range of new to experienced divers. On my very first dive here we spotted four wolf eels that survived the onslaught of two overzealous paparazzi divers and still managed to greet the rest of the dive team. At the time there were lots of juvenile lingcods, as well as small rockfish, one 6ft long octopus, and tons of invertebrates including anemones, and nudibranchs.

Z's Reef is a wall dive a lot like Sunrise Beach. What has made these small wall dive sites so great is that by making both areas protected marine preserves, the fish have had a chance to multiply in number, as well as grow in length. Which means that even on a bad day, these dive sites are great to dive, observe the life, and write about in your dive logbook. Rick Myers of *Bandito Dive charters* says he noticed a big difference in the amount of underwater life a mere six months after Z's Reef became a protected area. Rick Myers has been chartering dives here for going on 15 years. I asked him what keeps him doing boat charters and he simply said, "It's the life style. I enjoy what I do." Going to either of these dive sites you'll enjoy the diving experience too.

The ultimate boat dive site, when it comes to diving with currents and swift moving water, has to be right below the **Tacoma Narrows Bridge**. The original bridge built here in 1940 lasted five months before the center section twisted, bulged, and then fell into the waters below. During those few months it got the name of *Galloping Gertie* for the way it moved, twisted, then collapsed due to high winds. The underwater remnants of the bridge are home to various sea creatures. I've seen octopus here around the anchor blocks at 60ft. The deepest part of the ruins rest at 235ft.

One of the exciting aspects of this site is doing a drift dive starting near the bridge. You can sail along at several knots on a good tidal exchange and before you know it, you and your buddy are quite a ways from your starting point. You may end up someplace north in a back eddy area complete with sandstone ledges, tons of shrimp and clams galore. It's an awesome rush to fly so fast though the water and I recommend this experience to any advanced diver. The only problem with this site besides the currents, is determining how close the "most recent government rules" will let you enter the water near this area.

As for public access shore diving, Tacoma has some of the best. **Titlow Beach** has a good parking area, and artistic cement steps that lead down to an advanced dive site. The site has creosote pilings slated to be removed when state funds are available. It also has gentle slopes and lots of cracks and crevices in the sandstone portion of the substrate where you may encounter, crabs, clams, and octopus. This site should only be dove during slack tides.

Aaron Cummings, owner and manager of Tacoma Scuba believes the best-advanced dive in Tacoma is at **Day Island**. This wall dive takes you down 90 to 110ft and boasts multiple wolf eel sightings among other indigenous creatures. Parking here is limited and the site can only be dived when the currents are just right.

For beginners and experienced divers alike, the most hassle free parking site and the easiest entrance into the water has to belong to **Owens Beach**. This is a sand and gravel beach that gently descends to depth. It's a great place to practice you skills or look for small invertebrates. During a normal week you may only see a handful of divers enter the water here. During the Northwest Dive & Travel Expo and the Northwest Dive News treasure hunt, you may see a couple of hundred divers enter the water here.

All of what I have mentioned should make Tacoma eligible for the next issue of National Geographic. More importantly, for scuba divers, is that Tacoma is located right at the epicenter of some of the best boat and shore scuba diving sites in southern Washington. Tacoma is less than 31 miles from Seattle, Olympia, Gig Harbor, Bremerton, Port Orchard, and islands such as Vashon and Fox. This gives Tacoma a wide web of wondrous dive sites all within short convenient distances beneath the ever-present gaze of currently the tallest volcano in North America, Mt. Rainier. Great Dives.

The Hood Canal

It seems every year I make at least one pilgrimage out to the Hood Canal. When I lived east of Olympia, I was out here weekly and sometimes daily. One of my favorite west coast shore dives is Sund Rock just north of Hoodsport. It is a private beach area that you can enter after paying a small fee at Hoodsport 'n Dive scuba shop right in Hoodsport. The fee goes to the Sund family for access to the area, plus towards maintaining the portable restroom facility. A new wooden long bench has been added by the efforts of local dive club members. The Hood Canal Aquanuts from Shelton and the Kelp Krawlers from Olympia are both active dive clubs in this area.

During the week there are times when you and your buddy are the only ones down at Sund Rock. It's a good time to see the antics of the young bald eagles. Mid-week the harbor seals are more inclined to see what you are up to too. On the weekends it can get busy on the narrow strip of shoreline, but there is plenty of room to spread out underwater. Sund Rock is actually two different wall dives. The North wall has a sunken boat resting on an inclined sandy substrate. Over to the right and past 70ft of depth there is a rock wall that descends downward with ledges at various depths. This is where we once chanced upon a 14ft long giant octopus out in the open searching for the open crab bar. Here, you can go as deep as you are trained to dive.

The south wall starts at about 35ft and dips down to about 60ft at some locations. Here we have seen up to five wolf eels in various stages of growth on a single dive. Seasonally, lots of male lingcod here claim territory, guard white cottage cheese looking eggs, and work specific sentry post stations.

Just north of Sund Rock is Octopus Hole; a preserve sign from Mike's Dive Center marks it. On a high tide expect to walk down rock steps directly in the water. On a low tide you can walk fifteen feet or so down the beach towards the waters edge. Gear up and follow the fallen tree straight out until you find the beginning of a wall at about 35ft of depth. The wall heads south and there is usually an octopus or two here as well as a wolf eel. Plenty of nudibranchs and fish make this a nice leisurely dive site profile. Seasonally, there is usually one female octopus with eggs dangling on the underside of one specific rock. Parking is a difficult task on the weekends, but not during the week unless it's a holiday.

As far as boat dives go, my favorite dive site is Coleman's Pinnacle. Don and Diane Coleman run Pacific Adventures Charters out of Pleasant Harbor Marina up near Brinnon. I believe they still have the only full time charter working the Hood Canal, which incidentally is the southern most fjord in North America. Don and Diane usually pair this dive up with a dive over at Pulali Point. The pinnacle goes down to 150ft and starts 29ft underwater. If you dive down to around 80ft and start circling the pinnacle you should come across 3 mated pairs of wolf eels, at least one octopus, and a school of vermilion rockfish. It's a cool dive with plenty of creatures to discover and photograph. Even when the dissolved oxygen levels are low in the south end of the Hood Canal the animal life is thriving here in the Northern region.

Now when it comes to places to stay and dive, the number one destination has to be Mike's Beach Resort north of Lilliwaup on HWY 101. During the week I usually see Mike working on a project such as remodeling the cabins with hot tubs, or building new rails and stairways for divers to enter and exit the water. You'll also see tourists collecting oysters on the shoreline or setting crab traps off the end of the pier. On the weekends, it's all about the diving. Whether you have a group of forty, or a party of two, Mike's has accommodations right for you. Just a hint though: you can't beat the scenic views from the cabins where you are mere steps from the water's edge on a high tide. I don't know of anything more relaxing than this scenic combination, and associated sounds.

The last time I visited Mike's Beach Resort, Mike told me of a new octopus under a boat at 55ft of depth. I headed right towards the location and was greeted by a four-foot long spiny dogfish shark that promptly took off as soon as I raised my camera. I then headed down to the boat, and underneath it in a small crevice I could make out the sight of long tentacle arms and an eye staring back at me. She never even changed colors as I took a few photos. I think she was already used to seeing divers on a regular basis. Now there are a couple of resident octopuses at the resort as well as a few wolf eels. Another neat attraction here is the sea whip gardens down at 90ft, but the most unusual attraction of all has to be the cloud sponges found at the southern end of the resort. Normally, Cloud sponges are a rarity south of Canada. Weekends fill up fast at Mike's, so book well in advance.

Besides the changes between the weekdays and weekends, every three to five years roaming pods of killer whales come down into the Hood Canal to trim the harbor seal population. The orcas never get close to scuba divers, as they don't like the noisy bubble sounds emitted from our regulators. You can see the orcas a mile away, but that's as close as they've come to us, but this distance is close enough for a harbor seal to pop right out of the water next to you on shore. The seals can tell from the under water sounds if a killer whale is a transient seal eater or a local salmon eating orca. For the seal, the difference in sound signals life or death. Deep down I'm sure the orcas cull minions of squid too. For us, the orcas are just pretty to watch as they glide across the water.

If you decide too make a weekly, monthly, or annual pilgrimage out here, just be sure to pull over to the side of the road frequently, because with one eye looking out for river otters, one eye out for deer, and another one taking in the scenic beauty of forests and waterways, there's almost no way to watch where you are driving. Great Dives.

Whidbey and Camano Island
Wickedly Captivating Dives

When I lived in Edmonds, Washington, it seemed that every two months or so, we were headed across the Mukilteo Ferry on a dive trip over to Whidbey Island. Sometimes we went representing the local dive shop with training dives as our goal. Sometimes we went with a local dive club, while other times we went just for fun in groups of two's and threes. Other times we went by charter boat and dove next to the islands without ever touching shore. The diving is almost always outstanding around the islands. For every diver with advanced training or some threshold number of dives under one's belt, I recommend a dive or two at Keystone Park along **Keystone Jetty** wall. This boulder built jetty wall dive doesn't get much deeper than 60ft depending on tides, and should only be dove at slack tide unless you plan on carrying a passport and a *Capitol One* visa card. The folks at *Whidbey Island Dive Center* right behind Taco Bell in Oak Harbor can help you with the tide tables, air fills, and last minutes dive equipment adjustments or purchases. They know this dive site inside out. And to see all that's on this dive site, you'll have to carry a dive light even on a bright sunny day dive to see every inhabitant on this jetty inside and out too. You see, the nudibranchs, wolf eels, lingcod, and crabs are visible resting right on the rocks, but the giant pacific octopus prefers to hide back in the holes and crevices between meals. Shine a light back in the recesses, and you may get a glimpse of tentacled arms, a funnel, or a horizontal cat like eye peering out back at you. The size of the tentacle rings will give you a good clue as to how big the octopus is. Some of the octopus here I believe are more than 12ft long, others, not so much. Although octopus come and go during the year, it is always a special treat when you see them here. At the end of the wall the current picks up as if telling you that it's time to return to shallower depths. On a night dive expect to see an entire different cast of fish out here. Bioluminescent organisms are really lit up here because there is no city light glow to diminish the intensity of the bioluminescent spectacles. Just wave your hands through Keystone's waters at night and I'm sure you will agree. An advanced drift dive from the jetty will take you down to the old pilings just down the shore side. A line now runs from the southwest corner of the pilings over to the jetty and you can find it at around 42ft of depth. The line is not officially registered, but I think as long as it promotes dive safety and positional awareness, the rangers will let it retain its unofficial status and duties.

Some dive clubs stay at nearby Fort Casey State Park to spend a weekend diving Keystone. Some divers prefer to stay up in nearby Oak Harbor at places like *The Coachman Inn*. Others will dive here, then hop the Keystone Ferry over to Port Townsend and dive along the shores there too. Others, like we used to do many times, is dive Keystone at slack, then do a second dive south at the **Langley Tire Reef**. The Langley tire reef is home to fish and crabs alike. It is an easy dive with not much current. Last year during the Langley Marina sponsored Easter egg hunt they attached yellow polypropylene rope around the tire reef so divers would know the boundaries of the Easter egg "colored golf balls" hunt. The rope also acts as a safety barrier rope. From personal experience, I can tell you that beyond the ropes there is nothing but sand, fish bones…Oh, And more sand add nausea. Inside the tire reef there is lots of invertebrate life wedged in between the tires; including succulent mouthwatering Dungeness crab for those that are lucky and carry the right permits. Over the years, the fishermen, crabbers, and divers have developed a good relationship here. Local divers are respectful of immersed fishing lines and baited crab rings, and keep a respectful distance from the stockade walls that fishermen fish from. Divers have also retrieved escaped crab rings and lost fishing poles for said fishermen. This relationship with divers has led to the building of an out door shower to rinse off, and three new benches to stage dive gear. I heard that an outdoor hose might soon also be added to the bench stations. Langley is also the site of an historic and romantic getaway town with good eats and plenty of unique shopping establishments. You need a day or a weekend just to explore all the landside attractions here. Don't forget that there are many Bed & Breakfast Inns nestled in secluded or private settings; some with phenomenal seaside views.

Now one of my favorite dives of Whidbey Island is a boat dive at **Possession Point Fingers**. This wall dive has a set of finger like projections that have many crevices and ledges for sea creatures of all sizes to call home. It's one of those "bring your camera dives". For wreck divers, the remnants of the **Possession Point Ferry** are the place to jump overboard. Strong wicked currents and ship traffic restrict the monthly viewing times of this site or the adjacent site of piled timbers and other random cast off structures. Other boat dives include: **Deception Pass**, **Pass Island**, and **Strawberry Island**, and just about anywhere a boat crew can follow your bubbles on a slack tide. On a footnote, for some inexplicable reason, boats and divers left unattended inexplicably drift in opposite directions. And that's just another reason to dive these sites with a knowledgeable local charter boat operation. There are several boat charter operations that frequent this area from the San Juans, Anacortes, and even from down south. Other shore dives include **Ebey's Landing**, **Admiralty Beach**, and **Tire Reef**.

On Camano Island, Pat Ocean, the owner of *Whidbey Island Dive Center* recommends **Onomac Point**. It's a good artificial reef site with lots of sea life including plumose anemones, small invertebrates, and lingcod large and abundant enough to hunt by spearfishermen and women. On the other side of Camano Island are the waters of Port Susan. My buddies and I like to park at Kayak State Park on the mainland to dive these waters. At certain times of the year it is a great place to catch Dungeness crab. Near the pier I have recovered countless crab rings and once even a gold wedding ring. It just goes to show you that you never know what you may find on a dive. On Whidbey and Camino Islands, you may not find enchanted gold rings, but you will have a great time diving these captivating waters. Great Dives.

West Virginia
Mountain Diving Take Me Home!

West Virginia is like no other state in the union. It's the only state to secede from a Confederate State and join the Union side. Harpers Landing, where the Potomac and Shenandoah rivers meet, changed hands some 8 times during the American Civil War. Locals lost almost as many relatives on the Union side as they did on the Confederate side; 22-25,000 each, and the names John Brown, Robert E. Lee, and Stonewall Jackson will live on forever. Sure, Bob Denver wrote a song about West Virginia's natural beauty. West Virginia is the only state wedged completely inside the Appalachian mountain range as well as between five surrounding states, but the way its borders run gives it an extra strip of land going up into Ohio and preserves a seemingly intrusive strip of land from Delaware, giving West Virginia a rather unique stately shape. Add to this 4,863ft high elevations around Spruce Knob in the Monongahela Forest, and you have some very interesting dive sites, as well as some well known and favorite dive sites in the surrounding neighboring states.

So where to begin on a tour of West Virginia's dive sites? To start with, I spoke with Mark Allen, owner and operator of *Sarge's Dive Shop* and Mount Summerville Marina. Skin Diver Magazine called **Summerville Lake** "The Little Bahamas of the East". The vis is between 20-45ft, but this last September it was over 60ft even down at 100ft deep. The steep oligotrophic rock wall shoreline can run directly down to 100ft underwater and helps keep the water so clear. The water temp can vary from 68 t0 85° depending on the time of the year and the water level drops on purpose in September and is raised around the 3rd week in April to 1624ft in lake level altitude making Memorial day to Labor Day the best time to dive here. The US Army Corps of Engineers built the 2,280ft long and 390ft tall dam in 1966 by blocking the Gauley River. Below the dam the Gauley River supports class V whitewater rapids. The Lake actually rests on top of the inundated town of Gad near the present day marina, but the name "Gad Dam," was too much of a political/social hot potato, so the name "Summerville" won the day. Max depth is about 320ft. Under the cliffs and overhangs live catfish, walleye, and bass, but for the past 20years, the fish population has been declining. Five years ago when a gill net was used to catch walleye, I was told the net came up empty. I was also informed that the local fishing tournaments have taken their toll on nesting fish, because when the nesting fish are caught, they are released miles away from their nests and after being weighed, it is hard for the traumatized fish to find their way back along the 10mile long lake to their nest, so the eggs of the next generation are left unprotected. The lake is also currently not a "stocked lake", possibly because it is drained so low once every five years or so, but if officials stocked the lake and the fishing tournament schedules were tweaked, Summerville Lake could be booming with fish and become the envy of fishermen and scuba divers everywhere.

Right now Sarge's Dive Shop offers NAUI and ERDI instruction. The marina rents out boats, and has a pontoon boat that can hold up to 18 divers. Currently the marina has cruises that take about an hour to travel around to see the entire 60miles of cliff shoreline and the 2,790acres of the lake, but Mark would eventually like to get a large houseboat for 2hours evening cruises for visitors to enjoy the sun setting in the west.

Mount Storm Lake or Lake "Vepco" as the local call it, is the next big dive site in the state. This 1200acre lake is actually the cooling pond for the 3 operating units of the coal burning Virginia electrical power plant built in 1962. The altitude is around 3,200ft and the water temp between 50-85°. Max depth is 132ft deep. Catfish, bluegills and Mussels inhabit the lake that never freezes over. Platforms at various depths were once used by shore divers, but supposedly because of a dispute between boaters and swimmers hanging around the boat ramp have led to a ban on swimming and shore divers alike. You can now only dive from your own boat, and you must get an issued boat permit for this activity in advance from the power plant. Altitude tables or altitude-compensating computers are a must here. Charles Carroll Jr. of *Huntington Scuba* likes to view the animal life here such as deer and beaver. He also likes the picturesque scenery of the wind turbines that dot the nearby hills, but he's not so keen on the lightning storms that sometimes light up around the electric plant's tall spires. More importantly, because of the recent restrictions, it is just as easy for him and his past 7,000 students over the last 40years to go over to quarries in Ohio or lakes in Kentucky, which is just an hour away. He also instructs nearby along the banks of the Ohio River.

Dive Tech & Sports in Hernshaw has taken a different approach to local diving. They teach in quarries in Ohio, but, every spring and fall they plan a dive around the world, and at least once a month, they head on down to Florida to dive the springs. They teach cave and cavern diving on the spring trips. Since 1994, during the winter months, they teach NAUI instructors at their own career development center. As last reported, they have the only Nitrox fill station in the state.

Stonecoal Lake near Buckhannon comprises a mere 550acres, at 1,145 ft in elevation, 50-70° in temp, and only 60-70ft deep, but what makes this an interesting lake to dive even in low vis, is the chance to see a 50" long or 49lb muskie, 11lbs rainbow trout, 8lb golden trout, 41lb carp blue gill, crappie, bass, and catfish. It's all about the fish in this cold little lake, but it shows what you can do with the right fishing management team.

Tygart Lake near Grafton is at 1,094ft in elevation, has a max depth of 134ft. It may have little vis below 50ft, but it is also filled with a wide assortment of fish. It also has a couple of dive entry points to choose from such as Henderson Rocks, the swimming area, or the marina.

Lastly we have the **Upper Dog Run Lake** at 60ft deep or the **Lower Dog Run Lake** at 10-15ft deep. They may not be spectacular, but any day of diving beats a day at work.
Keep in mind that there are campgrounds, lodges, state parks, and other attractions located near these West Virginia dive sites

so Google the lakes and know before you go. There are some other local lakes that may turn out to be potential dive sites too, but more research and plenty of diving is required to check these sites out. In the meantime, Great Dives.

Wisconsin

Great Lakes, Great Dives

My great ancestor, a Naval Officer in the French Navy, first fell in love with this land of lakes when he acquired a homestead in Fon du lac, Wisconsin a few years back around 1798. This was right after the French had supplied a navy to help the colonies in their struggle against the King of England in the war that culminated with the Declaration of Independence some time in early July 1776. One of the first written encounters of the French in this territory was with their meeting with Winnebago Indians in Green Bay back in 1634. My ancestors eventually headed west on the Oregon Trail, and I grew up in Milwaukie, Oregon; Note the old spelling of the city name before the spelling of the name was changed back in Wisconsin by an early newspaper writer to Milwaukee and it stuck. I tend to think my ancestors would have gone no farther west than Milwaukee, Wisconsin had another French naval officer by the name of Jacques Cousteau brought to fruition the invention of the Aqualung regulator a mere 150 years earlier or so. The reason I think so is because all the great and little lake diving would have kept my ancestors too busy to think about heading out west, but so much for timing, and so much for the past history.

There really are two classes of lakes in and around Wisconsin, there are two fresh water seas, and a separate category for all the other lakes. The two major fresh water seas include Lake Superior and Lake Michigan. Many a ship have found they're resting place at the bottom of these two great lakes. Freshwater, unlike saltwater, preserves theses wrecks for decades and decades. The Wisconsin Historical Society has made 18 laminated maps representing historical wrecks such as the schooner **Lucerne** that sank in 1886 in 25ft of depth and the steamer **Sevona** in 1905 in 20ft in Lake Superior. Maps of wrecks include the schooner **Hetty Taylor** in 1880 at 100ft as well as the paddleboat **Niagara**, the **Louisiana**, and **Pilot Island**.

Modern wrecks in these two bodies of water include: the **SS Wisconsin**, built in 1881, was 48years old when it sank 6.5miles SE of Kinosha, Wisconsin. It went down November 29th, 1929. The steamship was just over 200ft long and carried iron castings, boxed freight, and 1929 era automobiles. If you anchor mid-ship and descend down the line you will come to an open hatch. Inside the compartment are an Essex, a Hudson, and a Chevrolet touring car. It's a penetration dive to tour the car show, so it definitely requires wreck diver training. At 130ft of depth it's best left for deep water or tech divers too. And like any dive on the lake, you have to be prepared for stray fishing lines below the surface and wind and wave action by the time you return to the surface due to brief changes in weather. Also, the surface temperature may be 80 degrees in the summer, but expect 55 degrees at depth. If the water dips in the 40's keep and eye out for Chinook and Coho salmon.

The wreck named **Straits of Mackinac**, not to be confused with the wrecks in the straits of Mackinac, ended its final voyage from Wisconsin to Illinois and was sunk as an artificial reef on April 11th, 2003. It rests 10miles NE of the Chicago Navy Pier in 73ft of water. This 1928 steel hull steamship is 204ft long. "The Mack" was a car ferry before the bridge over the straits of Mackinac was built. It's only 50ft down to the top deck by the smoke stack, making it readily available to divers who don't like to dive too deep.

The **Milwaukee Car Ferry** built in 1903 was 338ft long. She went down in 90-120ft of water with 25 railroad cars, including two loaded with bathtubs, one with cheese, etc, and 52 passengers on board. She has a sister ship in a Michigan museum and her story was portrayed recently on the Discovery Channel by The Under Sea Detectives.

The **Prince Willem V**, "The Willey", is a 250ft long Dutch freighter that sunk in 1954 at 93ft of depth resting on its starboard side. It's one of the most popular wreck dives off the coast of Milwaukee. Be sure and take a dive light along to peek inside.

As for the rest of the lakes, **Lake Wazee** in Jackson County at 355ft is the deepest inland lake in Wisconsin. This former iron quarry has several thermo clines depending on the time of year. While the surface maybe at 70°, at 30ft it may be 40°, and at 60ft of depth the temperature may be down to 34°. Lake Wazee is also known for it petrified forests and fish cribs, which are log cabin like structures filled with rocks. These structures give small fish a chance to hide and swim between the cracks and gaps and survive predation by larger fish.

Many of the divable lakes were quarries that filled in slowly with water, or filled in so fast that some of the original mining equipment can still be found at the bottom of the lake. And it's not just about the lake being deep, **Devils lake** in Baraboo is only 48ft deep, but it is surrounded by massive 500ft cliffs, and two sandy beaches. **Lake Owens** at a maximum of 96ft deep has an adjacent a national park and resort recreational area. Some lakes are known for ice diving in the winter and shallow lakes are known for warm waters in the summer. Most of the lakes mentioned are home to walleye, bass, black crappie, sunfish, northern pike, panfish, crayfish, and unfortunately for some lakes, the introduction of zebra mussels.

Wisconsin dive clubs like to spice up the lake diving experience by including group events. The southeastern UTS, *Urge To Submerge*, diving club enjoy good lake clean up followed by a Pirate festival at Lake Wazee. *Mountain Bay* has their annual quarry blast at a private quarry, but it is open to all divers that day. I should mention that *Badger State Dive Club* in Milwaukee is the oldest dive club in the state and enjoy many dive and non-dive activities. It's hard to go wrong joining a dive club that holds meetings above a pizza restaurant like *Eduardo's Natural Pizza*. Buccaneer's Dive Club an active dive club since 1970, hold their meetings right at Pirates Cove Diving Inc. on the south side of Milwaukee. Oh, and for great shore diving locations check out the maps on *Neptune's Dive Club* for northeastern Wisconsin dive sites.

Now you'll have to forgive me on some of the historical accuracy, as I'm not a professor of History like my Norwegian ancestor, before he came to America, but I do realize that my French ancestors left Wisconsin before the quarries were even dug or the current historical wrecks were even built, and this makes me only wonder what unrecorded artifacts slid beneath the waves during their days, and is now covered with a layer of silt and waiting for local Wisconsin divers to discover on their next underwater adventure. Great Dives!

Wyoming
Wet, Wild, & Geothermal

When it comes to hot spots to dive, they're few other places that compare in nature to Wyoming. This is the land of old faithful, Yellowstone Park, as well as lakes and rivers that can be frozen on the surface and have boiling hot water pumping up from the depths. Fish here thrive in some rivers even in waterways with higher than normal levels of arsenic, boron, or cadmium. River otters, elk, prairie dogs, buffalo, eagles, and brown bears seem to blissfully go about their daily tasks while ignoring the tourists, vacationers, fly fishermen, divers, and spouting geysers.

Yellowstone Lake is first on my list of dive sites simply because with 110miles of shore land and at 7,700ft, it is the largest high altitude lake in the USA. This lake is also the third largest geothermal vent system in Yellowstone Park. Most of the vents are in the northern part of the lake. The surface can be 64°, but some of the vents can burn a diver, so it's best to know where to go by asking a few questions at a local dive shop before you take a plunge. What's so cool about this lake is that 300ft off of Bridge Bay Marina in Mary Bay, you can explore underwater geysers and spires that rise above the substrate like stove chimneys. There are ancient fresh water sponges here as well as sunken small boats. Down at 100ft and in water 90°, some of these spires support an ecosystem of moss, shrimp, and a worm that has never seen before living in North America. This is also the land of cutthroat trout and game spear fishing is allowed in Wyoming. To dive here, you can obtain a permit from the Bay Bridge Park Rangers. Picnic tables and bathrooms are available at Mary's Bay. Local Diver Chris Hansen has a very nice map on the web listing several areas to dive provided you have access to a boat.

Fire Hole River is a tributary of the Madison River and runs 21miles from Madison Lake and joins the Gibbon River in

Yellowstone. This 8,200ft in altitude dive is a wild ride that should only be attempted by advanced divers. The waters are part of the old faithful geyser basin, and there are hot spots along the way. At least two spots dip down around 30ft of depth. What makes this a Buffalo Bill's Wild Ride is that at certain times of the year, the water is really rushing through steep canyon walls, and as the water churns and bubbles, you are left with less than 3ft of visibility. The air bubbles swarm around you giving you little time to react with upcoming rocks. To watch the trout pass by, some divers wedge themselves in a 35ft u/w cave for a moment or two. A hood is a safety item here, but not as much to keep you from hitting your head, as it is to keep the powerful water flow from perforating your eardrum. Fire Hole River is a popular site and expect to see other advanced divers either in front of you or quickly flowing past you to the exit point at the park swimming area where the vis improves substantially. So if you want the feeling of rock climbing in a hurricane, get your park permit, head down the one-way road that starts near Madison Junction, park near the stairway that leads down to bathrooms, and head on the path around the big rock or just follow other divers.

Buffalo Bill Reservoir is just east of Yellowstone Park and just west of Cody. The reservoir comprises 8,000acres of the Shoshone River. From Wapiti to the reservoir is a 9.5mile day trip for floaters. There are some class II rapids, but that's about all advanced divers or floaters will encounter as they pass by Yellowstone cutthroats, brown, and brook trout. The dam itself was built in 1910 and is 325ft tall, so weather you are floating, or diving at depth, you should find a dam dive site that fits your needs, desires, and dam diver abilities.

Yellowtail Reservoir, part of the Big Horn River and the Bighorn Canyon National Recreation Area, has 120,000acres of diveable water. This 50mile long reservoir has lots of small coves to dive and is home to carp, ling, walleye, and small mouth bass. The water temp can range from 65° to75°. Vis is 10-30ft. Since Billings is only 90miles north of here, expect to meet and greet many visiting divers from Montana.

Lake DeSmet in Johnson County is just north of Buffalo and 30 miles south of Sheridan. Randy Schmidt of *Aquatic Scuba Adventures* in Sheridan has been to this lake countless times. He teaches open water up to technical diving and even trains emergency response personnel. He recommends diving over by the 20-30ft underwater foundation ruins of the old Lake DeSmet Resort, which is complete with sidewalks currently leading nowhere in particular unless you're a fish. He also recommends checking out the old D9 Cat bulldozer by Barkley's Draw, or a swim under the sunken bridge 20ft deep.

Besides cliff walls and weed beds, Randy has also found four model-A ford cars hidden in this lake. The vis can reach 40ft, but it wasn't until the lake's level dropped about 30ft that a bronze statue of a mermaid was seen for the first time. They also say that there is a 40ft long sea monster called "Smetty" in the lake, but I digress . . . Anyway, your trip here won't be complete until you do a night dive when the crayfish, carp, trout, and perch are actively out and about. In the winter months, just like most of the other lakes in Wyoming, you can come here and try some Ice diving. Oh, and before I forget, every Labor Day, *Aquatic Scuba Adventures* and *Aloha Scuba* from Gillette have a Dive Fest here.

Flaming Gorge Reservoir in the Flaming Gorge National Recreation Area is next on the Wyoming dive list. This southwestern reservoir dips into the state of Utah so expect to read more about this dive area when I highlight the state of Utah. I will say one thing though, brown trout have been caught here at the record size of 25tlbs and 13oz and more than 34inches in length.

Other lakes that I would like to further dive and/or research in the future include Jenny Lake in Jackson County, which is 423ft deep, comprises 1,191acres, is 2.2miles long, 1.2miles wide, and is a glacier formed lake in the Grand Teton National Park. Lake Alcova near Casper is 130ft deep, and Glendo Reservoir south of Douglas could also be a promising spot to take a dip.

So there you go, hot geothermal vents, wild and rugged river rides, strange animal ecosystems, big fish where spear fishing is legal, ice diving, altitude diving, plus freshwater wrecks and ruins adorn this state and that's why Wyoming has something to offer just about any freshwater dive enthusiast, but don't take my word on it, bring a dive flag, and come and see these wonders of nature for yourself. Great Dives.

CANADA

9+1 Wonderful Wrecks
British Columbia Style

When it comes to quality and quantity of wrecks to explore, British Columbia Canada has to be at the top of the list. Warships, cargo ships, and wooden ships dating back to the 1800's give plenty of options and multiple adventures. But it's not just the ships that are so outstanding, but also the quantity of marine life each ship acquires with time and the types of marine life drawn to specific regions and habitats. The Artificial Reef Society of British Columbia, ARSBC, has to be the most active artificial reef society in the world, so it's no surprise that 8 of the wrecks I mention here are artificial reefs sunk on purpose for divers to enjoy and explore, and where fish can thrive and call home. Some of the best wrecks to dive include:

HMCS Mackenzie is a 366ft, 2900 ton, destroyer escort sunk in 1995 just north of Gooch Island and 4 miles east of Sidney. It sits at 100ft of depth and you can expect 25ft of visibility. It's in an area known for strong tidal currents so it's best to explore this wreck with a knowledgeable guide or charter operation. The original forward guns were dismantled and replica gun barrels made out of sewer pipes were put in their place, but the replicas appear real because of all the hard camouflage work done by encrusting barnacles and other small resident creatures. In addition, kelp covers the radar tower, wolf eels patrol the hallways, and all kinds of shrimp and nudibranchs man the decks and mortar well. Talk about hard working volunteers!

GB Church is a 175ft long coastal freighter sunk in 1991 off Portland Island near Sidney in the Princess Margaret Marine Park. She sets at 90ft of depth and expect around 35ft of visibility. The sinking of this ship turned underwater sand dunes into an oasis teaming with life. Sand alone could never support a thriving colony of copper rockfish, tubeworms, and red algae, just to name a few of the vivacious local residents. A short boat ride from the Sidney area and 17 years of marine life growth have made this reef, (former wreck), a very popular dive destination.

Xihwu Reef (pronounced 'key' quot") is the resting site of a Boeing 737: 60ft deep. The 100ft long plane sits on 11ft tall stands so it looks like its flying through the water and the added height also allows you to dive from underneath it into the cargo belly area. This may be the only plane in the world that you can board without first clearing with security even with a dive knife. Don't expect to find any pilots here. As many of us in the airline industry already know, most commercial airline pilots can't survive in an environment where they are not fed every 20minutes. (No offense intended towards pilot whales). Seriously though, this is the newest artificial reef site to date, but it doesn't take long to attract the initial members of a thriving marine community. The best part about diving any wreck over and over is being able to observe first hand the changes in the local sea life community over time and also how Mother Nature in general deals with the new artificial appendage.

All three of these sites can be reached by boat from dive shops as far south as *Ogdin Point Dive Center* in Victoria which has one boat stationed in Sydney just for these excursions, from local charters out of Sydney such as *49th Parallel Dive Charters*, or from nearby resorts such as *Cedar Beach Lodge Resort* on Thetis Island.

HMCS Saskatchewan is a 366ft 2900ton destroyer escort sunk in 1997 next to Snake Island. It's a classic dive where the main deck rests at about 100ft and advanced divers in good physical shape and good on air consumption can almost swim from one end to the other before having to come up and do a safety stop. There is lots of life on this structure, especially invertebrates. Currents here are usually mild, so it doesn't take long for most known species of critters to already have relatives living on, inside, or around this ship. Don't be surprised to find juvenile Puget Sound king crabs some 65ft up in the (crows nest) tower area, scallops on the main deck, and harbor seals off to portside.

FMG Cape Breton (fleet maintenance group) is a 411ft long 9500ton victory ship sunk in 2001 off of Snake

Island near Nanaimo on Victoria Island. It sits at 142ft of depth and when first sunk stretched up to just beneath the surface at 35ft. Because of its length and depth, this ship should be considered an advanced deep dive. It took over 18months to prepare this ship and less than 4minutes to sink her. She's the world's second largest diver-prepared artificial reef and it shouldn't take long before the marine life descends upon her like they have done so on the Saskatchewan a short distance away.

Ocean Explorers Dive Charters as well as many other local dive charters come out to these two sites several times a day. It's always a good idea to stay at the *Buccaneer Inn* who cater to divers and are conveniently located near an excellent pub and restaurants a short walk right across the street.

HMCS Columbia is another 366ft destroyer escort sunk off of Maude Island near Campbell River in 120ft of depth. Now, this wreck is tilted on its side, and if you get less than 20ft of visibility, your whole inner axis of vertical vs. horizontal seems to get thrown off kilter, but the angle doesn't seem to bother the marine life including the juvenile octopus living onboard in a cubbyhole at 90ft. The relative surrounding calm waters make this dive accessible year round.

Abyssal Dive Charters and Lodge, *Nautilus Explorer* and dive charters from as near by as Comox visit here on a regular basis. The problem with this shipwreck is that there are too many great dive sites nearby with 100ft plus visibility, to compete for your attention. It's like discovering a bar of silver in a sea of platinum and gold, but it's still an interesting dive.

HMCS Chaudierere "The Chaud" is yet another 366ft 2900ton destroyer escort sunk in 1992 near Kunichin Point, Porpoise Bay, Sechelt Inlet; off the sunshine coast of mainland BC. The stern sits at 55ft of water and the bow at 105ft. She tilts to her port and is home to thousands of orange plumose anemones, white tubeworms, glassy tunicates, and other critters make this a spectacular dive site. *Porpoise Bay Charters* and well as *Suncoast Diving* dive here on a regular basis.

SS Vanlene; a 8354 ton cargo ship carrying 300 Dodge Colt cars headed from Nagoya Japan towards America without any navigational equipment. The 29year old captain found land the hard way in 1972: Eventually, the ship broke into two pieces; the bow rests at 25ft and the stern at a max of 120ft. If you need some car parts, head out to Barkley Sound off Victoria Island. *Rendezvous Dive Adventures* can take you here and other great sites in the Barkley Sound.

SS Capilano. At a 125ft long and 235tons it's small compared to the other ships, and you cant go inside this vessel, but if you want to see how big 100yr old rockfish truly get, then you have to visit this 1915 wreck. The main deck sits at around 120ft so if the fish start to look bigger than you or speak with slightly slurred accents, ascend just a few feet to take in the full outline of the ship. Bring a light with you too, as it can get cold and dark in rockfish land. Bill Coltart and his team from *Pacific Pro Dive & Surf* in Comox can take you out to this "must see" site.

HMCS Annapolis. This 366ft destroyer escort weighing in at 3420tons has not been sunk yet. I just added it to the list to let you know what ARSBC is planning next. Commissioned in 1964 for submarine warfare and carrying a Sea King CH124 helicopter, this $31million steam driven vessel at one time could generate enough electricity for 18,000 homes. The ship has been to foreign ports such as Vladivostok Russia, Guam, and Hawaii, and will be spending its last days above water moored at Gambier Island for reclamation and environmental cleanup. Removing homing torpedoes is easy, but cleaning up paint, removing toxic waste, cutting out diver safety exits, and in general making the ship safe for fish and divers alike takes thousands of hours. The final resting site for the Annapolis is slated in the Howe Sound, the most southern fjord in western Canada, and an easy short drive from Vancouver, BC. But locations have a way of changing due to unforeseen circumstances, such as avoiding current and accommodating Coast Guard, fisheries, and Oceans regulations. I have photos of the 737 waiting months and months in Comox before the final word came down that it would be sunk near Sidney. The Breton was also scheduled at one time for another shallower location before assuming its final resting spot.

The ARSBC doesn't just sink ships; each artificial reef has guardians for life that care for the sunken habitats. Structures are continually monitored to make sure they remain safe for divers: checking for signs of loose wires, cable entanglements from outside sources, etc. Volunteers do biological studies such as track fish numbers and resettlement activities by marine species too. There may be an activity sponsored by ARSBC that might even interest you.

I haven't mentioned the minesweepers, battle class trawlers, or hundreds of other wooden ships and side-wheel steamers strewn around the bottom of Canada's shoreline. There are books that specifically detail many 100's of local wrecks. These are just some of the more prominent, if not the best, wreck dives to consider on your next expedition to British Columbia. And just like your mileage, your opinion on what are the best wrecks of BC may vary, but ultimately you'll come to the overwhelming conclusion that thanks to the hard work and dedication of a plethora of volunteers, sponsors, and devoted dive shops and non-profit ARSBC society members, wreck diving in BC is truly in a league of its own.

The Dive Industry of BC (DIABC) is a non-profit blanket organization that represents virtually all of the players in the province's dive industry. Check the web site, www.diveindustrybc.com, for articles and up to date information on diving in BC. This article is from my book *The Northwest Dive Guide* by Harbour Publishing. Great dives.

The Top 10 British Columbia Wrecks

HMCS Mackenzie is a 366ft, 2900 ton, destroyer escort sunk in 1995 just north of Gooch Island and 4 miles east of Sidney. It sits at 100ft of depth and you can expect 25ft of visibility.

GB Church is a 175ft long coastal freighter sunk in 1991 off Portland Island near Sidney in the Princess Margaret Marine Park. She sits at 90ft of depth and expect around 35ft of visibility.

Xihwu Reef is the resting site of a Boeing 737: 60ft deep. The 100ft long plane sits on 11ft tall; the added height allows you to dive from underneath it into the cargo belly area.

HMCS Saskatchewan is a 366ft 2900ton destroyer escort sunk in 1997 next to Snake Island. It's a classic dive where the main deck rests at about 100ft. Don't be surprised to find scallops on the main deck, and harbor seals off to portside.

FMG Cape Breton is a 411ft long 9500ton victory ship sunk in 2001 off of Snake Island near Nanaimo. It sits at 142ft of depth.

HMCS Columbia is another 366ft destroyer escort sunk off of Maude Island near Campbell River in 120ft of depth. Now, this wreck is tilted on its side, but the angle doesn't seem to bother the marine life.

HMCS Chaudierere "The Chaud" is yet another 366ft 2900ton destroyer escort sunk in 1992 near Kunichin Point, Porpoise Bay, Sechelt Inlet; off the sunshine coast of mainland BC. The stern sits at 55ft of water and the bow at 105ft.

SS Vanlene is an 8354ton cargo ship carrying 300 Dodge Colt cars. The bow rests at 25ft and the stern at a max of 120ft. If you need some car parts, head out to Barkley Sound.

SS Capilano is 125ft long and weighs 235tons. If you want to see how big 100yr old rockfish truly get, then you have to visit this 1915 wreck. The main deck sits at around 120ft.

HMCS Annapolis. This 366ft destroyer escort weighing in at 3420tons has not been sunk yet. I just added it to the list to let you know what will be sunk soon.
There are also minesweepers, battle class trawlers, hundreds of other wooden ships, and even side-wheel steamers strewn around the bottom of Canada's shoreline. For more details, see my book *The Northwest Dive Guide* by Harbour Publishing.

For non-wreck divers, I recommend starting at Port Hardy on the northern tip of Vancouver Island and working your way south over days, weeks, and years. British Columbia is truly blessed with some of the best diving sites in the world.

Saanich Inlet, BC
Kingdom of the Cloud Sponges

The Saanich Inlet is located on Vancouver Island less than 20miles from down town Victoria. The first nations people called the Saanich Peninsula "The land were it is good to be". This Peninsula is the driest region on the entire island of Vancouver. Douglas firs, western cedar, and hemlock grow here like no other region of the island. The bedrock here was ideal for making Portland cement, so cement and lumber became prime early commodities. Later, the cement factory and the adjacent timber cleared lands were converted into the now famous Butchart Gardens. Besides the gardens, the Victoria International Airport, and the Sydney Ferry Terminal where Washington State ferries carrying cars and passengers from Anacortes via the San Juan Islands are also located on the Saanich peninsula. The Anacortes boat ride is long and scenic and worth every minute of the passage. The other ferry route on the peninsula is from Brentwood Bay over to Mill bay and it is the oldest continuous ferry route on Vancouver Island; since 1924.

So now that you know a little about the land, lets talk about the adjacent water way. The Saanich Inlet is about 15miles long and 738ft deep in some places. At the north end of this fjord there is a shallow lip similar to the one down south in Hood Canal. The inlet was carved out of the earth by glaciers. When the glaciers receded, the exposed land filled with saltwater, plankton consisting of diatoms and dinoflagellates moved in and blossomed in numbers. Each night zooplankton such as copepods and pteropods rise up from the depths and feast. The plankton skeletons sink in the spring and combined with silt from the Cowichan river in the fall produces a layering effect that has been recorded and studied back to 13,000years ago. Herring who came in for the zooplankton have been dated back to 12,000years. Much later, predators such as hake, spiny dogfish sharks, salmon, and whales moved into the area. The Saanich Inlet is one of the most studied areas on the west coast. Now, the high lip on the entrance makes for smooth lake like conditions ideal for cloud sponges, but it also makes for anoxic conditions in the summer when hydrogen sulfide in deep basins builds up. You may find dense mats of chemosynthetic bacteria on the substrate. The more organic carbon they fix, the larger the mats get. Fall oxygenated river water from the Goldstream River and Oxygenated saltwater from the Haro Straights help bring the waters inside the Saanich Inlet back in balance. While other creatures may not be able to tolerate the wide oxygen concentration swings and therefore have had to periodically relocate, the undaunted cloud sponges have formed dense colonies in bizarre large shapes, and the colonies maybe hundreds of years old. I should add here that cloud sponges have tiny glass (spike-like) spicules inside them that cause an irritating rash if you touch them bare handed; the spicules also keep other creatures from eating them.

There are many dive sites where you can see the cloud sponges as well as the other resident sea creatures. Cloud sponges are usually between 80 to 100ft plus in depth. There are over 20 shore dives in the Saanich Inlet, and over 24 named boat dives where you may encounter cloud sponges. Some of the better-known shore dives include:

McKenzie Bight: In the Gowland Tod Provincial Park, a short hike from Mark Lane down the trail to Willis Point (south). It's a large wall dive near shore with boot sponges down at 100ft with plenty of life to keep a photographer busy, but sparse for those looking for massive amounts of life.

Willis Point: Towards the north end, and at the end of Mark Lane is a gravel path that leads to this shore site. The wall starts out at 35ft of depth and continues down to 130ft. More gumboot sponges, cloud sponges, octopus dens, at this site. The substrate then slopes slowly down deeper for tech divers. At 140ft there is a bathtub guarded by rockfish.

Henderson Point: To dive here you have to arrive early, as parking space is limited. This is a series of wall dives that go down past 130 feet. A wide variety of animal life lives here, due to the step structure of the walls; Lingcod on big boulders, and cloud and boot sponges hanging on walls at deeper end. In the summer time the vis can get low and the lions mane jelly fish count can get high.

As for boat dives, some examples include:

Repulse Rock: It's a rock pinnacle where a seal colony likes to hang out. The sites other name is "The White Lady" from days when cloud sponges were abundant here. Now fewer cloud sponges remain here. Cloud sponges are extremely fragile, and the touch of a glove can tear off or kill a hundred years worth of growth. Several colonies have appendages that have died and turned gray and this is due to some other unknown factors. There are lots of orange plumose anemones at this site.

Christmas Point: A buoy marks the spot. A wall dive starts at 70-80ft down with cloud sponges at around 100ft. An intermediate to advanced dive.

McCurdy Point: Dive through a layer of fresh water from the nearby falls. Stones turn into fingers until about 90 ft then you've reached a wall. Cloud sponges are between 100 to 125ft depending on where you are diving. Wolf eels, rockfish, and nudibranchs are found here along with colorful pink coralline algae. Also look for the massive stairs on the adjacent shoreline that lead to nowhere in particular. There is a great video on You Tube displaying this dive site.

Senanus Island: A dive buoy marks the spot to tie up. This is the homeland of cloud sponges. Cloud sponges of every sort and size. They start down at 85-90ft. Not much else here, but a plethora of cloud sponges.

There are other islands and artificial reefs just outside the Saanich Inlet to explore. So plan on staying a few nights to catch a glimpse of the most popular local dive sites. You can stay at The Brentwood Bay Lodge & Spa and be right next to the Rockfish Marina and Rockfish Divers Charter Operations with their boat "Loup De Mer". There are bed and breakfast inns such as The Inlet Beach House near the deep cove dive site. There are larger places such as The Best Western Motel located closer to Butchart Gardens, the airport and Sydney. Dive charters can be found in Sydney such as the Sydney Dive and Surf. Even boats from Ogden Point Dive Center regularly make their way into the Saanich Inlet. In the wintertime the vis can reach over 100ft, the summertime with plankton blooms, not so much, until you descend 20-40ft below the surface. So when is the best time to visit the Saanich Inlet? Answer: Several times a year. Great Dives!

Ontario Canada
Pristine Fresh Water Wrecks

Ontario is blessed with four great lakes as beachfront properties. Each lake is enormous, each lake acts as an independent fresh water sea, and especially during storms, each lake has claimed many a ship. Before we get into which ships were sunk, a quick background of the lakes will make it easier to understand why the wrecks ended up where they did. Lake Michigan, Huron, and parts of Erie sit on top of a bowl of limestone that is hundreds of feet thick and formed a coral reef area some 385 million years ago. Salt dried up from this early time was covered over by sediment. At 1750 ft below the current surface lays 35% of the world's mined salt. Fresh water is kept out of this deposit by layers of limestone. On Thunder Bay Island, scientists have found remnants of prehistoric brain corals. Add to this, glaciers five times the size of what we previously thought possible, gouged their way through basins following the path of ancient rivers beds and formed deep ruts and deposited boulders from far away north. We know the glaciers did this at least ten separate times, and when melted, formed the existing lakes of Michigan, Huron, and Erie a mere 12,000 years ago. Ancient volcanoes on the other hand, formed Lake Superior and Ontario, and that's why **Lake Superior** has a basalt-lined basin that descends almost 1300ft deep. Therefore, dive sites in Lake Superior are mostly inaccessible to recreational divers. Two of the more well know wrecks include the *Gunilda* at 270ft deep and the *Edmond Fitzgerald* at 530ft deep.

 Lake Erie on the other hand has lots of recreational dive sites including: the 200ft long steamer the *Tonawanda* at 45ft, the 105ft long slightly broken up wooden barge The *Finch* at 45ft, the tug wreck *Wilma* at 70ft, the 143ft long *Dupuis No 10 barge* at 85ft, the 136ft long barquentine schooner the *CB Benson* at 78ft, the 4-masted iron steamer the *Brunswick* at 85-100ft. the 200ft long steamship *Niagara* at 90ft, the 104ft long schooner *Stone Wreck* in honor of the cargo at 90ft, the 154ft long schooner *Carlingford* at 95ft, the 136ft long wooden schooner *George C. Finney* at 100ft, and 190ft long wooden steamer is at 130ft of depth.

Lake Ontario has the 135ft long schooner *George A. Marsh* that went down to 85ft in 1917, the 175ft long *Comet* paddle wheel steamer that sunk in 1851 at 80ft, or the 144ft long steel ferry the *Wolf Islander II* scuttled in 1985the at 85ft near Kingston. Actually there are many wrecks just around the Kingston area. There is the *Graveyard* where retired ships were unceremoniously and deliberately dumped. Other vessels include the *Munson, Frontenac, Effie Mae, Aloha,* and the *Cornwall..* Oh, and you'll need a permit to dive the Toronto Harbour. Even before you get to Kingston you'll have to stop in Picton and Prince Edward County for there are many a schooner that went down around the Main Duck Islands and Prince Edward Bay, such as the *City of Sheboygan.*

Moving on to the mother load of diving, we go to **Lake Huron** and **Tobermory**; the site of **Fathom Five National Park** on the Bruce Peninsula. This area is home to dozens of ships that couldn't make the final stretch to port. Here you can dive around the islands to do wall dives such as *Pablo's Hangover* or *North Otter Wall.* You can dive through two less than 15ft long passages into a 20ft deep grotto/pool area normally accessible only to hikers. The local natural erosion scenery includes what appear to be giant vases around *Flower Pot Island.* The wrecks of Tobermory include: the 1884 wreck of the three-masted barque *Arabia* at 110ft, the 1905 wreck of the freighter *Forest city* at 70-154ft, the *Caroline Rose, Sweepstakes, City of Grand Rapids, Minch,* and other various ships and tugs.

Following the course of the four Great Lakes, Ontario has the **St. Lawrence River** to dive into. **Brockville** used to be known for it's Ribfeast in August, but perhaps because of the fact that Zebra mussels have cleared up the river so much, divers have now found thousands of wrecks and thousands of islands along this stretch of fresh water. Check out the article on Brockville in Northeast Dive News by Rick Stratton to find out more about the *Lillie Parsons,* the *Musccallonge,* the *Henry C. Daryaw,* the *Keystorm,* the *Robert Gaskin,* the *Kingston,* the

Conestoga, the *A.E. Vickery*, the *America*, and the 140ft wooden drill scow *John B King* that sunk in 1930 after lightening set off some dynamite charges.

Ontario has lots of smaller lakes such as **Lake Simcoe** north of Toronto and east of **Barrie**, is used for ice diving in the winter and divers shore dive off of *Big Bay Point* and *Jackson Point* in the not so winter. The wreck of the paddleboat *J.C. Morison* is just off downtown Barrie.

Many divers use the quarries such as *Innerkip* near Toronto, *Sherkston Quarry*, and *Windmill Point Park* at Ridgeway. For a good drift dive, divers jump in the *Niagara River* up by Fort Erie. Uh, you get out way before the falls. **Barge X** is also in the Niagara River. Eastern Ontario has a few other dive locations that you may wish to consider.

Cris Kohl has several books out: *Dive Ontario*! 1995 or *The 100 Best Great Lake Shipwrecks* should be enough to get you started on your journey of exploring Ontario Canada. Keep in mind cold waters and thermo clines are available year long in some locations and 7ml or dry suits are the preferred fashion ensembles of the day. Ask the local dive shops and charters about local dive conditions both well in advance, and again just before you plan to dive.

Even 30 years ago, one of my friends from Cleveland, Ohio used to drive up here with the *Aqua Amigos* dive club to Tobermory via Michigan and Sault Ste. Marie as an annual event. Now, even more divers from New York, Pennsylvania, Illinois, and Maine have heard about the great visibility and diving up north and frequently legally cross the border packed with scuba gear and cash to support the local economies, and all for a chance to see some wrecks of which some are in pristine condition with cups and teapots still resting on tables or tools laying on work benches as if the day before the vessel went down. Other wrecks are the poster child of what massive power Mother Nature can bring forth at will and whimsy with china thrown about kitchens willy-nilly or buried in silt. All of the above make Ontario an awesome place to dive. Great Dives.

Mexico

Cozumel

Can you name an island continuously voted one of the top five destination values in the world? How about an island where a marine preserve ensures a never-ending plethora of fish and invertebrates? What about an island that hurricanes brush within 60 miles at least once every three or so years, yet this island has been a major tourist destination for the past 1500 years? If your first thought was Cozumel, then you may have just won a free ride on a sea horse (saddle not included).

The Mayans first set up Cozumel as a tourist destination around 300 A.D.; the same time the Romans were securing everlasting peace in the Middle East. For those in the Yucatan peninsula, a trip to the *Island of Swallows* and a pilgrimage to the temple of Ixchel (Goddess of Fertility) greatly enhanced one's chance of having offspring. Even today it could be reasoned that just walking hand in hand along Cozumel's beautiful sandy beaches increases one's chance of fertility.

So the Mayans visited and made pilgrimages until the early 1500's when the Spanish gave them an offer they couldn't refuse. It seems that for all the gold the Mayans really didn't need anyway, the Spanish were willing to trade Christianity, indentured slavery, and a healthcare plan that included a liberal deadly dose of small pox.

It's not surprising that some of the Mayans resisted such a tempting offer and with the aid of Gonzalo Guerro, a Spanish sailor, the Mayans, for a while, were able to strategically resist Spanish gracious intentions. In honor of Guerro the sailor, this type of diplomatic resistance was re-spelled and called Guerilla warfare. Eventually with the majority of the gold safely back in Spain and the majority of the local population wiped out by what could be termed germ warfare, the Spanish pretty much moved on to greener pastures and other gold bearing populaces in need of religious conversion.

From the 1500's until the invention of the regulator, Cozumel endured a deep downturn in tourism. Today tourists no longer arrive with ceremonial clay pots to drop in *Cenotes* (Holy Wells), but with masks, snorkels, fins, and beach towels. With the notoriety of *Palancar Reef* just minutes off shore, Cozumel is currently a thriving Mecca for scuba diving tourists. Some say it's easier to count the number of fish on the reef than it is to count the number of dive shops on the beaches, and the $5 or so fee tourists pay to dive the protected reef system ensures this scenario will continue for years to come.

Boat diving off Cozumel is strictly drift diving. It's a typical gentle drift that takes mere seconds to master and moves divers along at a slow leisurely pace. On *Palancar Reef* you can theoretically pass by a mile of reef attractions without moving your arms or kicking with your fins even once. I say theoretically, because you can't help exploring tunnels, passage ways, drop offs, walls, and other irresistible reef formations. These are the locations where spiny lobsters congregate, docile nurse sharks take a quick siesta, where sea turtles and stingrays glide by, and 6inch hermit crabs feel invincible: Formal dive site names include: Santa Rosa Wall, the Caves, Horse Shoe, La Francesca, and The Bricks.

Shallow dive sites less than 60ft in depth sustained damage from hurricane Wilma in 2005, especially areas with soft growths and finger coral, but in as little as 10 months after the hurricane evidence of coral growth was noted everywhere. It seems that hurricanes do for reefs what naturally occurring fires do for forests; they make way for a new generation of species to propagate. On the other hand, hurricanes take dive wrecks like the 40 seat DC3 resting right in front of La Cieba Beach Hotel and help to break apart the apparition a little more with each passing tempest making sites like this best to dive sooner rather than later.

There's a new wreck in Cozunel that's starting to attrack marine life. I predict that the Felipe Xicotencatl C-53, a former 190ft U.S minesweeper will become a major attraction once the corals take hold.

One attraction that you must see if you are into wildlife is the dolphin and human swimming pool at Chakanaab State Park. The adjacent Chakanaab Reef is another good spot to play name that fish and take pictures of flamingo tongue snails.

You need three days to see most of the local dive sites, but at least one day should be reserved for a short forty minute ferry ride to Playa Del Carmen and a visit to the Mayan relics and Cenotes.

When it comes to accommodations, it's hard to beat an all-inclusive resort such as the Occidental Allegro Resort on San Francisco Beach. There are several boat dives each day, an onsite dive shop, 3 restaurants to choose from,(Spanish, Italian, or Buffet style), plus all you can drink adult beverages while you are working on your tan next to one of the swimming pools or beach. The only problem with this hotel is that you may not want to ever leave. I had to pry myself away and skip a lunch just to go down town San Miguel for the day to shop and practice Spanish. The Allegro caters to tennis players and time-share owners too.

The Scuba Club Cozumel is a meal inclusive dive resort that has great reviews by divers; some who have been annual guests for the last 18 plus years. They have two restaurants including the Fat Grouper Grill, 7 dive boats, a 5 star PADI store (Scuba-Cozumel Dive Store), Wireless on site, and they really seem to be dedicated to divers. If obtaining free drinks isn't really a priority, but a diver friendly atmosphere is, Scuba Club Cozumel just might be your first choice.

Hotel Cozumel & Resort is all-inclusive and kids stay, play, and eat free. They have 3 restaurants, 3 bars, 2 hot tubs, child entertainment, and if that isn't enough, it's a 10-minute walk to down town. So if you have kids on deck or a spouse that would rather shop than plop in the warm water, you have covered all bases here. Hotel Cozumel & Resort uses the services of Dive Paradise (the largest independent dive fleet operation on the island boasting over 80 instructors. Fiesta Americana Cozumel Dive Resort is another hotel worth considering if you need a kids club, a bubble maker program, and activities for all family members. The fact is that there are enough hotels, on/off site dive shops, and independent dive charter operations to fill a phone book. Each of the hotels are just slightly different and unique, meaning there is at least one hotel that will fit your particular needs, and when it comes to dive operations, just remember that it's a good idea to check and see how many divers they take out at one time, size of the boat, how often they go out, and basically what's all included in the price of the dive as it all can vary between operations.

The water temp is 77-84°F depending on the time of year so just about anytime is a good time to visit. Hurricanes may alter shallow water habitats, but over all, Cozumel is still a great place to dive. On land, the locals appear to continue to put all their efforts and resources into amenities and accommodations for tourists. Perhaps this is why if a hurricane hits the island resorts, they rebuild immediately, yet, all those Mayan archeological sites are still in ruins. Either way, Cozumel has become the land of vacationing scuba divers and one of the top destinations for value hunters.

Cruising Down To Cabo San Lucas

I'd never been on a cruise before and I thought it might prove to be a good alternative way to take a 3yr old child on a vacation and still be able to get a few dives in along the way. Right up front I have to say that my daughter loved going on the cruise, attending camp carnival, and playing with all the other kids. Knowing what I know now, I think that the perfect age for a child to bring aboard a cruise is 8yrs old or above. The younger children tend to go to bed early, and unless you play tag team evenings out, you'll miss out on most of the adult evening events and nighttime activities, but whether you have children or not, a cruise might be a worthwhile experience.

Our particular Carnival cruise out of San Diego included one day in Cabo San Lucas and one day in Ensenada. I signed up for a certified diver two-tank excursion out of Cabo several months before the date of departure. The price of signing up for an excursion through the cruise line is more than if you just walked into *Underwater Diversions Dive Center,* in Cabo, but for the added price they had someone waiting for us on the dock ready to escort us to the dive shop. Because of a medical emergency stop in Ensenada, we we're two hours late arriving in Cabo, but when you are part of the cruise package, tour operators stand by until you arrive. Also as part of the cruise package everything is provided for you except for swimming attire. Upon entering the dive shop you sign some forms then the shop employees go in the rental room and bring out everything you'll need for the dive. They have you try on a (short-leg, long-sleeve) 3ml wet suit, buoyancy control device, fins, and mask. They pile all this on a cart along with tanks and regulators and off you go half way back along the U shaped harbor to board a dive boat.

Personally, I can't go anywhere without my basic snorkeling gear. But since you have to travel by plane or car just to get to San Diego to start the cruise you may have to limit what you take with you. If storage wasn't an issue I would have brought my Hydrooptix mask in it's case, but because of limited space I brought a frameless mask that I could stuff anywhere. One diver brought a large 20yr old mask, because that was his longtime favorite. I brought my own snorkel too because if there was any time to snorkel around afterwards or between dives, I wanted my Kapitol Reef which increases your air exchange while reducing your respiration rate more than any other dry snorkel currently on the market. For fins I brought a pair of Foil Force Fins. They weigh half as much as conventional or knock off brands of split fins, they were invented for long distance swims, and they easily fit in airline regulation size onboard roller bags. Hey, 3lbs could be all it takes to put a checked bag over the maximum allowed weight limit and that's just one fin with some manufacturers. The other reason why I like Force Fins is because with each kick they are literally *forced* on to your feet. Because of their recovery ability, (when they spring back into the natural curved shape), these fins actually push you through the water both on the up and down stroke. I know you've heard other manufactures say this too, but just undo the heel strap and kick with your current fin. If they fall off with the first few kicks as most brands do, you know that you are doing all the work for the fin. With Force fins, I've gone half a dive before someone's pointed out to me that my heel strap wasn't in place. Because force fins constantly work for you, (not the other way around), you could say that heal straps become a redundant artifact. I could go on and tell you also that the open toe configuration of force fins help reduce potential cramps, but you get the drift. Small powerful lightweight fins are the best type of fin to take on a trip and you could get by with full foot fins, but I like booties in case of rugged shore diving or sidewalk entrances even if booties take longer to dry before you pack them up to go home. In addition, you may want to take along a small knife, a small dive light to look in the crevices, and a wrist mounted dive computer comes in handy at decompression stops, but all the rest of the gear is not worth carrying with you for a few hours of diving on a five day cruise. The rental gear works just fine.

On this day there were just three of us from the cruise ship joined by Captain Chamara and Polo our divemaster. We took a short boat ride over to the right hand side of the bay and did two dives fairly close to each other. Polo gave a good briefing before each dive and He along with Captain Chamara helped us get ready for the dives.

On our first dive we went to **Neptune's Finger**. Hear we were greeted underwater by tons of big fish. Sand was running off the slopes and forming underwater sand falls. Schools of goatfish waited patiently for specks of food to tumble out into plain view. There was lots of soft coral at this sight and at least one puffer fish around every rock. Polo found a large stonefish blending in with the rest of the substrate. It was a nice dive, but not too spectacular.

The second dive was a few propeller spins away at **Pelican Rock**. This dive site near a Pelican rest area had tons of big fish and macro creatures. Polo descended and immediately pointed at a frogfish hiding behind a soft coral. I didn't see the fish until I closely examined the photos back on the cruise ship. Polo also pointed out an octopus wedged in a crevice while holding small stones in front of his tentacles so he could blend in with the reef; talk about intelligent life forms. We found several species of eels here including one big green moray as well as spotted and zebra eels too. Hundreds of tiny blue neon fish hung around a few big boulders. Polo pointed to one of the several fish that looked and floated like small leafs and we watched as it darted under the sand for safety. I thought that this site was hot with action and plenty to see for several dives to come. There are some other dive sites farther out where you can see hammerhead sharks, pinnacles, and whale sharks, but they will have to wait another day. Oh, and before I forget, if you want to do any UW photography bring a strobe or two, because the day I was there visibility was down to 30ft; where two days prior it was around 100ft. And if you bring strobes, bring a power outlet strip too, as there may be only one outlet in your ship's cabin.

After the dives, Polo and Chamara dropped us off back at the dock, which gave us plenty of time to shop, dine, or go back to the cruise ship. The only thing required to get back and forth from the cruise ship was a piece of photo id and our cruise ship room card. I went back on board to find my wife and she told be my daughter was busy coloring cruise shirts and playing with the other kids and their (assigned by age) activity directors, so my wife and I went back off the ship via the tenders (small motor boats) and shopped and walked some more around Cabo San Lucas.

The diving portion of the cruise went by fast, but I have to admit that it was definitely worth the effort. Taking a cruise is a great option for parents who dive and also have older kids. This way you can enjoy the nightly shows, fine dining, gambling, and other adult oriented events. Just remember to budget some $800 more than the cruise price for incidentals such as adult beverages, mandatory gratuities, and duty-free. Plus bring a spare roller bag for packing gifts and souvenirs. One reason why so many people like cruises is that there is no added hotel fee, daily restaurant fees, and car rental fees; it's all-inclusive except for adult beverages. You may still have a taxi or shore excursion to pay for, but that's strictly up to you as it would be with any land adventure. So a cruise may be a viable option and your ticket to traveling with or without children and still fitting in a dive in here or there. Now that I've done the cruise to Cabo San Lucas, my only problem is wondering when I can return to Cabo to dive and explore even more. I hear the *Nautilus Explorer* hangs out here between trips to Revillagegedos and Socorro Island; perhaps joining one of their cruises is the next logical step on a quest to continue diving these warm southern waters. Great dives.

WORLD WIDE HOT SPOTS

Bon Dia Bonaire

As a pale dive instructor in the Pacific Northwest, students step up and ask you all kinds of questions, and when they ask me what's my favorite place to dive and take photographs in the Caribbean, I answer without skipping a heart beat "Bonaire." Bonaire is part of the Dutch Antilles just some 50 miles north of Venezuela, 30 miles east of Curacao, and 68 miles from Aruba. Bonaire may not have the busy nightlife of Grand Cayman or the ancient Mayan ruins of Cozumel, but Bonaire has the oldest marine park system and that means lots of fish and other macro sea creatures who have grown up in a world void of spear guns and who view divers as a passing curiosity and not something to run and hide from.

The waters of Bonaire are teaming with protected sea life from Pilot whales down to sea horses. A marine park orientation at 9am where you learn first hand about local conservation efforts, fill out a form or two, and pay a $25 annual dive park tag fee is first on the list of things to do before you can go diving here. After the orientation you do a fun, yet required, shore dive, then you're allowed unlimited access to Bonaire's national park waters which start at the high tide line and go down to 200ft all around the island. The shore dive is really just to make sure you are not over weighted and will not accidentally plummet down and harm the fringing reefs full of elegant yet fragile corals. This dive is also a good time to check out and make sure your gear is still working properly and you have enough weight so you don't just float on the surface while watching everyone else dip beneath the surface and swim around the corals. We used this orientation dive to follow a rope down a coral laden slope and swim around the 35ft wreck called the *Machaca*. The boat is filled with coral colonies and small fish to photograph. This was our first dive and we already had spotted a Fingerprint cowry. We continued on and followed the rope down to 113ft; the rope continued another 27ft before ending near another small wreck. We planned to go down to 100ft, but with the water so warm and clear we were surprised that we had already made it down so deep. The water was 81°F and the vis was 80-100ft.

Before I forget, the park fee collected is used by members of CURO (the Council of Underwater Resort Operators of Bonaire) in conjunction with STINAPA and the Bonaire Marine Park to install new mooring buoys and maintain buoys where a single boat can tie up without disturbing local reef inhabitants; a system first pioneered by Captain Don Stewart back in 1962; currently there are over 70 permanent buoys. The Bonaire Marine Park is so well organized and operated that when I devised my own P.A.D.I approved Marine Reserve Specialty course for divers in Washington State at Edmonds Underwater Park, I based much of my course outline on Bonaire.

Great numbers of fish and beautiful reefs are only part of the overall advantages to diving Bonaire. The island has some 100 painted and numbered rocks positioned along the roadsides designating that this is a great place to pullover and do a shore dive. Using a guide map or book, you can look up the rock number and see what the dive site is called or perhaps get an insight as to what you will find at a specific dive.

Caution, Hotels and Charter boat operations can keep you fairly busy, so it may be difficult to squeeze time in for extra shore dives. Sometimes the roadside dive sites and the boat buoys converge and you'll see divers coming from shore and divers jumping off a boat all heading for the same dive site. "**Oil Slick**" is one such dive site. Reef ledges make this area a great spot for turtles (usually hawksbill or loggerhead) to rest against and Caribbean squids love to hover above gorgonian corals in search of pry or just to e-mail one another via awesome displays of chromatic body color changes. **Oil Slick** was named after a number of cars and trucks couldn't quite make the sharp turn in the road in wet weather conditions and ended up on a short sea cruise. You won't find any cars at this dive site, but if you're looking for horsepower, check out the base of coral branches for red, yellow, or brown sea horses.

Just a few minutes boat ride away is the small-uninhabited island of Klein Bonaire. You may see flying fish or the resident school of porpoise who circle Bonaire Island just about once a day. Turtles lay eggs just under the surface of the small sandy beaches of Klein Bonaire. Some of the dive sites here were barely touched by the last hurricane. Traditionally, Bonaire and Klein Bonaire are below the hurricane belt, which makes them a great haven for divers year round. We saw lots of seahorses out here at the dive site **Mi Dushi**, once the Divemaster pointed out what to look for. We also saw hundreds of flamingo tongue shells, yellow arrow crabs, and pederson shrimp. On a night dive nearby at **Bon Ventura** we saw spanish and slipper lobster, a caribbean reef octopus, spotted eels, lettuce sea slugs, and heart urchins that looked like hairy coconuts plowing through the sand.

One dive site you hear a lot about is the town pier. Fifteen feet under the dock there are a lot of small creatures and corals and you might even see a frog fish, but you'll first have to get permission from the Harbor Master to dive this site as the harbor can be a busy place for both boats as well as divers. I spoke to an Italian tourist couple that did a night dive here and they really liked it.

If you are in to wreck diving, the 230ft *Hilma Hooker* at about 100ft depth is a great place to dive, but the nearby mushroom caped coral reefs may compete for your attention. There are many other well-known and marked dive sites in the neighboring vicinity accessible by land or sea. From this area you can see the salt evaporation flats and a salt conveyor belt that juts out into the sea.

For shallow water diving and snorkeling you'll have to try a day at the park and swim through the elkhorn or staghorn coral at the Washington–Slagbaai National Park.

On the surface, you'll find small stores and towns with friendly natives who may speak English, Dutch, Spanish, or the local all-inclusive language called Papamiento. The capital city Kralendijk is a colorful boldly Dutch painted town with many tourist destinations, gift shops, open-air bars and restaurants including at least one ice cream and one pizza parlor. The local food is the culmination of many nations and goes well with Dutch beer.

There are many hotels that cater to divers and some hotels such as Captain Don's Habitat can keep you so busy with shore dives and boat dives, that you may never get a chance to rent a car and visit the roadside dive sites. I do recommend renting a car for at least a day though; to tour the small towns, pass by a small herd of wild donkeys, or to stop and watch at the iguana crossings. Other activities you might want to try include mangrove kayaking, caving, or limestone cliff rope climbing. The ride to Washington Park is very picturesque, but you'll need 4-wheel drive to enter the park for the day.

Two hotels I highly recommend are Captain Don's Habitat for the ultimate dive experience with three dive boats and multiple dive destinations to choose from each day, or Buddy Dive Resort which now boasts a fleet of five boats and is located adjacent to Captain Don's Habitat. There are several other great resorts on the island, but these two resorts are located a few feet from great short diving, both have friendly staffs, good food and more.

A couple of reminders: voltage is 127v 50hz so some appliances may run hot. A $10 dollar departure fee is collected at the airport before departure.

I can't say enough good things about Bonaire; perhaps that's why you have to show your return ticket upon entry into the country. Otherwise, I might have purchased a one-way fare and stayed forever. I often wonder what it would be like to be a dive instructor with a great tan.

Captain Don's Habitat

We arrived late in the evening at Captain Don's Habitat on the Island of Bonaire. We had to change planes three times to arrive direct from Seattle. After a few minutes of checking in and tossing our bags in a clean and updated air-conditioned room, we went straight for Rum Runners restaurant; we were starving. When you go to Captain Don's you have try the salmon, spinach, and blue cheese pizza. Drinking cold Dutch beer, eating outstanding pizza, and sitting at a table near the ocean surf with a breathtaking view of the sunset is the perfect way to wind down after a long flight and officially start one's vacation.

Back home several divers told me that if you ever get a chance you have to go to Bonaire and stay at Captain Don's Habitat. I have to admit that the home of "Diving Freedom" is a very well organized operation. Full scuba tanks are lined up near the dive shop and you are free to take one anytime you like day or night. A perfect shore dive is just a few steps away. Next to the entry and exit points are a large rinse station and a locker room area (bring your own lock or buy one from the shop) and outdoor showers to rinse off. I should mention that they also offer dive courses and instruction up to and including actual dives using Draeger Rebreathers.

You can snorkel near shore and take pictures of southern stingrays, peacock flounders, and silvery tarpon. By diving down to 30ft you can shine a light in a reef ledge and spot spiny lobster. With total diving freedom you can be a non-stop diving machine, or you can just kick back and relax at the Deco Stop Bar, or work feverishly at becoming a really tanned reclining recluse.

We actually got to meet Captain Don Stewart at the welcome party that they hold weekly for new arriving guests. Captain Don was one of the early pioneers in reef conservation. Because of him and other people and organizations that followed in his footsteps, Bonaire is surrounded by an unparalleled marine park system with over 350 species of fish

and invertebrate species waiting for your arrival. Captain
Don's crew can take you out to the dive sites on one of three
roomy pro-42 dive boats, which as far as I'm concerned are the
ultimate warm water dive boats. Each guest is given a dive
number, and you sign up for daily boat dives by placing your
assigned number next to any of the dive sites listed on that
day's schedule of events. The boat dives are so much fun that
it's easy to forget to rent a jeep and drive to some of the 100
shore dive sites.

The resort staff was friendly and the dive staff went out of their
way to make sure everyone had a good time. The pizza never
tasted quite as good as it did that first evening, but that might
be because it had to compete with baby back ribs, and fresh
catch of the day the rest of our stay. If you are fond of diving,
then you'll enjoy Captain Don's Habitat. If you love diving,
then one trip to Captain Don's will never be enough to satisfy
your passion; another trip back will definitely have to be
planned.

Cayman Islands

In 1503 on the last voyage of Columbus the crew spotted two islands that they promptly named the *Tortugas* after the resident population of turtles. In 1523 the name of the islands was changed to *Lagartos* in honor of the abundant saltwater alligators. By 1530 the name was changed to *Caymanas* after the Carib Indian word for crocodile. You won't find any Caymanas any longer in the currently called Cayman Islands. It seems that Sir Francis drake, in 1586, mentioned to some quite ravenous sailors that the Caymans were edible and now, along with notable pirates and Dodo birds, the saltwater reptiles are just a footnote in history. You may not find any *Caymanas* on the islands, but you will find plenty of Iguanas, 120 species of birds, and millions of photogenic fish.

The Cayman Islands geographically are the three exposed summits of the Cayman ridge. Bordering the north and west sides of the islands is the Yucatan Basin. On the south and east sides of the islands lies the deep Cayman trench. The steep drop off below the surface into the deep trench and basin gives the Caymans some of the best wall dives in the world. Some walls start in as little as 25ft underwater and drop down 1000's of feet. Each of the Islands has is own famous wall dives and with over a 100ft of visibility there's a lot to see on any dive. Terms like walls, pinnacles, sand chutes, arches, tunnels, canyons, grooves, spurs, and caves, cover the dive site maps.

Grand Cayman, where over 90% of the local people live, has 220 moored dive boat sites in addition to a plethora of shore dive sites. Grand Cayman is also home of Hell; a limestone formation of jagged rock where postcards can be sent from . . . you know where. On the other end of the island is the famous sea turtle farm, soon to be renamed *Boatswain's Beach*, a marine adventure park. Along *Seven Mile Beach* you will find the major shopping areas for passengers from port calling cruise ships and local hotel and resort guests.

Cayman Brac is 70 miles away from the main island and is home of *Bloody Wall*. Along this elongated structure was a major pirate battle a few centuries ago. People still search the caves in the Island's 140ft tall bluffs just to make sure the pirates such as Blackbeard and Edward Teach didn't leave any Spanish gold pieces of eight behind.

Little Cayman is 5 miles from Cayman Brac and is home of the famous *Anchor Wall*, the Russian destroyer *Tibbits*, and a world-class bird sanctuary. The island's highest point is only 40ft above sea level. Just over 100 people live permanently on the island so it's the perfect spot to unwind from the rest of humanity, do some great diving, and just relax.

The Cayman Islands are very distinct. The population is just over a total of 44,000 people yet the Islands have 40,000-registered businesses and 600 banks. Not only is the average income over $35,000 and the language English, but also the locals are friendly. In addition you'll meet lots of (loving the sun) Canadians working here in the dive industry. The Cayman dollar is worth $1.25 US and the locals seem to take either currency as well as credit cards. Taxi drivers don't seem to mind wet dive gear (I always ask first) and they are so easy to hire that you may never get around to renting a car and driving on the left side of the road. Water temp is between 77-82F and I recommend taking a 3ml wet suit with you. Not only does a 3ml keep you warm at the end of the week when you are finally adapting to the local climate, but also it protects your skin from sunburn and jellyfish or other such wandering creatures. The electricity is 110/60 so bring all your camera and electrical gear. Some resorts have free Internet service. There are big and small dive shops all over the islands so if you forget something, chances are you can buy or rent it there. The Costco Kirkland brand of batteries seems to be everywhere too. You'll need a passport coming from the U.S.A., $13 for a departure Fee, and roundtrip airfare. It takes 1.5 hours flight time from Miami and 2.5 hours from Houston on Cayman Airways.

Sunset House, Grand Caymans
Going the extra mile to make divers smile☺

On Grand Cayman Island there is a dive resort "for divers by divers and is known world wide as Sunset House. A group of us from the local dive shop booked a trip to Grand Caymans, but I couldn't wait to set fin in warm water so I flew off two days ahead of the rest of the group. I arrived late at night and by the next morning I had signed up for two days of boat diving. Sunset House has five dive boats that they rotate according to the dive destination in mind. I think over the course of the week I dove off every boat, but I would have to say that the 45ft *Manta,* which they use routinely on the north and east coast of the island, is my favorite boat.

The very first dive I went on was called *"Hole in the Wall."* This site is 110 feet deep, but the water is so clear that at that depth you can still see the boat floating on the surface. A group of us went up inside a naturally formed tunnel and came out at 60ft of depth to a sandy area where small fish, corals, sea fans, and assorted invertebrates waited to have their picture taken. This location is a great Multi-level dive site.

The wreck of the *Oro Verde*, 52ft deep, made a great secondary dive site. Hundreds of Garden eels watched us from their sandy homes as we glided over towards the wreck. Schools of fish swam through the wreck while a few Great barracuda monitored their movements from stationary positions not too far away. This first day of diving was awesome, but over the week I was impressed time and again with the sea life from the huge silvery Tarpon fish, goliath Jewfish, and abundant Green Sea Turtles, down to the artistically captivating allure of the Fingerprint shell. One day of diving here was all it really took to put this Island in my top ten list of places to dive in the Caribbean.

You hear a lot about great dive destinations, but what set this dive adventure apart from the rest was the resort staff I met. From the moment I got on the dive boat they remembered my name and made me feel like a long lost friend. From that point on whether I was walking to or from the boats or just going over to "My Bar" for a quick snack between dives, one of the staff members was always calling out "Hi Mike", and you know what, it wasn't long before I was greeting them back by calling out their names too. I bring this point up not only because I felt welcomed at Sunset House, but also because of what happened next.

After two days of great diving, the rest of my group was arriving on the island. Three people of the group were significant others that I had never met before. That afternoon I was walking over to Cathy Churches photography studio, which is located in the main area of the Sunset hotel, to pick up a video copy of the dive I went on the previous day. I had accompanied a group of divers to *Stingray City* where we all in a circle on a sandy bottom at 15ft and hand fed Southern Stingrays pieces of fish by hand. Twenty to thirty Stingrays of various sizes glided around us in search of food. I once saw 55 million year old fossils of their ancestors at an airport exhibit. Stingrays have changed very little over time except that these stingrays were very smart. Some where down the history line they have discovered that if they nibble on the head of a woman with long flowing hair, there is a good chance that she will suddenly release all the fish food she is holding in the palm of her hand. The stingrays then swoop to the point of food releasement and gobble down the free-floating pieces of fish.

While we fed stingrays and touched their skin, which felt like wet mushrooms, one of the staff members videoed our adventure. It was for a copy of that video that I was now strolling over to Cathy Church's studio to purchase. As I turned the corner of the building I heard a "Hi Mike" from one of the staff members so I called back a hello with his name. Some 30ft away a tall attractive blonde watched as the two of us casually returned greetings. I saw that she was standing next to a friend of mine from the dive shop back home. He was distracted by their luggage and didn't notice me until I called out. "Can I help you?" He looked at me and asked me if I knew where his room was located. I said, "It's right over there." And pointed in the general direction of a little pathway then added, "How are you John?" as I shook his hand. "Do you know him?" The lady in question asked John as she looked from him to me. "This is Mike Hughes, he's part of the group." "No he isn't. He works here." She replied. She thought we were trying to put one over on her. John laughed and I smiled, but deep down I did wish I worked at Sunset House. It took her a few seconds before I could convince her that I truly was part of John's and her dive group.

I felt right at home the minute I arrived at Sunset House. The diving was great and so were the dive staff. I recommend Sunset House to all my friends and dive students and there are many a day when I wear my red souvenir Sunset dive staff T-shirt and wish I was back again diving the Cayman Islands.

Saint Somewhere
9 Saintly Dive Destinations

To start with, if you've never been to the Caribbean, then I highly recommend setting this article aside and leaving on the next space available flight. Divers who visit the Caribbean on a regular basis may have told you about reef sharks, barracuda, snapper, grunts, porgies, chubs, tangs, parrot fish, puffer fish, file fish, and so much more. It's an eye opening experience when you come face to face with painted animals such as the orange and white spotted Gaudy Clown Crab, Thor anemone shrimp, or the purple and white spotted anemone shrimp. The neon blue azure vase sponge looks surreal, squids radiate seemingly electrified color shows, and the whale shark with thousands of small teeth inside a massive 10 ft wide mouth, 50ft long white spotted and lined brownish gray body, and 5ft tall dorsal fin just looks humongous. As you gain a few dives under your belt you soon find that you're able to point out the blue spotted peacock flounder, tongue cowry shells with their leopard spotted mantles clinging to purple gorgonian sea fans, and with a little more developed observational skills you'll see seahorses and frog fish clinging to corals and rocks. At first it took local divemasters to point these creatures out to me. As you become familiar with the fish species, you'll find that some fish look like different species, but in fact, they are the same species, just the same fish at different stages in life. Drum fish only have a few stripes across their body as juveniles, but have spots and extra faded brown-black lines as adults. French angle fish as adults are gray oval shaped fish with tiny yellow spots, while juveniles are triangular gray fish with yellow stripes. Who would have thought that they were even remotely related?

The Caribbean diving encompasses more than the incredible creatures and sometimes you need a quick peek, or a small sample, before you can select which island may have the best suitable diving for your particular needs and desires and that is why I've compiled this loose list of 9 islands. Whether your favorite dive fetish is wall dives, wreck dives, photography, boat dives, or pristine shore dives, one of these saintly islands should not only satisfy your diving needs, but it's probably calling out to you right now.

Saint Croix: Let's start with the "American Paradise" United States Virgin Islands (USVI), which consists of St Croix, St Thomas, and St John. St Croix, 28 miles long and 7 miles wide is the largest of these 3 islands as well as home to a spectacular 7-mile long wall dive. Off of Cane Bay you can start at as little as 20ft of depth and descend down to some 3200ft. Columbus discovered this island in 1493, which must have been quite a surprise to the local Carib natives. We, the USA, bought it from the Danish in 1917 for $25 million and a promise to keep the waters safe from Axis maritime aggression. When not diving the wall or the town pier in Frederiksted, visit the old Whim Plantation or the dungeon at the 1794 fort above Christiansted. The steeple Building has a good exhibit on Carib and Arawak Indians. Off shore and great for snorkeling, is the Buck Island Reef National Monument. For those that want to relax, you can't beat a bar on the Cane Bay beachfront that literally is called "Off the Wall". I should add that liveaboards such as the Nekton vessel "Rorqual" travel around St Croix too.

St Thomas is for wreck divers. It's home to the *Miss Opportunity,* a 350ft long Hospital ship, the *W.I.T Shoal*, a 400ft freighter sunk in 80ft of water and a dozen other last century wrecks. It's amazing how fast coral and sea life can take over a sunken ship. St Thomas and St John are both just 40 miles north of St Croix.

St John: 3 miles east of St Thomas 2/3 of this island is national park area. With plenty of offshore rocks, shoals, and cays, you'll find 30-70ft deep dive locations everywhere. *Cow and Calf Rocks* are notable as swim through sites. The main attraction out here however, is not even in the USVI, but over in the British Virgin Islands. You can take an all day boat trip over to Salt Island. This is the home of the 1867 wreck *RMS Rhone.* This iron hull royal mail steamer ship is not famous because it tried to out run a storm that turned out to be a late season hurricane, nor is it famous because only 23 of the 146 onboard survived the event, the main reason it is so popular is that the wreck was the setting for the movie "The Deep." If you look towards the bow, 75ft deep, you will see the hatch that Jacqueline Bisset swam thru wearing not much more than a scuba tank and a wet tee shirt. The Rhone originally broke into two pieces, but the Royal Navy decided the stern section at 20ft of depth was a maritime hazard so they blew it up in the late 1950's . . . so much for historical preservation. The 15ft wide brass propeller sits on the bottom looking up at the surface. Checkerboard pattern tiles lie where once stood a galley, and wrenches are still encrusted in their original secured compartment. The nearest Tee shirt is back at the dive shop.

St Kitts: 400 years of European ships fighting in the bays and surrounding offshore waters has left this island with some of the oldest wrecks in the Caribbean. If you want to dive and see encrusted cannons, cannon balls, plates, uniform buttons, and other artifacts, this is the island for you. *Coconut Tree Reef*: 40-200ft, *Black Coral Reef*: 40-70ft, the 144ft long *River Taw* Wreck, and *The Caves* of Nevis Island at 40ft with swim thrus and grottos are just some of the other attractions waiting for you to experience. On land, Brimstone Hill Fortress has plenty of dry historical artifacts. Depending on the time of year you may see 6ft long 1300lb leatherback turtles come ashore at Barry's Beach to lay clutches of oversized white ping-pong ball like eggs in the sand.

St Martin/St Marteen: is home of the 1800 British man-o-war wreck *HMS Proselyte* in 50ft of water with 13 encrusted cannons. Other dives include *The Maze:* a swim thru, *Moon Hole:* a crater 20ft below the surface that opens up to 60ft of depth with walls, open corridors, and caves. *One Step Beyond*: is 2 pinnacles at 70ft. Wrecks include the *Gregory* at 55ft and the *Fu Shen* at 120ft. there are also many other reefs as well as the artificial reef created by the remnants of the old Simpson Bridge. One of the popular dives is the *Shark Awareness Dive* at *Big Mamas Reef*. Here you can sit at 55ft of depth and watch trained professionals feed big Mama and her sharp-toothed cartilaginous cousins.

On the surface this island has been co-habited and co-governed by the Dutch and French for the past 350yrs. They literally drew a line through the island and one side is Dutch with the capital of Phillipsburg, 120volt/60cycle electrical current, and uses Netherlands Antilles Florins as well as US dollars as monetary currency. On the other side we have streets right out of Paris with the capital of Marigot, 220volt/50cycle, and Euros. Must sees include Fort Lois built in 1767 and the Marigot Museum with some native Arawak artifacts dating back to 1800BC and ceramic artifacts dating back to 500BC. Suffice it to say that the Arawaks were culturally thriving until the Caribs discovered them and the Caribs met a similar fate when discovered by the Europeans.

St Barts/St Barths/Barthelmy: Supposedly named in honor of Columbus's brother. I'm not a history buff, but I believe that the French exchanged this island with Sweden in 1784 for trading rights and a free day pass to Sam's Club. France repurchased the island in 1877, so on the surface you'll see Swedish names on signs, but the island is French in almost every other way. You might have heard Robin Leach espousing this island on the TV show *Life Styles of the Rich and Famous*. The Rich do come here, but don't expect to see them out by a hot dog stand. With so many excellent French chefs concentrated on one patch of land, many visitors prefer to have meals catered in their private villas. To save a little money on airfare, you might want to bring your own yacht. The local marina is a favored transit station while island hoping and can hold up to 500 yachts at one time although 50 or so are typically in port.

The island itself is formed by ancient coral reefs and boasts more white sand beaches than any other Caribbean get away. Diving is by boat around surrounding rocks and shoals. The marine reserve is set up into 6 zones and marine life has made a major comeback because of concerted efforts. There are over 15 noted dive sites, 4 wrecks, caves, and reefs to choose from. Remember to bring bagfuls of dollars to exchange for a few fistfuls of Euros. This is the place to enjoy champagne boat dreams and caviar dive wishes.

St. Lucia: At 27miles long and 14miles wide this island is home of the Soufriere Marine Management Area as well as the famous Chastnet Reef. Shore diving goes from 20-140ft. *Superman's Flight* is an awesome drift dive in front of the Petit Piton. The *Key Hole* is actually a set of 4 pinnacles or seamounts. You can already guess what you'll see at *Turtle Reef:* Hawksbill and Green turtles. On the east side you'll find *Piton Walls*, and *Coral Gardens*. Plus they have the wreck *Daini Koyomaru* at 108ft max depth and under 300ft long. As diving goes, this island has a lot of bang for the buck.

Above ground Mt Gemie is 3,117ft high. Rain Forests are everywhere. You can visit a dormant sulfur springs, waterfalls, forts, and former pirate sites. Leatherbacks go ashore at Grande Anse Beach. What more could you ask for?

St Vincent: 18miles long and 11miles wide. Mount Soufriere, an active volcano, ascends 4048ft. This is a land of black sand beaches, drift dives, wall dives, and an underwater photographers haven. It called the critter capital of the Caribbean, but it's really not fair to compare it to other single island nations as St Vincent includes 32 islands; the Grenadines. Some famous dives include *Coral Castle* and *Bat Caves (*yes, you swim right up under small bats*)*. 30 some other sites and wrecks make this an ideal dive destination. Above the water line there is Fort Charlotte on Berkshire Hill, rain forests, and Old Hegg Turtle Sanctuary.

Hopefully I've given you just enough information to wet your regulator and make you want to seek out additional information about these saintly islands on your own. There are videos on the Internet as well as still pictures that say more than I ever could even if I wrote a book on each island, but why say more about these Caribbean saints when instead we should be diving them?

St Kitts & Nevis
Ship Wrecks, Tropical
Jungles, Picturesque Beaches

The "ships to reefs program" is not something necessarily new. From 1493-1825 some 400 ships settled beneath the waves around the islands of St Kitts and its sister island Nevis. Columbus first discovered these islands on his second voyage, which must have been as big a shock for the folks back home in Spain as it was for the thousands of local Carib Indians who were currently residing on the islands. Arawak Indians first settled the islands 5-7 thousand years ago. They were a peaceful people that seemed to spend all their spare time carving graffiti on black lava rocks now known as Petroglyphs. Some 1200 years before Columbus spotted the shorelines, the fierce warlike Carib Indians had moved on up to the east side and taken over the islands. From the Carib Indians we acquired words like "canoe, hurricane, and cannibal". Under Spanish influence, influenza, involuntary work programs, and irrepressible musket fire, the Carib Indians were heartily persuaded to vacate the Island of Nevis by the 1700's. In 1626 the separate English and French colonies joined forces and massacred the Carib Indians on St Kitts. Apparently they claimed the Carib were massing to massacre them first. **Bloody Bay Reef** near the location of the massacre and named after the historical event is a well-known dive site with colorful coral, sea fans and small caves where you might discover some spiny lobsters.

With no more Indians to fight, the European settlers were free to fight against each other from time to time, sink ships, import slaves from Africa, turn the Island of Nevis into the greatest profitable sugar region in the world at that time, attract Pirates such as Kidd William, and enjoy a typical European colonial lifestyle. Needless to say, they did do a lot of fighting and sinking ships and this is why St Kitts and Nevis

322

have become a wreck diver's paradise. If you enjoy looking at cast iron cannons, coral encrusted anchors, musket balls, old pipes, and other assorted artifacts such as the ones they have found at **Paradise Reef** just within range of the cannon balls from the 38acre Brimstone Hill Fortress considered the Gibralter of the West Indies, then these islands are made to order. It's said that out of the 400 wrecks that only a dozen have been uncovered and verified. A recent hurricane revealed a 1740 vintage troop transport ship in **White House Bay**. This wreck is one of the top 3% best preserved historical wrecks in the world and was most likely lost during the Battle of Frigate Bay in 1782. Over 300 artifacts were recovered including buttons from 11 different English regiments. 29 French ships fought against 22 British ships in that battle and although Admiral Hood performed brilliantly, the odds were on the French side. He soon had to disengage and Brimstone Hill Fortress with only a 1000 men defending against a force of 8000 French soldiers soon fell as well. It appears the British already had their hands full with rebels in the American Colonies who were under the leadership of a certain General Washington. The French gave back St Kitts and Nevis to the British the next year at the treaty of Paris. Many of the historical artifacts are on display at the St Kitts National Museum and at the Brimstone Hill Fortress. It's hard to go on a dive or do just about any other activity here without thinking about past historical events that helped shaped these islands.

Now if you've seen enough copper spoons and porcelain plates to last a lifetime, then I suggest you dive one of the three modern day wreck attractions. The **River Taw** is a 144ft long freighter that rests in 50ft of water. It was broken into two sections by hurricane Hugo to form a nice swim through. **M.V. Talata** freighter rests at 70ft. The tug **Corinthian** lies intact at 72ft of depth near a group of cordial garden eels. There is also the inter-island ferry Christina that went down with some 320 people in 1970. With this tragedy fresh in the minds of the 90 survivors and a painful memory to the relatives of dead or missing, this is not a scheduled dive site by many tour operators.

Nags Head is a drift dive where you may see large pelagics as well as stingrays and turtles. **The Caves** is a popular dive off the west coast of Nevis; this series of coral grottos and swim throughs lie only 40ft below the surface. Hot water vents are another unexpected find while diving around these islands. Southern stingrays, black and white spotted stingrays, 3ft long porcupine fish, reef sharks, nurse sharks, Greenbacks, Hawksbill, and Leatherback turtles make up a good percentage of the larger sea creatures. Fishing has thinned out the ranks of other large fish. Macro photographers will not be disappointed with the abundance of smaller sea creatures. Colorful eels include black and white spotted, purple mouth, golden chain, and black and white banded snake eels.

There are 40 moored dive sites and other dive sites waiting to be explored. Most of the diving is done on the Caribbean side where the water is calmer than on the Atlantic side. The water temp is usually around 79 degrees. It's recommended that you wear a full 3ml exposure suit just to play it safe with fire worms, sun burns, and generally keeping you warm on longer dives or when you are just sitting still and slowly loosing heat while gazing at some amazing reef creature.

The first recorded group of tourists to stay for a 5 day all-inclusive package was in 1607 when Captain John Smith and his party layed over at the hot springs on Nevis before continuing on and founding a colony in Virginia. It wasn't until 1778 that Nevis had its first hotel built over the hot springs. Today the biggest luxury resort is **St Kitts Marriott Resort &The Royal Beach Casino** on St Kitts. Their web site has a running show highlighting the hotel facilities as well as the scenic beauty of the pool, beach, and ocean in the background. It's a great web site to view anytime you need a break from the rain, snow, or the daily mundane.

There are a handful of dive operations on the island. *Dive St Kitts* is the only dive shop connected to an all-inclusive dive package resort; **The Bird Rock Beach Hotel**. *Pro-Divers* is close to **The Ocean Terrace Inn**. *Kenneth's Dive Centre* and *Turtle Beach Dive Shop* are also located on St Kitts. On

Nevis dive operators include *Dive Nevis* at **Mt Nevis Hotel & Beach Club** and *Scuba Safaris* at **Oulie Beach Club**.

Non-diving activities include horseback riding, golfing, tennis, shopping in downtown Basseterre, eco tours, hiking 4000ft up Mt. Liamuiga; a dormant volcano, or just viewing tropical flowers and the green Vervet monkeys who inhabit the tropical forests and who are said to have been brought to the islands by French soldiers over 200 years ago. As you can see there are lots of things to do or not do in your spare time. If you still need more to do, come January thru April and watch and listen for the return of the Humpback whales. From March thru May tours go out to spot 6ft long Leatherback turtles returning to beaches they same way they have for over millions of years.

As you can see, some traditions are old on these two islands; others are just a few hundred years young. If Christopher Columbus had been a scuba diver, he may never have left St Kitts and Nevis and gone back to Spain to tell them what he discovered. Perhaps it's time that you discover St Kitts and Nevis too.

POTPOURI OF DIVE STUFF

10 Popular Dives Off New Jersey, Maryland, and Delaware

Some say that there are over five thousand wrecks off the coast of New Jersey, Maryland, and Delaware. So how can I come up with the top ten dive sites? I can't. It's like picking the best ten marshmallows from an unopened bag while blindfolded. What I can do though is pick a random sample of dive sites that hopefully will give you a feel for diving off the Atlantic coast. So here we go with a random sample:

The most popular wreck is the **USS Bradford:** DD-968. This artificial reef was sunk August 10, 2011. The destroyer Bradford is 26 miles off shore or so depending which state and which boat harbor you start your excursion. The ship is 563ft long, the top deck is at 70ft of depth, and the bottom rests on the substrate at 140ft of depth. Although the ship was cleaned of artifacts and local sea creatures are still moving in to the neighbor hood, divers never the less, still clamor for a chance to dive this newly submerged vessel.

On the other side of the coin, you have vessels that went down by natural causes that still have tons of artifacts to find and peruse like the 360ft long **Washingtonian**. This American-Hawaiian Steamship Company vessel was a steam-powered freighter built in 1914. She was carrying 10,000 tons of raw sugar when she collided with the **Elizabeth Palmer** January 26, 1915. She now rests at 100ft of depth. She left Honolulu December 30th, passed the Panama canal January 19th only to sink in 10minutes off the east coast of Delaware. One man was lost, and two 11ft long Ivory tusks with silver end caps were never officially recovered from the wreck site. She is currently a great place to spear big fish and hunt for lobster. The 300ft long five-mast schooner, Elizabeth Palmer, sank two days later at 90ft. This was the second and last time she sank another ship.

The African Queen oil tanker bow section, which is south and in blue waters some 15miles offshore from Maryland, is still a very popular wreck. While the stern section was towed to dry dock after running aground, the bow section became a natural wreck with lots of life with reliefs 30 to 70ft deep. Lobster and big tog "tautog" are found here.

Fenwich Shoals is an easy 20-30ft dive with an upper thermo cline. From mid-June to September you can easily get by wearing a 3ml suit when you dive here. This last July the Vis was around 30-40ft. There are several wrecks out here covering more than an acre of substrate. Some of the wrecks on the outer Fenwick Shoals include the steamship *Brinkburn*, the Norwegian *Siam*, and on the inner Fenwick Shoals rests the 300ft long *BoilerWreck*. Lots of fish make this a popular site for spearfishing.

The Marine Electric has been described as one "Bad @ss Wreck". The former coal carrier sank in 1983, 32miles out from Maryland to the sand at 130ft and the top is at 70ft of depth, but at 605ft long, it will take several dives to see it all. One charter Captain would like to mention that spear fishing and catching lobster is the number one sport in the Mid-Atlantic and at this site you can catch black bass, cobia, amberjacks, and jack crevalle, but in the summer months when the warmer waters slide up, you can spear mahi mahi, and blue fin tuna here.

The 582ft long tanker **Stolt Dagali** sank Nov 26, 1964 after a collision with the Israeli liner *Shalom* and now rests 18 miles out at 130ft of depth. Jim says that on artificial wrecks, everything of value has been removed to pay for the sinking, while on natural wrecks you may find a lighter personally marked that formerly belonged to someone from the past. The divers out here find artifacts and catch fresh seafood and enjoy the atmosphere aboard the boat; it's a small price to pay for by having to wear drysuits and using wreck reels.

The 250ft long **Delaware** sank 75ft July 9th, 1898.Capt Dave found the leather of a woman's size 7 shoe with the stitching disintegrated. After preserving the leather, he re-stitched it to see what the fashion was at the time. He also found a pewter spoon and cup on this wreck. He says that wreck diving never gets boring, and that fewer miles out is better, as bottom time is everything; when you are searching, sifting, and looking for artifacts.

The 194ft **Pinta** was a freighter from the Netherlands that sunk May 8th, 1963. The bow was salvaged, so the wreck is 142ft long and rests between 65 to 130ft deep on its port side. Paul has found lots of old stuff digging around wrecks including a brass capstan with a brass base 3ft in diameter and 3 1/2ft tall and 18 pairs of cowboy spurs from around 1854.

The 445ft long oil tanker **R.P. Resor** sank in 125ft of water after being torpedoed by U-578 Feb 27, 1942. It rests 30miles off shore and is lightly defended by lobster and a 6inch gun mounted on the stern foyer.

As you can see, some of these ships are immense in size while others are small and quaint. Some still give up treasures or small souvenirs, while others were cleaned before they went down or have been picked almost clean over the years by long gone treasure hunters, but remain great destinations for lobster hunters. Some of these sites are great places to spear fish, while others sites are naturals for underwater photography. During the summer season warm waters enter the area along with tropical fish and larger pelagic creatures. At times the visibility can reach over 100ft in some locations and less than 40ft in other locations. Yet to be confirmed and named, while others you can read about their long history, the cargos they carried, the day leading to their particular disaster, and even the layout of the ship before you ever descend upon it. You can dive with a group that are all newly certified and just going out for the fun of it, or you can find a charter where many of the divers have been to specific sites before and have certain goals in mind on their return trip to these wrecks. Your time out to the sites will vary depending on from which of these three states you started your expedition, but most of the local charter operations can cover all of the mentioned above dive sites. Charter Captains are still marking newly discovered shipwrecks on their personal maps, and who knows, you may be on board one of these vessels when a random secondary dive site may turn out to be the next major discovery. In the mean time though, enjoy some great dives.

Virginia, North & South Carolina Top 10 Dive Sites

Although there are hundreds of dive sites to choose from in North Carolina, South Carolina, and Virginia, these tops ten sites offer something for everyone including: tons of sea life, historical artifacts, spear fishing, photography, plus tech and wreck diving opportunities.

Starting with the most northern state of Virginia we have the 423ft long Liberty ship **John Morgan**, built and launched the 4th of May, filled with war cargo destined for Iran, and sank to 100ft June 1st in 1943 after colliding with the SS Montana. The motorcycles are cool to look at, but the best feature has to be the tanks that are upside down, right side up, and with barrels bent. There are also Willy Jeeps, tractors, a ford truck, machine guns, P-39 airplanes, and various types of ammunition littered everywhere.

The 448ft freighter **Lillian Lucanbach,** which sank in 1943 after colliding with the SS Cape Henlopen rests on her port side at 105ft of depth. She was carrying war goods such as tires, and airplane parts with 50calliber machine guns still attached to P-40 wings.

In North Carolina, the Graveyard of the Pacific, the most famous ship sank to 240ft of depth while being towed in the middle of a storm off the coast was the **USS Monitor**. With only twin 11inch guns based on a turret, the Monitor faced off, and stale matted in battle against the 10 fixed guns of the ironclad *CSS Virginia* "the remodeled *USS Merrimac*". Items recovered from the Monitor can now be seen at the Mariner's Museum in Newport News, Va.

U-352 is probably the most well known submarine sunk off the coast of North Carolina. The hull is in relatively good shape and the plethora of sea life makes a great backdrop for underwater photos. It rests at 90-110ft in waters that range from 75 to 80° in the summertime. Commander KL Rathke fired 4 torpedoes at one ship that never hit or detonated. A few days later he fired two more torpedoes with the same effect on what turned out to be the Coast Guard Cutter *Icarus*. After five depth charges, the U-352 surfaced to abandon ship and Rathke gave orders to scuttle the already damaged vessel on 5/9/1942. *Dale A Hansen*, a diver from Discovery Diving in Beaufort has made a CD with pictures of the U-352, the prisoners taken, video clips of the wreck, and photos and names of many tropical species of fish that inhabit the wreck. He also has a book at the dive shop on some of the major wrecks in the area including what they looked like, and what the wrecks look like now from a diver's perspective. Several charter operations frequently run dedicated trips to this site.

U-85 near Nags Head and the Bodie Island Light House can have warm water at the surface but is can cool down to the 50's at the 100-110ft depth of the wreck. This submarine has more items removed from it than the U-352. A hatch from the U-85 is displayed at the Cape Hatteras Lighthouse museum in Buxton. Two oak boxes with enigma code machine parts were recovered from inside the wreck in 1997. It's the only VIIB class sub in American waters. It sunk 3 ships before the *USS Roper* depth charged and destroyed it on 4/14/1942. The *R/V Go Between* makes two runs a week out here when weather is favorable.

U-701 sank 9 ships before a Lockheed Hudson A-29 drooped 3 depth charges and sank the u-boat on 7/7/1942. Commander KL Degen sank the small-armed trawler YP-389 with his 88mm deck gun on 6/19/1941. The trawler rests in 300ft of water off North Carolina. Degen also sank the tanker SS William Rockefeller. The U-701 remained hidden under shifting sands north of Diamond Shoals until discovered in 1989 by Uwe Lovas. His crew kept the site a secret for 15years. By 2004 the site coordinates became public and looters soon took a heavy toll on the structure and resting spot of many crewmen; 17 crewmembers escaped the abandoned vessel, but the coast guard picked up only 7, including Degen. The conning tower, the stern, and deck gun have been exposed above the sand for quite some time. The vessel lists on its side by 45 degrees. Amber Jacks and sand tiger sharks frequent the wreck. Strong currents make this site at times undiveable.

So you are not a fan of wreck diving? No problem. North Carolina has miles and miles of 5 to 20ft tall underwater ledges full of coral and fossil artifacts. **Fossil Ledge** is famous for divers finding 6.5inch teeth from prehistoric 60ft long sharks that used to patrol these waters. Fortunately it's safe to go back in the water now and with a little luck you may find a fossilized tooth that doesn't quite fit in the palm of your hand. Dive trips to fossil sites vary greatly and you have to shop around to get the best price. Also, they don't guarantee that you will come back with a large prehistoric tooth, you just have to keep your eyes open, but even if you come back toothless, it still is a great dive experience.

As far as shore dives go, the most famous beach dive is **Radio Island** near Beaufort. It's a jetty dive with up to 43ft of depth. You have a good chance of seeing dolphins playing on the surface and stingrays just beneath.

In South Carolina one of the favorite dive sites in the area is the **Bill Perry Reef System**. There are quite a number of things to dive here. The Bill Perry is a tugboat sunk 21 miles off shore at around 65ft of depth, but near by it rests 44 New York subway train/cars, a navy landing craft, and a shrimp boat. This collectively makes this reef system a must dive destination. Small fish like to embark and disembark the subway trains in finicky fashion, groupers seem to conduct the movements of schools of fish in harmonious headings, and between soft corals, agile algae, and the occasional policing the area by small bands of barracuda, typical subway graffiti has never been an issue.

For the record, some of the best black water diving is found in South Carolina. What you will get for you efforts are finding prehistoric Megalodon shark teeth, mammoth and giant sloth bones, Native American Indian pottery chards, bottles, Civil War and Revolutionary War buttons, buckles, and bullets. Case in point, the **Cooper River Underwater Heritage Trail** has 2 miles of underwater sites from the old 1781 British military *Strawberry* shipwreck to remnants of the *Mepkin* plantation dock pilings. Other rivers have also given up artifacts to hobby artifact divers, it's not surprising when you remember that hundreds of skirmishes between British & Loyalist troops and later Union and Confederate soldiers.

I hope this short list gets you motivated to dive these three great states. There are hundreds of other local reefs and wrecks to choose from and it could literally take you years to see them all, but that's what makes scuba diving such a great adventurous sport. Great Dives.

Top Ten West Coast Dives

There are many great dive locations here in the Wild West, but if some adventurous divers come out here where the sun finally sets, for their very first visit and travel time is not an issue, then these are the top dives I would like to show them in reverse order.

10. Clear Lake, Oregon. No other dive site in America has a 3,000-year-old volcanic eruption field that you can dive and glide across. If it weren't for ancient petrified tree stumps and wayward trout in crystal clear water, you would think that you were floating over the lunar surface. This site is east of Salem past Mill City. This is a summer time dive only as the roads get clogged with deep snow. It best to call ahead and see if the area has been cleared. There are some rental cabins nearby, you can also tent camp, or just drive over for the day from Salem or Eugene.

9. Keystone Jetty, on Whidbey Island. In the rock crevices that form the jetty you may spot some fairly impressive giant octopus or wolf eels. It's a marine preserve so expect to see lots of fish and other sea creatures. At the edge of the jetty it drops down past 50ft of depth and here the currents can pick up considerably. So I recommend being advanced diver trained to deal with the water conditions. Also be sure to carry a knife and scissors as some fishermen don't know what a marine preserve is. There are changing areas complete with hot showers that work with quarters. Fort Casey is right up the hill, so don't miss touring the world war two gun mounts and underground bunkers. The Keystone jetty goes over to Port Townsend and you can get some great scenic photos during the ferry ride.

8. Port Townsend/Port Angeles. Hudson Point, one of the most popular dives here is right at the end of the Water Street. It used to be a submarine tender station, now its home to photogenic fish and octopus. For 80year old bottle collecting I recommend anywhere along the shoreline of the old town

section. For advanced divers that don't mind fast currents and kelp beds, then Tongue Point at Salt Creek County Park just past Port Angeles is the place to show off a variety of marine animals and tide pool critters. The tides and currents here are similar to Race Rock in Victoria, Canada. Tongue Point reminds me of Hawaii, but only with pine trees instead of palm trees. To get to both Port Angeles and Port Townsend, take the Keystone ferry, or follow Highway 101 by Hood Canal and you'll see the signs. Stop by the Marine Life Center in Port Angeles to see and learn more about what you will see underwater.

7. Mukilteo. Whether you like 200ft deep dives or just catching crabs by the hundreds, this dive site has it all. There actually three places to dive here. You can go extremely deep by the boat ramp in the adjacent Mukilteo Sate Park, deep or shallow in front of the Silver Cloud Inn motel, or you can do long swim 40ft shallow dives by the oil dock and come home with a large bagful of crabs. I've seen sea lions, Gray whales, harbor seals, and even tiny stubbly leg squids no bigger than your thumbnail swimming in the waters here. Lot's of new divers are trained right in front of the Silver Cloud and the currents and visibility are usually favorable here. Parking is right on the side of the Silver Cloud, and there is a nice walkway built for divers leading right to the beach.

6. Tacoma Narrows Bridge. Here you can either search for giant octopus around remnants of Galloping Gerdie Bridge or you can do a fast exhilarating drift dive and be spit out near clay walls, shrimp infested ledges, and the filtering protrusions of endless clam beds. This is strictly a boat dive. As for shore entrances, don't even think about it. Several charters frequent this area. While boating to the dive site don't be surprised if you spot dolphins swimming right under the Tacoma Bridge heading into the South Sound.

5. South Sound: Zee's Reef or KVI Tower. At Zee's Reef you will find lots of south sound critter residents at less than 50ft of depth including wolf eels, lingcod, starfish, and anemones. It's an easy mild current boat dive and a great place to take photos since it is a protected area. Now, if you are searching for giant octopus or deeper waters, then the KVI

Tower artificial reef is the best southern sound boat site to visit. Right in front of the radio tower is a sandy/gravel bank that descends at less than a 60-degree angle with giant cement pillars randomly strewn on the substrate making it a perfect sanctuary for multiple octopus gardens in the shade There's a small boat down at around 90ft.

    4. Seacrest. Cove 1 has plates and glasses at 20ft. Cove 2 has several man made objects and lots of sea life at 50ft, a giant resident octopus at 110ft, and six gill sharks are occasionally seen at various depths. Cove 3 sports a small boat at 35ft, crabs, and pile perch. Cove 1 is right next to Salty's Seafood Restaurant on Harbor Ave SW. Cove 2 is on the south side of the fishing pier. Where you can get fresh clam chowder at the pier restaurant or change in and out of your dive gear at the outside restrooms. Always carry a knife and scissors at these dive sites as fisherman are pulling in 2-3ft long salmon right from the nearby fishing pier. You'll see lots of beginner dive classes at cove 1 & 2. Advanced and tech divers pool around cove 2: as depth is pretty much unlimited. This area has a great view of Downtown Seattle and the especially the Space Needle.

    3. Bruce Higgins Underwater Trails in Edmonds. 100's of sunken boats, 1000's of rocks, countless voluntary man hours, and millions of fish and invertebrates have made this the biggest and best marine preserve on the west coast. No two dives are ever the same due to the natural migration of marine life. To visit some sites you may require a long swim on the surface to the site, but the destinations are definitely worth the effort. From beginners to advanced divers, the underwater trails with thick ropes and cinderblocks holding them in place make it easy to get around. Stop by the Edmonds Underwater Sports dive shop on Railroad Avenue, two blocks south of the park, and purchase an underwater map of the park with all sites listed. The proceeds from the maps go to sinking more boats, dive friendly artifacts, as well as enhancing and maintaining dive sites within the park and adjacent buoy markers.

    2. Hood Canal. The only natural Fjord south of Canada, this inland sea has orca whales, harbor seals, and nuclear submarines. It descends past 400ft in some locations and is the

only known site south of British Columbia to contain cloud sponges: at Mike's Beach Resort. The "Pinnacle" is a must do boat dive where you will encounter multiple families of wolf eels and vermilion rockfish. Sund Rock and Octopus Hole are two of my favorite Hood Canal shore dives. Both are marine preserves. There is a small fee to dive Sund Rock, but there is a port-o-potty down by the beach area and a new bench makes gearing up here even easier than before. The fee can be paid at Hood Sport n' Dive on Highway 101 in Hoodsport. Divers of all ranks and levels come to the Hood Canal for it's usually good visibility, mellow currents, and abundant sea life. Local wine outlets, otters, bald eagles, deer, and other wildlife add to the mix whether you are camping in one of the many nearby state parks, or enjoying the amenities of one of the local resorts.

1. The San Juan Islands. How can you ever spend enough time diving 170 different Islands? There are only 50 to 100 published dive sites with names from Strawberry Island to Dawn's Bottom. Visibility is usually 40 to 100ft. From thousands of swimming scallops, to three pod families of salmon feeding orca whales, it's hard to see them all. Suiting up is hard to do when you are watching deer and eagles on nearby islands. Safety stops become extended exploration periods and the last thing anyone wants to do is go back aboard the dive boat no matter how nice the captain and crew are. On top of all this, some of the islands are farther north than parts of the Canadian border, so the abundance of sea life is almost matched by the sheer diversity: Gray whales, purple sea stars, red urchins, and yellow nudibranchs. Here on deep dives I believe I've even seen pink mermaids. There are a plethora of bays, inlets, and rocks to swim through, wrecks to explore, and deserted islands to set foot on. The larger islands are great getaway vacation spots. My family enjoys spending time back at port in Anacortes. Besides the great diving, there are great restaurants here, outstanding local micro brews, and scenic outdoor parks and marinas.

So now you know my top picks for west coast diving. I have added even more information on these sites in my book, "*The Northwest Dive Guide*". Most of the diving out here is done wearing flexible drysuits or not so flexible 7ml wetsuits. A tune up dive with a local professional may be a good idea if you want to visit an unfamiliar spot while also getting acquainted with unfamiliar dive gear. Sure the water is colder out west, but the abundance of sea life is a direct by product of the water's temperatures. Where else can you see a giant octopus, a gray whale, a harbor seal and a wolf eel separately, or all on a single dive? Also, what ever you do, even though the diving at these locations is some of the best on the west coast, please don't invite your friends to come out here all at once, because if you do, there might not be a parking space or a spot on the boat left for me! Great Dives.

Deep Down, Diving's Delightful

On this dive you are feeling a little excited. You already have slowly descended deeper than you have ever gone before. The visual spectrum of colors has been reduced to mere shades of blue. It's darker down here and you realize that it's a good thing you brought along a dive light. You check your gauges more frequently on this dive. You are extra careful with your air supply. You see in front of your face a gloved hand form the "are you OK?" sign. You smile because you are feeling warm and elated. You are with your dive instructor and this is your fourth dive below 60ft. As trained, you answer back with your own hand signal "I'm fine". But you know you are feeling the effects of nitrogen narcosis or "rapture of the deep". Your instructor signals for you both to go up a few feet and you immediately feel those strange sensations magically evaporate. You are given a slate with mathematical calculations to solve. It seemed easier to do in the classroom. You finish the math problems and look at your gauges. Your air supply has gone down faster than you expected.

As a deep diver, you are following the rule of thirds: One third of air in your tank to go down and explore, one third to ascend back up, and one third left in reserve. With a third of the tank depleted, your instructor signals that it's time to slowly ascend to your planed decompression stop. Your buoyancy has greatly improved on this dive. At first it was difficult to regulate your buoyancy at depth because it took so much more volume of air to make you evenly buoyant at depth. Then you had to expel all that extra air just to keep from rising too quickly at the end of the dive. At first it seemed like a complicated procedure, but now you are getting the hang of it.

Back on shore you are excited. After several dives you have completed the deep diver course. More than just a certificate, you personally experienced working at depth with buoyancy, felt the effects of nitrogen narcosis, and witnessed first hand how quickly air supplies diminish at depth.

The instructor answered your questions concerning alternate air sources including different size pony tanks, pony tank attachments and clip on locations, and even working with argon gas to keep you extra warm during deep dives and what seem like extended durations of stationary positioning during practice and real decompression stops.

The instructor was also helpful with discussing dive lights in general and especially which dive lights might be best suited for your personal needs. Such as one high power light, one small light clipped to a D ring on your buoyancy compensator and a small signal light on the back of your tank. The instructor may have one of those small strobe lights that can signal planes six miles away on a clear night, and other lights you may someday wish to own.

You really learned a lot during this course, and had fun doing it, even though you were a little apprehensive at first. Ok, although you don't normally do math calculations during a dive, the math calculation experiment did make you realize that nitrogen narcosis can indeed impair your mental faculties and more so than you first would have thought possible. Some dive instructors use puzzle cubes or flat sliding puzzles, and there are many other ways to demonstrate the effects of rapture of the deep.

Some divers may never dive deep unless they go to warm tropical destinations, but like any dive activity, training at home means that all your dive time on vacation is spent on pure enjoyment. There are no dive police placed around the for corners of the world that enforce rules or say you can't dive down to 130ft unless you are deep diver certified or face going to pinniped "fin-footed" prison or derelict diver jail. It's just common sense that dictates only diving down to the depth to which you are trained to penetrate. Traveling to any other depth would be taking a risk where none need be taken.

A word of caution: trained deep divers tend to dive deeper on more dives, and enjoy more wonders, wrecks, and wildlife. Some deep diver graduates enjoy descending to depth so much that they eventually enhance their training and become tech divers and descend well below the recreational dive limits.

When it comes to scuba diving, the level of training and type of future experiences are decidedly up to you and paradoxically the limits are almost bottomless. This is why I recommend a deep diver course to every diver as soon as physically, psychologically, and practically possible. Great dives.

Dive Flags

There are many dive flags and float systems on the market. If all you are trying to do is fulfill a county or state requirement, then the easiest option is to get a relatively inexpensive flagpole with a styrofoam float. They do the job (of warning boaters to stay away from the divers below) in calm water, but never use them with an underwater scooter as they will be pulled down underwater and the styrofoam will crush below 50ft of depth. How do I know? Don't ask, but they do make nice furrows in the sand.

Inflated flag buoy systems fair a little better, but not all are created equal. My favorite is the Pocket Buoy. This one can be inflated with a party balloon and assembled in a minute. This float has an internal frame and the flag sticks up high. Plus, the collapsible fiberglass flagpole can be taken back down in less than sixty seconds. You can store and travel with this flag buoy anywhere. The Pocket Buoy can also come equipped with a White sign with black letters that reads "DIVERS BELOW." This comes in handy in places where being a boat operator does not require any knowledge of what a dive flag looks like, just the ability to read. This makes the Pocket Buoy my favorite "personal use" flag float system.

Now you can build a flag buoy system by yourself with a milk crate, a rubber inner tube, some polyester boat rope and a flag on a pole stick. This model type lets you use the inside portion of the milk crate for weights, crab storage, and can be seen from far away, but does not generally give you any place to hold on to in an emergency situation, and it takes up lots of trunk space. A place to hold on to and a float system that can handle a diver's weight is paramount when instructing new student divers; you need a bigger float system altogether for teaching abilities.

The middle of the road float model is a buoy dive flag system that has fabric covering a large inner tube with a zip able compartment in the top side central portion with a flag on a fiberglass stick sticking through a grommet and pointing skyward. This float system has fabric woven handhold rings for up to four different divers at one time, and is popular with dive instructors who need to own their own flag flat systems. With this configuration you can stow equipment inside the zippered area and you can either let the air out at the end of the dives or keep it inflated: as the nylon fabric typically dries out fast and the sheathed inner tube can be thrown in the back of a pickup truck, flag and all.

Now if you have deeper pockets and desire a sturdy system, the Cadillac of all surface support floats is the Diver's Platform. This ultimate design has a one-inch aluminum tube bar going all around the float so divers can latch on any side: 360degrees. It can be used with the *raptor auger* system that can bore through anything apart from solid rock, or the *broad head auger* for securing the float to mud and sand substrates. Either auger attaches the float to the substrate by means of a 5/8inch poly braided anchor rope. This is why I classify Diver's Platform as the ultimate flag float system.

So there you have it. Simple mouth inflated buoys to air pump inflated inner tubes with fancy nylon covers and/or aluminum outer skeletons. At times I've had four different flag float models. One for hunting crabs and hauling gear, One for teaching students and giving them a place to hold on to when necessary, one for fun dives just to let boaters know I was there or for county rules, and one I kept for spare parts. You may not need four flag systems, but one for your personal needs or local requirements can be a very handy piece of safety gear as well as save you expensive local or state fines if applicable for diving without a flag. Either way, dive flags float systems come in many varieties, some with blue flags for international waters and others red with a diagonal white stripe for North American waters. Ask your friendly frequented dive shop about state and county regulations and local dive practices, and then maybe you too can find a favored float flag system that best floats your own flag.

Dives Knives

Dive knives come in all sorts of shapes and sizes. I prefer the flat edges ones as apposed to the pointed end ones because those pointed ends were made to poke holes in things, such as my drysuit. Sharp pointed knives do look cool though, so if you get one as a gift, I recommend strapping it to the inside seam of your lower leg area. That way it will look cool and not get entangled as much with kelp and other floating debris. I've never used my big pointy knife in 30 years of diving, and maybe that's why it never has rusted.

One of the first things that comes to mind when new divers think about what they will use a dive knife for is to use it in self defense against a shark. The problem with this thought process though is that poking a shark and causing it to bleed is like chumming the water to start a shark frenzy. In reality, most sharks run away at the first sight of a diver. If one were to become aggressive, the metal from a flat-ended knife rubbing against their body should freak them out enough to make them steer clear of you forever. Any further aggression on their part and I would say it really is time to get out of the water.

So why do I like flat ended knives so much? Because, you can use them to pry open oysters, abalones, scallops, or use them as a screwdriver to tighten things before making the plunge. Some flat-end knives are actually slightly curved and come with a serrated edge blade as well as a built-in line cutter.

So is one knife all you need? No, I recommend carrying at least three in assorted sizes, plus one pair of scissors for tough modern fishing line that some knives just can't seem to cut through.

Besides the big knife on my leg that I could use in self-defense against husked coconuts, I recommend a smaller knife hooked on or permanently attached to the chest region of the BC. It's all about mobility, and say you were stuck in a fishnet or kelp bed: you could have limited mobility. You may not be able to reach down to your leg region, but you could reach your chest, waist area. I also like to carry a zip or line cutter blade on my wrist for fast fish line cutting. I put a knife and scissor combo on my BC shoulder strap and I have been known to attach other knives in pre-designed areas on my BC waist or pocket area. Makers of knives have arranged new fastener systems to complement prefabricated BC holes for permanent or temporary placement setup points. Quick snap on carabineer clips also make the knives convenient to place almost anywhere that you think will come in handy.

There are many more styles of knives including flip open and butterfly knives, but such feats of dexterity needed to open these knives is best left for warm water divers who don't need to wear thick gloves to maintain warm and dexterous hands.

Also keep in mind that all knives are not created equal. Some rust easily while others with 18 percent nickel and a hardened steel base could keep their stainless steel appearance for 50 plus years. Titanium blades may remain sharp for decades, but could break if used inappropriately. Ceramic blades may last a thousand years, but I seldom cut tomatoes underwater, and I still like the multi-purpose ability of a steel blade to cut, pry, and shine in the sun at would be rescue planes.

So which knife is best suited to your dive needs? The one, or combos of knives, that you can most afford. Scissors and knives have many different uses including: a handy bottle opener. Even an old rusted knife could come in handy if need be. The point is that I would never want to be on a dive without a dive knife. I've dove marine preserves where there shouldn't have been any fishing line, yet mysteriously there was. I've also come to the surface to find not so sharp people fishing next to "No Fishing" signs. From these edgy encounters I have determined that the time when you don't have a knife is the time when you may need one the most. On land a dive knife may have little value, but when confronted underwater with kelp beds, fishing line, shredded rope, lost nets, and other miscellaneous human debris, a dive knife is priceless.

Drysuits 101

When considering purchasing any new item, it's a good idea to weigh the benefits: positive versus negative. With a drysuit, the positives are added warmth, comfort, and maneuverability. The only down side is the extra cost compared to a wet suit. For some drysuits the extra cost may only be a few hundred dollars. For other drysuits the extra cost may exceed a thousand dollars. It all comes down to material used and the amount of time and labor required to make a particular product. The thing all dry suits have in common is that they trap a layer of air around your body instead of a layer of water like a wet suit. You can wear fleece, polyester, or other outfits underneath the drysuit shell including: a tuxedo, airline uniform, or Halloween costume. Your choices are unlimited, the only thing to remember is that the more layers of warmth you add, the greater will be your total volume and the amount of weight needed to make you neutrally buoyant will have to be adjusted accordingly. Most drysuits only require a few extra additional pounds of weight than a wet suit. The benefit of a layer of air is noticeable underwater, but it's those intervals between dives where you really feel the difference over wetsuits. Anytime you are wet, you are drawing heat away from your body. Long surface intervals; say while boating to another dive site, or while eating lunch could leave you feeling cold towards your next dive in a wetsuit. Most dive instructors wear drysuits because they have to sit so long in one place while waiting for students to repeat dive skills. Photographers like dry suits to keep warm during inactive periods underwater. Also, because you are warmer in a drysuit, your urge to use a bathroom will be reduced to some degree and contingent on many other factors.

Apart from warmth, the greatest advantage of a drysuit is flexibility. A typical 7mm wet suit will have your arms fill like they were pinned in place like a bendable rubber toy Gumby. Sure, you can bend, but it takes noticeable effort. A drysuit can give you full range of motion somewhere between what it's like while wearing a windbreaker or heavy overcoat. Laminate drysuits and crushed neoprene drysuits tend to flex the most. Latex rings around the neck color and wrists are able to twist and turn greatly without any water leakage. Plus the latex seals are easy to cut to the right size for maximum fit and minimum pressure against your neck and wrists.

Some drysuits come with preinstalled boots, and others require rock boots to go on top of fitted feet tips. I like wearing rock boots, because of the reduced air in the boots so you don't need ankle weights, but other divers like being able to slip into their drysuits and slapping on ankle weights while I'm still lacing up my boots. The caveat being, once I'm dressed in my drysuit, I have no need to take it off for the rest of the day. You can zip it down between dives to cool off or use certain facilities, but to fully remove it is the last thing I do before leaving a dive site unless it is a super hot day. On cold snowy days, I've just gotten in my car with a towel on the seat and drove away while wearing my drysuit. Oh, did I mention that once you have a drysuit, weather may no longer be a determining factor whether you go diving or not? Excluding storms of course. Not many wetsuit divers can use the phrase "Oh, it's snowing!" while entering extra clear winter waters. If you do dive with such a brave soul, give them first rights on the use of hot water when they get back to the beach.

Zippers are found in different locations on drysuits. If you always dive with a buddy, it doesn't really matter where the zipper is located. If you are a certified solo diver, you will want a front mounted zipper as not all limbs on trees are the right height to help zip you up completely. And if a dive buddy helps you zip up, it's always a good idea to check their work and make sure you are sealed up all the way; especially if they are a wetsuit diver. It's not that they want you to be as cold as they are; they just might not notice the subtle nuance of the end of the zipper since they don't own a drysuit. But deep down in their heart and especially underwater, I know they would love to own a dry suit. In the end, saving for a drysuit could save one lots of long lost warmth.

Enriched air is a gas!

Hospitals and airlines administer oxygen to patients and passengers to make them feel better, reduce headaches, and reduce mental or physical fatigue. But pure oxygen is not so good at depth so scuba divers do basic training using air, which is 21% oxygen, 78% nitrogen, and a small trace of other gasses. During a dive, some of that nitrogen accumulates in your tissues. For small amounts of nitrogen build up we follow dive tables and expel the gas accordingly. For deeper depths and/or longer dive times, we use safety stops to decompress and expel residual nitrogen that has accumulated in out tissues and airways. By adding just a little extra oxygen to our scuba tanks, called blending and usually done prior to or while filling the tank, we can increase the amount of oxygen in the tank usually between 32-40%. The reduced amount of nitrogen 68-60%, allows us to stay down longer at depth without the additional amount of decompression time required by diving with air: 78% nitrogen. Note: most divers call air enriched with oxygen "Nitrox". I guess nitrox sounds better than calling it "Reduced Nitrogen Air". Plus, it's the partial pressure of oxygen that ultimately determines your maximum depth limit, hence the lean on the name towards the oxygen percentage. This is one of many things you learn about during a typical nitrox course.

In real life a good example of how nitrox can expand your dive time is to compare air dive times to nitrox dive times. Air at 60ft will allow you to stay at depth for 47 minutes without a safety stop. Using 32% oxygen will allow you 70 minutes and 36% will give you 89 minutes without a safety stop.

At 90ft you can dive on air for 21 minutes before you need a safety stop. On nitrox at 32% oxygen, you could stay down there for 29 minutes. Using 36% oxygen you could stay down for 35 minutes without a safety stop.

Your tank might not last that long at depth, for either of these dives on either mixture of nitrox, so you might end up staying down at depth for less than the stated maximum time, but this still would give you a great reduction in the amount of residual nitrogen in your system compared to diving on air, and this alone could prove a bonus when calculating the surface interval prior to and/or the bottom time of your next dive.

The only downside to either of these nitrox gasses is that at 36% nitrox, you can only go down to 90ft without contingency plans or only to 90ft on 32% nitrox without decompression stops. It sounds tricky but when your dive instructor explains it on the beach or in the classroom, it will sound more reasonable as well as less complicated. I should note, that as a recreational diver I'm big on dive profiles that don't require safety stops. As a technical diver I only like safety stops and decompression stops when I have multiple independent sources of air or nitrox in other pony or (not so staged) redundant travel tanks complete with alternate regulators.

Available dive tables are already set for certain gas blends such as 32% and 36%. Modern dive computers can be set for just about any blend and this makes then very attractive for divers who don't want to carry around extra tables or plan to dive profiles with gradual slopes or who like to move up and down along walls and reefs.

Personally, I like diving with nitrogen because I feel more energetic at the end of a dive. However, disappearing headaches and reduced fatigue could be signs of a dive that is occasionally skip breathing or holding their breath for periods longer than they would normally do while walking. If you still feel better after a nitrox dive and you are certain that you are breathing normally, only then can you truly tout the benefits of nitrox gas.

As an instructor going up and down in the water column multiple times, I want to reduce my nitrogen intake as much as possible. Greater amounts of dive time at depth, reduced mental and physical fatigue, and less, in tissue, nitrogen accumulations all demonstrate why not only is nitrox a gas, but why it's the preferred choice for many thousands of satisfied divers. This is also why so many resorts and charters operations offer nitrox to their guests.   My advice, take an enriched air or nitrox course as soon after you get your open water certification. The sooner you do it, the less nitrogen you'll accumulate during each dive and the more energetic you may feel after your nitrox dive experience is all said and done.

The Gulf Oil Spill
One Year Later

I'm not going to sugar coat it and say everything is back to normal. The local populations of animals and humans have been put through devastating circumstances since the 10million dollar cost savings route to installing an oil well proved to be so deadly and so long lasting, and the lawyers and lawsuits will take longer to disperse than the pockets of crude oil still remaining thousands of feet below the surface or in the still standing oil puddles in the marshlands of Louisiana.

A year after the spill, the government has declared the local seafood good to eat again. The beaches off Alabama are white again, and the dive visibility is back to spectacular. Most of the local dive charter operations and dive shops are gearing up for what could be a great dive season. Most of these organizations can't discuss how they were affected by the oil spill as they just about all have lawsuits pending. Some areas along the panhandle had no oil wash ashore. Some areas had just a few tar balls wash ashore over a few days. Some areas such as off shore islands were completely covered with oil, yet all areas suffered the loss of tourism equally. The dive businesses are able to say that bookings are up for the spring season and they expect to dive boats to be filled by the time spring break hits, so make your reservations as soon as possible.

I know the folks at *Down Under Dive Shop* will be taking charters out to the **USS Oriskany** almost every Saturday and possibly twice each week; weather permitting. This 911ft long attack aircraft carrier is one of the most popular dive sites in the panhandle region. By spring the waters are 70degrees warm and by summer 80degrees. The flight tower is around 70ft, the flight deck down at 140ft, and for tech divers, the ship rests in sand at 212ft of depth. With lots of resident fish, and occasional swim by's by pelagics, it's no wonder that this is one of the top must dive sites in the area.

Now I know that if you have been following the news, you've probably heard that thousands of coastal birds died from the oil spill, over 600 turtles perished, and recently *USA Today* reported that 48 dolphins have washed up on the shores in the last two months alone. 29 of which were fetal sized calves and may or may not have been still born or died before their first breath of air. Previously it was common to find 2 dolphins washed ashore before the oil spill. There were many immediate casualties of wildlife and some of the over all affects may not be known for years to come. At this point it is difficult to tell which animals fell victim to the oil spill and which animals fell victim to the oil spill dispersants, which are known to have a mortality effect on coral larvae.

The Valdez disaster lead to a crash in the herring run five years after the accident and the herring have yet to recover in the area. At least one pod of killer whales never regained pod status. Thousands of bird, otters, salmon, and seals were decimated. As a marine biologist, I hope nothing like this happens to the gulf region, but expect to hear about even none-oil contaminated crashes such as in the oysters beds around Louisiana as fresh water sent down river to keep the oil tainted saltwater at bay and out of more marshes, killed many beds of oysters who were not able to tolerate a fresh water habitat for such a critical period of time.

As a diver, you too can help monitor the future of the gulf. It is as simple as noticing the changes in numbers of aquatic creatures on your dives. On the positive side, a diver from *Dive Pro* in Pensacola, Florida told me that the required fishing restrictions over the last year has taken a lot of pressure off the fish populations and because of this, divers can expect to see more fish on a typical dive. A spokesperson for *Panama City Dive Charters* told me the goliath grouper are already returning from their deep water spawning grounds and you can now see them on the local wrecks and reefs. Besides the changes of "back to normal" fish populations, other changes might be noticeable such as the behavioral changes as witnessed by Bruce Flareau, a PADI Rescue Diver with over thirty years of scuba diving background and 50plus logged dives a year has described. He notes that since the oil spill, he has encountered whale sharks closer to the shoreline. Whether they have moved in because of food supply or because of the colder water temperatures near shore lately has yet to be determined. The fact remains is that now whale sharks are more abundant and easier to find closer to shore than ever before. It would be interesting to gather data on the behavioral and population changes on dolphins and sea turtles in the local dive areas as well.

I started writing this article in my hotel room in Tampa Florida. This is the first time I got a room overlooking the Tampa Bay waters. I could see past the swimming pool and low dense brush land leading to exposed mud flats at low tide. A white crane was wading ankle deep in the water for a fish to stray too near. The waters were clear and the bird had no idea what had transpired a year earlier. For the bird, life in the gulf was as it had always been. You can say the same for the divers that come here for the diving this spring. It's not until you see the marshes and islands off Louisiana or the mats of oil thousands of feet below the surface that you know that all has not been restored and put back to right. It will take time to discover the true effects of the dispersants and the oil itself. The oil on the surface waters has deteriorated by sun, weather, and has been eaten away by voracious microorganisms. The oil thousands of feet deep remains relatively unchanged. Weather can't play a vital role this deep and due to temperature, pressure or microorganism activity at depth, the killing fields at depth may continue for quite some unspecified period of time.

I am finishing the final draft of this article while sitting in hotel room in Houston. On a flight to Houston a year ago I met a tall unassuming man wearing blue jeans, long leave shirt, and a baseball style cap which read, "Department of the Interior". Ken Salazar was on a fact-finding mission for the President's administration. I had a brief moment to talk about scuba diving with him. The administration and scientists around the world will be studying and investigating the BP oil disaster for years to come. In the meantime civilians like us can enjoy scuba diving the local waters knowing that Mother Nature has already been doing her part to restore the local environment.

New Diver Briefing

Congratulations on your new or renewed "C Card" open water diver certification card. Now what do you do? Just by reading this article in Northwest diver news puts you well on the road to diving success. The calendar of events in the front section is just loaded with dive clubs and events. The advertisements give names and numbers of charter boats and resorts, and the articles highlight dive sites and other activities; but more about this later.

Your local dive store where perhaps you initially learned to dive should be your next stop. Dive shops post fun dives, shop sponsored dives, and/or shop club dives. You can meet lots of divers going on outings this way. Dive shops also offer continued diver education such as advanced diver classes that usually use more than one dive site or location to meet their class needs. People you meet in an advanced class or higher up classes can become life long dive friends, and what's more, you personally know that they are trained up to your current level of diving activity. Dive shops also offer specialty courses that may take you out of the local region and other interesting locations. Such as a wreck class up in Canada, boat dives in the south Puget Sound, rescue classes at Mukilteo, deep diving at Hood Canal, or a marine reserve diver specialty at Edmonds underwater park. The point is that with each class or dive shop related event, you learn a little more about diving and are introduced to new dive sites and adventures.

Joining a dive club is another good way to meet other divers and try out new locations. Some clubs are affiliated to dive shops while others are independently run with presidents, elected officials, and so forth. Some operate better than others, but all give you access to more diving. You don't have to join the biggest clubs to get the most bang for the buck. (Clubs usually have very small joining fees.) A small club with active members could keep you busy year round. Large clubs may have small in house groups or clicks that prefer a certain style of diving. You might want to hang out with the night divers, or buddy up with the digital photo divers. Dive clubs usually have a calendar full of local dives, dive trips, and perhaps even a yearly Caribbean trip, ect. Besides all these activities, some dive clubs have culminated relationships with officials that give them access to diving sites normally off limits to the rest of us. They may do dives in conjunction with agencies to collect sea creatures for educational purposes, fishing pier clean ups, or help with underwater creature studies. These are all considered fun dives that club members look forward to on a yearly basis. Charter boat diving is another viable option. If you can't find a buddy, they can either pair you up with another lone diver, or they might even be able to arrange for a guided tour by a divemaster if you arrange so in advance. A good divemaster may know a location like the back of their hand and may be well worth the extra money to experience a private tour of a new dive location and view the local attractions. Plus, it's just fun to go boat diving. You're practically guaranteed to meet other enthusiastic divers, and dive some interesting sites. This should be enough information to get you started. Another rule of thumb is buddy up with someone that knows the dive site. What ever you do, never dive alone. A new diver in a new place without a buddy is a recipe for disaster. Solo diving should be left to trained tech divers with redundant tech gear and to those specifically trained by diving agencies as solo certified divers. Solo diving is also illegal in some locations due to local city ordinances. Ok, it's time to thumb back through Northwest Dive News, make some calls, and start marking on your calendar. I'm running low on air so I hope to see you down under soon.

Sound Dives & Clean Activities

If you ever hear about a dive club, or a dive shop sponsoring a clean up dive, drop everything and sign up before all the spaces are filled or before the deadline for any pre-dive paperwork has passed. At first you might be hesitant, but the opportunity embraces much more than picking up underwater litter and hauling it back to shore, this is an opportunity to meet new divers, buddy up with seasoned professionals, and dive and explore areas normally restricted or off limits to scuba divers.

Years ago when I first joined Emerald Sea Dive Club, I signed up for a clean up dive at Edmonds Fishing Pier on the waterfront of downtown Edmonds Washington. It was one of those events where you had to sign up well in advance so the city of Edmonds could have all their required information documented before the actual day of the dive. On the day of the dive the beach master marked off our names and in most cases we were paired off according to skill level. We geared up and were given a ride to the far end of the fishing pier on an inflatable zodiac. The pier had been partially closed off just for the day's cleanup activities. It was my first time on a zodiac and my first time out to this particular pier and the adjacent tire reef. The pier itself is very popular with fishermen, especially during salmon season. Needless to say, when we dropped down 35ft we found plenty of snagged fishing line, a few relatively new fishing poles, and tons of fishing lures in various stages of degradation. Anything that could have fallen from the pier sank swiftly to the bottom and that also included crab pot rings, rusted cat food cans whose contents were used as bait, and also a large selection of chicken bones. All divers carried at least one sharp knife and a pair of scissors that could cut through just about anything. We collected everything under the pier and put it in our net bags. The fishing poles we just had to hold on to as best as we could. Attendants up above lowered plastic crates, which we filled with the contents from our net bags. Beach masters and surface attendants separated the salvageable items from the junk while we went down to collect more debris. We cleaned up the far section of the pier first, then on the second dive we cleaned up the remaining section. At the end of both dives we did a little exploring on the tire reef and wherever we went we found fishing lures embedded in, around, and between the tires. We also found lingcod, cabezon, and lots of red rock crab. The lures in good condition, we sold back to the fishermen and pooled the money for charity purposes as most dive clubs are nonprofit organizations.

Other dive clubs may clean up other locations on an annual or semi-annual basis. They may call it a clean up dive or give it a fancy name such as Trashfest 2022. The clubs or local city may also have different requirements to complete before you can join on one of these dives. Also, the type of clean up work may be different or unique to each site. Cleaning up around the pier at Kayak State Park in Washington you'll find lots of crab pot rings, but not much else. Some of the rings look brand new and they might be, because you can't leave the crab traps set up over night here. Eventually a park official will discover the crab pot lines left forever and cut the lines from the pier. Considering how many crab rings you can find here you can only surmise that there are a great number of people who either can't read or just ignore the ubiquitous and very easily legible park signs. Probably the most important ring I ever found at this site was a gold wedding ring, an amorous couple lost the previous weekend. They were happy to get the sentimental ring back. The ring was sitting almost upright in the sand in less than twenty feet of water.

Over at Mukilteo you'll find items that have fallen overboard near the boat dock and discarded bait traps close to the oil tanker dock. Cleaning around swimming piers such as those along Lake Washington you'll find old wallets, floating dollar bills, abruptly deactivated cell phones, and brand new Swiss army knives. It makes you wonder if they had all this stuff in their pockets when they jumped in to the lake, or did they just leave it all next to the edge of the pier waiting to see if it would fall in on its own? I've also picked up trash around

Potlatch State Park on the Hood Canal. Here you mostly find picnic items that went gone with the wind; including items such as beach towels t-shirts, and cut off shorts.

Occasionally you might find a new camping water bottle perfect for storing dry goods. I guess this leads to the question as to when are you no longer collecting trash and have become a certified souvenir collector? Anytime you find an old antique bottle such as the ones commonly found off the piers of Port Townsend and you set it for display at home to show off to your friends, after you have made sure no tiny residents such as an octopus inhabit the bottle, then you are a collector. Anytime you pick up trash on a dive to make the dive site look better for other divers, but have no intention using the items for personal use or for putting the discovered items on the mantel or letting them even enter your personal abode, then you are truly a good Samaritan that has become part of the pollution solution. I can't say that I pick up and collect every piece of rubbish I encounter on every single dive, but I do help out when I can and maybe that's all it will take to keep our waterways clean; in practice, just a little help from each diver seems to go a long way.

I must add that working around fishing line is not without risk, so divers cleaning such sites should be very comfortable with their gear, emergency diver skills, and extremely buddy team oriented. Exploring less frequented dive locations and cooperating, as a team of clean up divers, can be very rewarding as well as a lot of fun. You will also gain some great dive adventures and experiences as well as clean up and shine while you gain bottom time. Although the fishermen may never consider how you saved their line from future entanglement, and most of the public may never see what objects sank to the substrate, you, your dive club, and/or your dive team members, will still feel a sense of pride and satisfaction in knowing that your diving practices and group activities are part of the proactive solution to global pollution.

OysterFest
Written 4 years ago

Mark your calendars for the first full weekend in October. This is the weekend of Oysterfest held by the Skookum Rotary Club Foundation at the Mason County Fair Grounds in Shelton Washington. Now I don't usually write articles on events that offer a smorgasbord of savory seafood specialties, wonderful local award winning wines, and a bountiful bevy of adult beverages in a banner bound beer garden. As difficult as it maybe, try to look past the smoked salmon linguini, the bacon wrapped smoked Oysters, and the crab topped muffins. I'd like to turn the OysterFest spotlight on an exhibit set up by a very dedicated group of dive club members.

OysterFest is going on its 29th season and for the last 25 years the Hood Canal Aquanuts, a dive club based in of Shelton, have participated in this event by selling various bite size treats as well as setting up cold water aquariums for land lubbers as well as potential future scuba divers to view inhabitants of the local salt waters. John Tupper, a long time Aquanut club member, told me that through trial and error they have honed their skills to the point that they currently only sell crabwiches (lightly toasted muffins complete with crabmeat and cheese). The rest of their time and energy is spent the weekend displaying some eight or so assorted sized glass aquariums filled with anemones, barnacles, and crabs. Besides these basic abc groups of invertebrates the Washington Department of Fish and Wildlife lends them critters such as large geoducks to display. The Aquanuts are currently co-hosting this event with the Kelp Krawler Dive Club based in Olympia,WA. Besides going out diving and collecting all the critters on the Thursday before Oyster fest, the co-mingled volunteer teem sets up the tanks, talks to OysterFest attendees about the creatures in the tanks, and helps the public obtain a hands on experience with sea life through their touch tank exhibits. Club members also tell the public what it's like to dive in the northwest, and answers any other questions curious spectators may have. Sunday evening after Oysterfest officially closes the gates, club members take down the whole exhibit and store it until next year's festivities. Since the Hood Canal Aquanuts are a non-profit dive organization, any proceeds from the annual event are used for charity purposes as well as mini-scholarship programs. At the last Aqaunut Dive Club meeting I attended, they voted to buy copies of *Return of the Plankton* video by Still Hope Productions, Inc. and donate them to local schools to help promote awareness of the local annual underwater life cycles.

Most dive clubs are non-profit organizations and many do charitable work in the local communities such as fishing pier cleanups and local monetary donations in addition to just being great groups to hang out and go diving with. Dive clubs usually cost relatively little to join and the rewards can be great, both to you and to the local community as well. I strongly encourage all divers to join a local dive club. Seasoned dive club members seem to know all the hot spots to dive and there always seems to be at least one club member ready to go diving just about anytime of day or night.

Local dive clubs may be associated with one or more dive shops or they may be completely independent. You can find out about the dive clubs in your area by contacting your local dive shop, checking out the activities section of Northwest Dive News or just by asking fellow divers. As for dive clubs like the Hood Canal Aquanuts and the Kelp Krawlers, members from their clubs are easy to locate, buti if you like to procrastinate, just wait until next October when you can ask them about their clubs while perched over a touch tank filled with starfish or while waiting for the timer on the crabwiches to count down to zero. Oh yes, and enjoy the rest of the OysterFest too. After all, you haven't had the full Hood Canal experience until you've attended this annual event. Great Dives.
www.oysterfest.org.

WRITING FOR
DIVE NEWS NETWORK

At last year's Northwest Dive and Travel Expo in Tacoma Washington I gave a seminar on how to become a writer for Northwest Dive News, which is part of the Dive News Network that currently covers most of North America. You don't have to be Clive Cussler, Earnest Hemmingway, or JK Roland to get your articles in our magazines; our staff can even help polish your writing if you like. What I covered in the seminar were tips to make the whole process easier and more understandable. We covered photo images, article guidelines, article planning, and article writing benefits.

Because an image is worth a thousand words, I tell every potential writer to carry a minimum 3meg pixel camera. Because I'm so bad at photography, I take three images of everything. I vary the light, speed, and distance as much as possible. This way, at least one of the images should turn out good enough for publication. Your results may be better than mine, and that's why I'm a **writer**/photographer, and not a **photographer**/writer, if that means anything in the big scheme of things.

As far as fish go, get closeups of heads not tails. If taking far shots, get a diver in frame for perspective. Action shots of divers gearing up and going overboard work well. Images of people wearing dive gear in the water, having fun, and smiling are great shots.

Keep in mind that 60% of the images appearing in magazines are of landscapes and above water shots such as the front of the hotel, the rooms, the dive boat, shoreline, funny tourist signs, and other unique landmark features. If you forget all the above, just carry a camera at all times and snap away like you're CIA.

As for article guidelines, while some magazines like articles of 200 words in length plus an image, Dive News Network prefers local articles between 800-1200 words. On each page this gives half a page of space for 400words plus images, and the other half of page for ad space. We have currently a two month lead time which may soon be extended to three months, so staff articles due May 1st, will be featured in the July issue. Unsolicited articles are selected as they fit in the scheme of things; more on this in a minute. Keep in mind though, that the more ads generated per issue, the more articles can be utilized per issue.

As for article planning, because articles may be due two or three months before printing, writers are always working on future projects. You may find yourself working on "Night Diving" in June for an October issue when the nights are longer. You may write a story on Cozumel for a spring edition and tropical articles for winter getaways or annual roundups. On the other hand, if you wrote an article in June on how to stay warm, you may not see it go in to print until a cold winter month issue like January or February. If the article involves a charter boat, you may need to go on the boat six months out and then write up and submit the article two months before its due date. Long lead times are also needed when certain dive sites are only diveable at certain times of year due to weather or currents; ice diving would be a good example. Diving with migrating species like salmon might be another reason to dive a particular place at a particular time of year. You get the drift.

Finally, some of the benefits for writing include: Just another reason to go diving and a chance to meet and go diving with other divers. You meet dive shop owners, charter captains, and industry leaders, try new gear before the masses, go on charter trips (scheduled and unscheduled), go behind the scenes, at aquariums, resorts, quarries, and dive expos, possible future job positions and pay prospects, work on future book material, and just learn more about diving and dive sites around the world.

Now as part of the Dive News Network, you can also write articles for our Northeast Dive News edition, our Midwest Dive News edition, and/or our Southeast Dive News edition. As you can see, there is plenty of room for expansion and a wide variety of States and Canadian Provinces to explore, dive, and cover in related topics.

Finally, I didn't say that writing it all up would be easy, but the outcome is extremely self-rewarding, and the entire process is just one more step along the road to discovering, enjoying, and logging dives in an expanded form; great diving destinations and great dive adventures.

END

www.ingramcontent.com/pod-product-compliance
Lightning Source LLC
Chambersburg PA
CBHW060241100426

42742CB00011B/1599